大学英语特色课系列教材

总主编 董金伟

英语文学名篇欣赏

Appreciating Literature in English

主　编　周　芳
副主编　葛静萍　Quinn Nicholson
（按姓氏笔画排序）
编　委　陈　静　周　芳
栗　萍　葛静萍　Quinn Nicholson

科学出版社
北　京

图书在版编目（CIP）数据

英语文学名篇欣赏 / 周芳主编. —北京：科学出版社，2013.12
大学英语特色课系列教材 / 董金伟主编
ISBN 978-7-03-039423-1

Ⅰ.①英… Ⅱ.①周… Ⅲ.①英语-阅读教学-高等学校-教材 ②世界
文学-文学欣赏-高等学校-教材 Ⅳ.①H319.4:I

中国版本图书馆 CIP 数据核字（2013）第 309857 号

责任编辑：阎　莉　常春娥 ／ 责任校对：郑金红
责任印制：赵德静 ／ 封面设计：无极书装

科 学 出 版 社 出版
北京东黄城根北街 16 号
邮政编码：100717
http://www.sciencep.com

骏杰印刷厂 印刷
科学出版社发行　各地新华书店经销

＊

2014 年 1 月第　一　版　开本：787×1092 1/16
2014 年 1 月第一次印刷　印张：15 3/4
字数：450 000

定价：35.00 元
（如有印装质量问题，我社负责调换）

总　序

随着经济全球化的飞速发展、信息技术的广泛应用和网络社会的日益兴起，知识经济不断得到拓展和深化，使得高等教育国际化成为势不可挡的世界潮流。作为一所国际化特色鲜明的教学研究型大学和华南地区国际化人才培养及外国语言文化、对外经济贸易、国际战略研究的重要基地，广东外语外贸大学（以下简称广外）一直以培养国际化人才为目标，即秉承培养全球化高素质公民的使命，着力推进专业教学与外语教学的深度融合，培养具有国际视野和创新意识、能直接参与国际合作与竞争的国际化人才。在广外现有的八大学科门类（即文学、经济学、管理学、法学、工学、理学、教育学、艺术）中，全日制在校本科生两万余人，其中，非英语类专业学生占四分之三，约15 000名。大学英语作为我校非英语专业学生的必修课，其教学贯穿一、二、三年级的六个学期，修读学生人数最多，影响面最大。

为了加强大学英语的教学与研究，广外自2001年以来一直致力于大学英语教学改革与创新，遵照"分级教学、分类指导"的大学英语教学指导原则，努力构建"国际化、校本化、个性化、立体化、人性化"的大学英语教学体系，凸显"分层次教学、专业英语教学、网络自主学习、教师专业发展、课外延伸学习"的广外教学特色。经过层层申报和严格评审，2011年3月，我校顺利成为教育部第三批大学英语教学改革的示范点；同年6月，我校的大学英语系列课程被评为"广东省精品课程"。

作为大学英语教学实施、改革和创新的重要环节，教材的作用不容低估。因此，教材建设，尤其是特色课程的教材建设一直是我校大学英语教学改革的重要内容之一。在新时代大学英语教学改革中，有一套适合国际化人才培养的特色课程系列教材是非常必要的。根据教育部颁布的《大学英语课程教学要求》，针对培养具有跨文化交际能力的国际型英语人才的需要，我校组织长期从事一线教学的中、外籍教师，早在2006年就相继编写、出版了一些大学英语特色教材，供我校一年级和二年级学生使用。经过在长期教学实践中的不断修改、丰富和完善，并结合兄弟院校使用的反馈意见，我们对现有的教材进行了认真修订和改版，使之成为一套更加科学、系统、前沿、实用的大学英语特色课系列教材。该系列教材包括影视英语、新闻英语、文学文化三大版块，共6本，各版块相互衔接、合理分布，旨在从不同侧面和不同角度出发培养学生在跨文化交际中的英语语言实际运用能力。教材的编写从教学实际和学习规律出发，设计循序渐进、灵活多样的教学活动和练习形式，以达到外语课程教学的最大成效。

众所周知，英语教学中，文化与语言密不可分。在长期的教学中我们发现，学生乐于了解西方文化，渴望能够用英语流畅、准确地就身边的社会文化现象与外国人进行交流。然而，语言产出能力的欠缺和文化层面知识的不足，常常导致学习者交流困难，甚至产生误解。本系列教材的特色之处恰是能够帮助师生在英语课堂上通过视、听、说、读等方面的训练，模拟、复制、创造文化语境，从而有效提高学生跨文化交际的英语实际应用能力。教材内容取材于原汁原味的英语新闻、电影和文学文化作品等，保证语料真实、语言地道、内容有趣，既增强学生的学习兴趣，又拓展学生的国际视野；既涵盖当代大学生关注的社会热点和热门话题，又辐射西方文化、社会礼仪和风土人情的各个领域，从整体结构到局部细节都精益求精，将知识的传授、能力的训练、方法的指导、习惯的培养、文化的意识相结合，构建起一个较为系统的整体培养体系。

我们真诚希望，通过这套特色课系列教材的使用，能够进一步推进我校的大学英语教学朝着"国际化、校本化、个性化、人性化、立体化"的方向发展；使我们"分层次教学、专业英语教学、网络自主学习、教师专业发展、课外延伸学习"的广外大学英语教学特色结出丰硕的成果；使我们的"教育部大学英语教学改革示范点"真正起到全国示范的作用；使我们的"大学英语系列省级精品课程"建设在广东省独树一帜，成为品牌。同时，我们也希望，此系列教材的出版，能为全国兄弟院校开展大学英语特色教学提供一些有益的启示，为他们在教材的使用上提供一种选择。

借此机会，再次感谢科学出版社领导和同仁，尤其是胡升华主任和阎莉编辑慧眼识珠，在我们修订、完善此系列教材的过程中给予专业指导、真诚帮助和大力支持。广外英语教育学院前任院长霍海洪教授生前也曾出谋划策，给予了悉心指导和大力支持，让我们以此系列教材的出版告慰他的在天之灵。

是为总序。

总主编　董金伟

2013年10月

前 言

文学的魅力，只有在阅读中才能体会。阅读的方式很多，我们可以有目的地"苦读"，也可以无目的地"闲读"；可以为了内容而读，也可以为了形式而读；可以用心灵去阅读，也可以用大脑去阅读。本书精心选择了在文学思想和文学价值上堪称一流的丰富多样的英语文学作品，向读者展示了一个美丽多姿的文学百花园。着眼于文学作品的精选、作者介绍、文学知识及写作技巧介绍、详细的注解和大量的富于启发性的问题，本书旨在引导读者进行多种方式的阅读，在更自信、更自由、更自觉的阅读中体会文学的魅力，并在文学作品中获取知识和智慧，提高文学欣赏能力。

基于已出版的英语文学欣赏和文学选读类书籍，本书尝试从以下方面有所突破：（1）本书的主题编排以人的成长轨迹为线索，纵阅全书，自然引发读者产生共鸣，使读者在阅读文学作品的同时联系到个人人生旅程，激发积极思考。（2）本书除了选编传统意义上的经典作品外，也选编了一些优秀的当代作品，同时选编了如歌词等鲜为收录的作品。其目的是引导读者突破迷信经典的心理，打破狭隘的文学界限，鼓励读者接受更广泛意义上的文学作品。（3）本书所选的作品以英美作家的作品为主，也包括其他国家如俄国、德国、法国、瑞典、尼日利亚、中国等国家的英译作品。向读者介绍不同国家、不同文化背景的作品，旨在帮助读者开拓阅读视野，丰富读者的文化体验，并激发读者在比较中进行深入思考。（4）本书附有详尽的文学知识注解，每篇作品后附有大量由浅入深的思考问题，既便于教师教学也便于学生自学。（5）本书在选编作品和设计问题时，始终考虑到读者的中国文化背景，有意选编了中国文学作品，在思考问题中也包含了不少中外作品对比和中外文化思想对比的问题，旨在引导读者在阅读和思考作品时立足于本土文化，同时也从异域文化的角度对本土文化进行批判性的思考。（6）本书每单元附有与本单元主题相关联的名画，意在拓宽读者的视野，并激发读者借助不同的艺术形式对同一主题进行思考。

本书包括介绍单元和6个主题单元。这6个主题单元分别为：第一单元，自我认知（Identity）；第二单元，心灵历程（Spiritual Growth）；第三单元，爱（Love）；第四单元，家庭（Family）；第五单元，人与社会（Man and Society）；第六单元，人生思索（Contemplations）。每个主题单元包括文学作品、作者简介、注解、文学知识介绍、思考问题、推荐书目、推荐电影和插图，有的单元带有附录。

本书适合英语或非英语专业大学专科和本科二年级以上学生、英语及非英语专业研究生使用，也可作为英语文学爱好者阅读和自学的教材。

　　本书由广东外语外贸大学英语教育学院的部分教师编写而成，以主题为线索的编排思路由周芳和Quinn Nicholson提出并形成。参加本书编写的人员有：周芳、Quinn Nicholson、栗萍、葛静萍和陈静。本书的编写得到了广东外语外贸大学英语教育学院李海丽教授、霍海洪教授、董金伟教授的大力支持和崔华、陈冬梅等老师的热心帮助。中山大学区鉷教授对本书提出了宝贵意见。科学出版社编辑阎莉、常春娥精心设计本书的编排，并进行了耐心细致的校对。本人在这里代表本书的全体编写人员向他们致以最衷心的感谢！

编　　者

2013年10月于广州白云山下

目 录

Introduction
What Is Literature and How to Read Literature

In the broad sense, literature includes anything that is written down. A story, a letter, a song, a document, a survey, even a math problem can be called literature. Usually, people tend to use literature in a narrower sense of the word. We tend to exclude practical writings from the sphere of literature. A letter, a document, or a survey will not become literature unless they are so well written that some aesthetic value is acquired. A math problem is less likely to become literature unless it is used by some writer in some postmodern writing experiment. A song is closer to literature in the strict sense, but again, only the really good ones are considered to be real literature.

It seems that it is form that makes literature. Literature in the narrow sense possesses a kind of form. It is partly the literary form that helps create aesthetic value which differentiates literature from other kinds of writing which are read mainly for their practical value. Paradoxically, the traditional reading of literature focuses mainly on the meaning, the content of it, rather than the form. Plato, the Greek philosopher, rejects poets from entering his ideal republic, because poetry "feeds and waters the passions", creates division and unsteadiness in the heart, or frivolous laughter, and produces the opposite of civic virtue. To Plato, Homer and Hesiod① and the dramatists②, instead of representing God as good and the source of all good, give us a flirtatious, quarrelsome, deceitful, jealous and revengeful crowd of deities. Plato's attitude towards poets suggests that it is the content of poetry and drama that he is mainly concerned with.

Plato's student, Aristotle, marvels at the great power of tragedies on the same basis. To Aristotle, the hero of a tragedy must be a man of high rank or social position, and there must be a turn of fortune for the tragic hero (from prosperity to calamity). So when the audience watch a great man fall from prosperity to obscurity, they are shocked into thinking about his own fate, and the great power of catharsis③ is produced. Though to both Plato and Aristotle, the great power (polluting power or the purifying power) can't be achieved without the help of a certain form, content is their major concern. This attitude towards literature carries on to today. To read for meaning is still most people's practice.

For some people, the value of literature as well as other forms of art lies not in the content but in the form. "There is nothing new under the sun," as the Bible says. We may have heard or experienced the same story many times without giving a bit of attention to it. But when the same story is presented in a certain literary form, it becomes a different thing. A certain distance or awareness is created. Though the story sounds familiar, there is something new, something exciting, and something uncertain about it. We are forced to look at the old story in a different way, and the familiar story becomes unfamiliar. Accordingly, we become more curious, more sensitive.

The same magic happens to other forms of art. A pair of shoes is a familiar sight, so familiar that we often can't tell one from the other. But when we look at it when it is presented in an oil painting by Vincent van Gogh (see the painting attached), we are shocked by it. We are shocked by the size, by the color, by the coarse skin, and by the way the laces tangle. We are shocked at every detail of it

---

① Hesiod: an ancient Greek poet, living around the time of Homer, the author of *Theogony* and *Works and Days*
② dramatists: Here refers to the ancient Greek dramatists, such as tragedians Aeschylus, Sophocles, Euripides, comedian Aristophanes, etc.
③ catharsis: purifying, especially of the soul

and we wonder about its history, its master, and what journey it has made, etc. A pair of shoes is no longer a pair of shoes. It becomes an object of great interest, an object of contemplation, a source of imagination. It is the way it is presented, the form, that creates meanings for it.

The world is full of things, but most of the time, we can't see them. In order to make people see things, the artists defamiliarize things (to ravel them with unusual forms) so people feel they are looking at the things for the first time. Their eyes become curious, their senses sharp and their reactions strong. In this sense, art not only resurrects things but also resurrects human beings. Because of art, things begin to exist. Because of art, human beings are born again as babies. The world is totally new and awaits their discovery. Since people will soon get used to one art form and their eyes become blind again and their senses dull, art has to forever innovate. One art form is soon replaced by another to ensure the defamiliarizing effect.

So in addition to read literature for its content, we shall also read literature for its form. What form is applied? How does the form enhance meaning, create meaning? What effect is achieved? What meaning is created? What new perspective do we acquire because of the defamiliarizing effect? Do we like this new perspective? Literary forms include elements like structure, narration, language, music, etc.

Still, literature can be read from critical stance. With this stance, people read literature to criticize how certain issues are approached in literature. Common issues for critical approaches are: gender problems, racial problems and social problems. For gender problems, people read to find out how women are presented in literature. Are the women characters relatively important or unimportant compared with the men characters? Are they in an obedient position? Are they distorted or simply stereotypes? Is the language of the writing male-oriented? Or critics read women writers to show how women writers write in a male-dominated society, or what perspective women take to look at the world, or to discover what is specifically female in terms of language, feeling, or perspective. For racial problems, people ask similar questions: are certain races ignored or unjustly treated in literature? Is the image of a certain race distorted or stereotyped? Is the tone favorably biased or unfavorably biased towards a certain race? If we call reading for content emotional and didactic reading, and reading for form aesthetic reading, then this approach to literature can be called political reading. This approach is popular with people who are politically conscious or who are interested in certain issues.

When people read literature for its meaning, for its form or for a political purpose, they presuppose that the structure of the literary work is stable and thus what is revealed is relatively stable too. What if the stability of the structure itself is to be doubted? Is there any definite meaning then? This is the poststructuralist stance to a literary work. The poststructuralists think that the structure of the literary work is not solid but a chain of signs with no sign dominating the other. When you start defining one sign, you have to use other signs which again need to be defined. You start a chain of infinite meanings. Like waves stirred by a stone, meaning is forever diffusing and expanding, evading your grasp. In this sense, the poststructuralists declare the "death of the author". Since language and the so-called meaning produced by language refuse to be controlled, the author has no authority over his work anymore. Meaning becomes the interaction between the text and the reader for a short time being. The reader has to arbitrarily cut the flow of meaning for a moment and get a relatively stable meaning for a time being. So in a sense, it is both the author and the reader that create meaning together.

Poststructural reading, like poststructual writing, is interesting as a radical experiment, a revolution against the traditional way of thinking. As anything that is radical, it can't hold the dominant position. For most readers and critics, literature has a stable structure, from where they can read for content, read for form, and read for discussing problems.

A Pair of Shoes
Vincent van Gogh, 1887.

▶ APPENDIX 1

A Poem by e. e. cummings

```
1    l(a

     le

     af

     fa

5    ll

     s)

     one

     l

     iness
```

STUDY QUESTIONS

A> *Recalling*

1. How does the content of literature affect you? Please give examples to illustrate.
2. What is the significance of literary form?
3. What are the common issues for political reading?
4. What is the basic assumption for the poststructuralist reading?

B> *Interpreting*

5. To what extent can form contribute to the meaning? Please illustrate with e. e. cummings' poem which is given above.
6. Do you believe that the meaning of a piece of literary work is free of the author's control? Why or why not?
7. What is the role of the reader in a piece of literary work?
8. Do you believe that there is difference between male and female writing? If there is, what is the difference?

C> *Extending*

9. In your understanding, what is the boundary between literary and common writing? Should there be any boundary?
10. How has literature affected you? Do you welcome this influence?

FURTHER READING

Hans Bertens, *Literary Theory: The Basics*
Terry Eagleton, *Literary Theory: An Introduction*

MOVIES RECOMMENDED

Dead Poets Society (1989), directed by Peter Weir
The Blood of a Poet (1930), directed by Cocteau
The Legend of 1900 (1998), directed by Giuseppe Tornatore
Lust for Life (1956), directed by Vincente Minnelli and George Cukor

Unit One   Identity

I. *I'm Nobody! Who are you?* by Emily Dickinson

▶▶ ABOUT THE POETESS

 **Emily Dickinson** (1830-1886), was born in Amhcrst, Massachusetts on December 10, 1830. Emily lived secluded in the house she was born in, except for the short time she attended Amherst Academy and Holyoke Female Seminary, until her death. Only ten of her poems were published in her lifetime. Today Emily Dickinson is universally acknowledged as a poet of the highest order. Her odd and inventive poems helped to initiate modern poetry.

I'm Nobody! Who are you?

1   I'm Nobody! Who are you?
Are you—Nobody—Too?
Then there's a pair of us!
Don't tell! They'd banish us (advertise) —you know!

5   How dreary—to be—Somebody!
How public—like a Frog —
To tell one's name—the livelong June—
To an admiring Bog[①]!

▶▶ STUDY QUESTIONS

 Recalling

1. Who are the "pair of us" and "they" in this poem?
2. What does "an admiring Bog" refer to?

 Interpreting

3. In what way is "Somebody" comparable with "a Frog"?
4. What is likely to be "Somebody" according to the poem?
5. Does the speaker enjoy being "Nobody"?

 Extending

6. Do you want to be "Nobody" or "Somebody"? Explain.
7. What is the real self ? Is it the one content with his or her own private world or the one who throws him or herself into the society?
8. Discuss the form of the poem. How does the form of the poem contribute to the meaning?

---

① bog: soft, wet, spongy area

▶ LITERARY FOCUS

❯ *The Speaker and the Poet or Author*

The speaker is the voice, or mask or persona (Latin for "mask") that speaks the poem. It is usually not identical with the poet or author who writes it. The author counterfeits the speech of a person in a particular situation. Emily Dickinson invented an "I" who prefers to be "Nobody". We call "I" the speaker in the poem rather than the poetess herself. The speaker's voice does often have the ring of the poet or the author's own voice, and to make a distinction between speaker and poet or author may at times seem perverse, because some poetry (especially contemporary poetry) is highly autobiographical. Still, even in autobiographical poems it may be convenient to distinguish between poet or author and speaker: the speaker is Emily the lonely woman, or Emily the curious and naughty woman, not simply Emily the poetess.

▶ THINKING ABOUT SPEAKER OR POET

In the poem *I'm Nobody! Who are you?*, what kind of person is the speaker? Who is the speaker addressing to? Why does the poetess invent this speaker?

II. *Song of Myself* by Walt Whitman

▶ ABOUT THE POET

Walt Whitman (1819–1892), generally considered the first national poet of America, together with Emily Dickinson, he is regarded as America's most significant poet of the 19th century. He sings enthusiastically about the spacious geography of the country, the free spirit of an individual and about love of people of all kinds. His masterpiece *Leaves of Grass* received mixed claims at his time because of the openness about body and sex and the innovative style. Now *Leaves of Grass* becomes one of the world masterpieces. Whitman is often called "the father of free verse".

From *Song of Myself*

16

1   I am of old and young, of the foolish as much as the wise,
     Regardless of others, ever regardful of others,
     Maternal as well as paternal, a child as well as a man,
     Stuff'd with the stuff that is coarse and stuff'd with the stuff
5   that is fine,
     One of the Nation of many nations, the smallest the same and the largest the same,
     A Southerner soon as a Northerner, a planter nonchalant and
     hospitable down by the Oconee① I live,

---

① Oconee: a river in Northern Georgia

A Yankee[1] bound my own way ready for trade, my joints the limberest[2]

10   joints on earth and the sternest joints on earth,

A Kentuckian[3] walking the vale of the Elkhorn[4] in my deer-skin
leggings, a Louisianian[5] or Georgian[6],

A boatman over lakes or bays or along coasts, a Hoosier[7], Badger[8],
Buckeye[9];

15   At home on Kanadian snow-shoes or up in the bush, or with fishermen
off Newfoundland[10],

At home in the fleet of ice-boats, sailing with the rest and
tacking[11],

At home on the hills of Vermont[12] or in the woods of Maine[13], or the

20   Texan ranch[14],

Comrade of Californians, comrade of free North-Westerners, (loving their big proportions,)

Comrade of raftsmen and coalmen, comrade of all who shake hands
and welcome to drink and meat,

A learner with the simplest, a teacher of the thoughtfullest,

25   A novice[15] beginning yet experient of myriads[16] of seasons,

Of every hue[17] and caste[18] am I, of every rank and religion,

A farmer, mechanic, artist, gentleman, sailor, quaker[19],

Prisoner, fancy-man[20], rowdy[21], lawyer, physician, priest.

I resist any thing better than my own diversity,

30   Breathe the air but leave plenty after me,

And am not stuck up, and am in my place.

(The moth and the fish-eggs are in their place,

The bright suns I see and the dark suns I cannot see are in their place,

The palpable[22] is in its place and the impalpable is in its place.)

---

[1] Yankee: the nickname for the native of New England or northern states
[2] limber: flexible
[3] Kentuckian: a native in the state of Kentucky
[4] Elkhorn: a place in California
[5] Louisianian: a native in the state of Louisiana
[6] Georgian: a native in the state of Georgia
[7] Hoosier: a native in the state of Indiana
[8] Badger: a native in the state of Wisconsin
[9] Buckeye: a native in the state of Ohio
[10] Newfoundland: a large island on the east coast of Canada
[11] tack: to sail in a zigzag way
[12] Vermont: a state in New England
[13] Maine: a state in the northeast
[14] Texan ranch: a big farm in the state of Texas
[15] novice: a person who is new to the circumstances or work
[16] myriads: a great many
[17] hue: color
[18] caste: class
[19] Quaker: a popular name for a member of a Religious Society of Friends
[20] fancy-man: a person, esp. a man, who connects between the customers and prostitutes
[21] rowdy: a rough, disorderly person
[22] palpable: tangible, obvious

▶ STUDY QUESTIONS

A ▷ Recalling

1. What is the speaker's age and gender?
2. Is the speaker a Southerner or Northerner? What is his profession or trade?
3. What kind of person is the speaker?

B ▷ Interpreting

4. What does "stuff'd with the stuff that is coarse and stuff'd with the stuff/that is fine" mean?
5. How can the speaker be both "of old and young, of the foolish as much as the wise" and "maternal as well as paternal, a child as well as a man"?
6. What does it suggest that the speaker is at the same time a Yankee, a Kentuckian, a Louisianian, and a Georgian?
7. What does it mean that "I resist any thing better than my own diversity"?
8. What does it mean that "(I) Breathe the air but leave plenty after me"?
9. What kind of personality is the poet singing about?

C ▷ Extending

10. Compare the "I" with the "I" in *I am Nobody! Who are you?* What is different and what is similar?
11. What kind of personality would you sing about? Do you like what you are?
12. Please discuss the form of the poem. Does the form agree with what it intents to say?

III. *Theme for English B* by Langston Hughes

▶ ABOUT THE POET

Langston Hughes (1902–1967), was one of the most important writers and thinkers of the Harlem Renaissance, which was the African American artistic movement in the 1920s that celebrated black life and culture. His literary works helped shape American literature and politics. Hughes, like others active in the Harlem Renaissance, had a strong sense of racial pride. Through his poetry, novels, plays, essays, and children's books, he promoted equality, condemned racism and injustice, and celebrated African American culture, humor, and spirituality.

Theme for English B[①]

1   The instructor said,

Go home and write

a page tonight.

And let that page come out of you—

---

① English B: second-level English class

5   Then, it will be true.

I wonder if it's that simple?
I am twenty-two, colored, born in Winston-Salem[1].
I went to school there, then Durham[2], then here
to this college on the hill above Harlem[3].
10   I am the only colored student in my class.
The steps from the hill lead down into Harlem,
through a park, then I cross St. Nicholas,
Eighth Avenue, Seventh, and I come to the Y,
the Harlem Branch Y, where I take the elevator
15   up to my room, sit down, and write this page:

It's not easy to know what is true for you or me
at twenty-two, my age. But I guess I'm what
I feel and see and hear, Harlem, I hear you:
hear you, hear me—we two—you, me, talk on this page.
20   (I hear New York, too.) Me—who?
Well, I like to eat, sleep, drink, and be in love.
I like to work, read, learn, and understand life.
I like a pipe for a Christmas present,
or records—Bessie[4], bop[5], or Bach[6].
25   I guess being colored doesn't make me not like
the same things other folks like who are other races.
So will my page be colored that I write?

Being me, it will not be white.
But it will be
30   a part of you, instructor.
You are white—
yet a part of me, as I am a part of you.
That's American.
Sometimes perhaps you don't want to be a part of me.
35   Nor do I often want to be a part of you.
But we are, that's true!
As I learn from you,
I guess you learn from me—
although you're older—and white—

[1] Winston-Salem: a city in North Carolina
[2] Durham: a city in North Carolina
[3] Harlem: a section of New York City, in the northeast part of Manhattan, which is inhabited mainly by black people, thus the word "Harlem" becomes a byword for the black people, the black community or culture.
[4] Bessie Smith: a blues singer
[5] bop: a kind of Jazz
[6] Bach: Johann Sebastian Bach, German organist and composer. He is often called "the Father of European music".

40   and somewhat more free.

This is my page for English B.

▶▶ STUDY QUESTIONS

Recalling

1. What is special about the speaker?
2. How does he feel about his teacher's assignment?

Interpreting

3. Why to the speaker "It's not easy to know what is true for you or me"?
4. The speaker asks "will my paper be colored?" How will you answer this question?
5. Why does the speaker say "You are white — /yet a part of me, as I am a part of you."? Can we be part of each other?

C > Extending

6. In this poem the speaker describes his feeling and experience in college at age 22. He says he is not sure if it is easy to tell what is true at his age. Do you feel you can tell what is true about yourself or your teacher?
7. Compare this poem with *I am Nobody! Who are you?* and *Song of Myself*. What have you found out?

Where Do We Come from? What Are We? Where Are We Going?
Paul Gauguin, 1897.
Museum of Fine Arts, Boston.

IV. Two Songs by John Lennon and Paul McCartney

▶ ABOUT THE SONGWRITERS/ROCK MUSICIANS

As half of The Beatles, John Lennon and Paul McCartney were one of the most successful songwriting teams of the century. Together they wrote dozens of hit tunes, ranging from *Help!* and *Ticket to Ride* to *Penny Lane* and *Let It Be.* Lennon's romance with Yoko Ono was a major influence on his post-Beatles career, and he collaborated with her on everything from avant-garde noise to the modern pop hymn *Imagine.* After The Beatles, Lennon's solo career was marked by unpredictable records and his public pleas for world peace. After a reclusive five years as a family man, Lennon released an album with Yoko in 1980, *Double Fantasy.* As their new song, *Just Like Starting Over* was reaching the top of the charts, Lennon was shot to death outside his New York home by Mark David Chapman, a schizophrenic fan.

Song One

Nowhere Man

1   He's a real Nowhere Man,
Sitting in his Nowhere Land,
Making all his nowhere plans for nobody.
Doesn't have a point of view,
5   Knows not where he's going to,
Isn't he a bit like you and me?

Nowhere Man, please listen,
You don't know what you're missing,
Nowhere Man, the world is at your command.

10   He's as blind as he can be,
Just sees what he wants to see,
Nowhere Man can you see me at all?

Nowhere Man, don't worry,
Take your time, don't hurry,
15   Leave it all till somebody else lends you a hand.

Doesn't have a point of view,
Knows not where he's going to,
Isn't he a bit like you and me?

Nowhere Man, please listen,

20　You don't know what you're missing,
　　Nowhere Man, the world is at your command.

　　He's a real Nowhere Man,
　　Sitting in his Nowhere Land,
　　Making all his nowhere plans for nobody,
25　Making all his nowhere plans for nobody,
　　Making all his nowhere plans for nobody.

Song Two

Eleanor Rigby

1　Ah, look at all the lonely people
　　Ah, look at all the lonely people

　　Eleanor Rigby picks up the rice[①] in the church where a wedding has been
　　Lives in a dream
5　Waits at the window, wearing the face that she keeps in a jar by the door
　　Who is it for?

　　All the lonely people
　　Where do they all come from?
　　All the lonely people
10　Where do they all belong?

　　Father McKenzie writing the words of a sermon that no one will hear
　　No one comes near
　　Look at him working, darning his socks in the night when there's nobody there
　　What does he care?

15　All the lonely people
　　Where do they all come from?
　　All the lonely people
　　Where do they all belong?

　　Ah, look at all the lonely people
20　Ah, look at all the lonely people

　　Eleanor Rigby died in the church and was buried along with her name
　　Nobody came
　　Father McKenzie wiping the dirt from his hands as he walks from the grave
　　No one was saved

25　All the lonely people (Ah, look at all the lonely people)
　　Where do they all come from?
　　All the lonely people (Ah, look at all the lonely people)
　　Where do they all belong?

---

① rice: Rice is spread on wedding ceremony as a symbol of fertility.

STUDY QUESTIONS

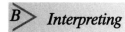 A Recalling

1. In the first song *Nowhere Man*, what makes the man a "nowhere man"?
2. What is Eleanor Rigby's life like?
3. Please interpret "wearing the face that she keeps in a jar by the door" in the song *Eleanor Rigby*.
4. What does Father McKenzie do? What is his life like?

B Interpreting

5. Do you think the characters in the song *Eleanor Rigby* have a "purpose in life"? Should they?
6. Both Eleanor Rigby and Father McKenzie are lonely people according to the poem. Are they somewhat different in their loneliness?
7. What makes these people lonely?

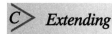 C Extending

8. The Beatles' songs talk about people who don't seem to have a place in life. Do you feel like you have a "place" in life—or are you more of a "nowhere man"?
9. Is purposeful life more valuable, or is purpose merely a way of comforting ourselves? What gives life purpose?

LITERARY FOCUS

A What Is Poetry?

It is difficult to define. We have been more successful in describing and appreciating poetry than in defining it. Poetry might be defined, initially, as a kind of language that says more and says it more intensely than does ordinary language. William Wordsworth defined poetry as "the spontaneous overflow of powerful feelings, recollected in tranquility." Poetry is the most condensed and concentrated form of literature, saying most in the fewest number of words.

B Reading the Poem

Here are some useful suggestions as to how to read a poem. (a) Read a poem more than once. (b) Keep a dictionary by you and use it. (c) Read so as to hear the sounds of the words in your mind. Poetry is written to be heard: its meanings are conveyed through sound as well as through print. Every word is therefore important. (d) Always pay careful attention to what the poem is saying. (e) Practice reading poems aloud. Ask yourself the following questions: (i) Who is the speaker and what is the occasion? (ii) What is the central purpose of the poem? (iii) By what means is the purpose of the poem achieved?

THINKING ABOUT POETRY

People's attitude towards poetry is divided. Some people don't like poetry on the basis that poetry is difficult to understand; poets are insane people and they intentionally complicate things and they are excessively emotional. These people think we don't need poetry in our life. Other people think poetry is the flower of language, the essence of literature, the best that is ever said and thought; it provides guidance to our life; it nourishes our spirits and it helps us find the truth. What do you think? Do you love poetry? Why or why not?

V. *Dumplings* by Yi Sha

▶▶ ABOUT THE POET

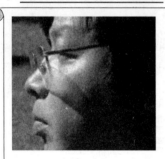

Yi Sha (1966–) Born in 1966, Yi Sha graduated from the Chinese Department of Beijing Normal University in 1989. Since the publication of his first collection *Poets Starved to Death* in 1994, Yi Sha has become an influential figure in the Chinese poetic landscape both for his uncompromising commitment to *kouyu shi* and for his love of literary polemic. His poetry is frequently confronting, and occasionally seems to be more intent on upsetting than providing delight to readers, but he has already assembled a core of work that tries to get poetry to acknowledge the realities of day to day existence. Poetry was always too pure to be found in the mundane world: it existed in rainbows and dreams and worlds of intense private feeling. Yi Sha seeks to counteract that tendency: signs of his life loom large in his work, starkly at times, and without the warm glow of self-glorification.

<table>
<tr><td colspan="2" align="center">饺　子</td><td colspan="2" align="center">Dumplings</td></tr>
<tr><td colspan="2"></td><td colspan="2" align="center">*Translated by Simon Patton*</td></tr>
<tr><td>1</td><td>大年三十那天
他和父亲埋头在地里
干了一整天的活儿
所以他在往家走的途中</td><td>1</td><td>on the last day of the year
he spent the whole day with his father
hard at work in the fields
for this reason he can still see in his mind's</td></tr>
<tr><td>5</td><td>记准了蛇年
最后一轮夕阳的模样
回到家中
母亲端上了
热气腾腾的饺子</td><td>5</td><td>eye
the sun setting for good on the Year of the
Snake
as he walked home
when they got back</td></tr>
<tr><td>10</td><td>吃过之后他就睡了
因为第二天
他和父亲还得下地干活
必须这样做
因为他每年的学费</td><td>10</td><td>his mother served up
hot dumplings
after eating them he went to bed
because the following day
he had to go and work in the fields again</td></tr>
<tr><td>15</td><td>就是（也只能）
从地里刨出来
一位来自
乡村的大学生
在我的课堂上</td><td>15</td><td>with his father
he had no choice
because the money needed to pay his
tuition fees each year
could (and could only)</td></tr>
</table>

20	做口头表达的练习时	20	be dug up out of the ground
	向大家讲述		a university student
	他如何过年		from a village
	在五分钟的过程里		explained to us how he spent the New Year
	他叙述平稳		in class, as an exercise in oral presentation
25	语调冷漠	25	in the five minutes it took for his talk
	只是在说到		his account went smoothly
	饺子一词时		his tone of voice was deadpan
	才面露微笑		it was only when he mentioned the word "dumpling"
		30	that his face betrayed a hint of a smile

STUDY QUESTIONS

A> Recalling

1. Please point out the images in the poem.
2. Who is the speaker of the poem?
3. Please think about the choice of words in both the Chinese and English version. Which word or line do you like best? Why?

B> Interpreting

4. What does the student's indifferent tone in presentation indicate?
5. Why does the student smile at the mentioning of "dumpling"?
6. With what kind of tone does the speaker narrate this story?
7. What is the poem about?

C> Extending

8. Please compare the Chinese poem with the English translation. Which one do you like better? Why?
9. Think about the line-dividing in both the Chinese and the English versions, what are the specific reasons for the division?
10. Besides the division of lines, what makes the passage a poem instead of a prose?
11. What kind of language is used in the poem? Do you think poetry should be written with special language? Why or why not?

LITERARY FOCUS

> Image

Image is a concrete representation of an object or sensory experience. Or to put it in simpler words, image is whatever appeals to any of our senses (including sense of hearing as well as of sight, smell, taste, touch and sound). For example, image "red leaves" appeals to the sense of sight; image "the waves are roaring" appeals to both sense of sight and sense of hearing. Image "the water is cool" may appeal to sense of touch and image "the plum is delicious" appeals to sense of taste. Images are either "literal" or "figurative". A literal image is something that represents a thing in the "real" world, or it is seen as its own thing, divorced from the burden of representing anything other than itself, for example, "the sunlight in a lemon/makes me wince". A figurative image does not follow the literal meaning of the words exactly and is standing for something else, for example, "how dreary—to be—Somebody!/How public—like a Frog—". "Frog" here is more than a frog. It represents something else.

▶ THINKING ABOUT THE USE OF IMAGE

How are images used in the poem *Dumplings*? What kind of effect do they help achieve?

VI. "Hamlet's Soliloquy" from *Hamlet* (Act III, Scene 1) by William Shakespeare

▶ ABOUT THE PLAYWRIGHT

William Shakespeare (1564–1616), "the Bard of Avon", English poet and playwright. He was born on April 23, 1564, in Stratford-on-Avon, a charming little village in Warwickshire. Shakespeare wrote 154 *Sonnets* and numerous highly successful often quoted dramatic works including the tragedy of the Prince of Denmark, *Hamlet,* and *King Lear, Othello* and *Macbeth*. Shakespeare is a great master of the English language and he is universally acknowledged to be the summit of the English Renaissance, one of the greatest writers the world over.

▶ THE SUMMARY OF *HAMLET*

Hamlet is the son of the late King Hamlet (of Denmark), who died two months before the start of the play. After King Hamlet's death, his brother, Claudius, becomes king, and marries King Hamlet's widow, Gertrude (Queen of Denmark). Young Hamlet fears that Claudius killed his father to become king of Denmark and this fear greatly angers Hamlet. Two officers, Marcellus and Barnardo, summon Hamlet's friend Horatio, and later Hamlet himself to see the late King Hamlet's ghost appearing at midnight. The ghost tells Hamlet privately that Claudius has indeed murdered King Hamlet by pouring poison in his ear. Hamlet is further enraged and plots about how to revenge his father's death.

In his anger, Hamlet seems to act like a madman, prompting King Claudius, his wife Gertrude, and his advisor Polonius to send Rosencrantz and Guildenstern to spy on Hamlet and figure out why he is acting mad. Hamlet even treats Polonius's daughter Ophelia rudely, prompting Polonius to believe Hamlet is madly in love with her, though Claudius expects otherwise. Polonius, a man who talks too long-windedly, has allowed his son Laertes to go to France (then sent Reynaldo to spy on Laertes) and has ordered Ophelia not to associate with Hamlet. Claudius, fearing Hamlet may try to kill him, sends Hamlet to England. Before leaving, however, Hamlet convinces an acting company to reenact King Hamlet's death before Claudius, in the hopes of causing Claudius to break down and admit murdering King Hamlet. Though Claudius is enraged, he does not admit murdering. Hamlet's mother tries to reason with Hamlet after the play, while Polonius spied on them behind a curtain. Hamlet hears Polonius, and kills him through the curtain, thinking the person is Claudius. When finding out the truth, Hamlet regrets the death, yet Claudius still sends him to England, accompanied by Rosencrantz and Guildenstern with orders from Claudius that the English kill Hamlet as soon as he arrives.

After Hamlet leaves, Laertes returns from France, enraged over Polonius's death. Ophelia reacts to her father's death with utter madness and eventually falls in a stream and drowns, further angering Laertes. En route to England, Hamlet finds the orders and changes them to order Rosencrantz and Guildenstern to be killed, as does occur, though Hamlet is kidnapped by pirates one day later. The pirates return Hamlet to Claudius (for a ransom), and Claudius tries one last attempt to eliminate Hamlet: he arranges a sword duel between Laertes and Hamlet. The trick, however, is that the tip of Laertes' sword is poisoned. As a backup precaution, Claudius poisons the victory cup in case Hamlet wins. During the fight, the poisoned drink is offered to Hamlet, he declines, and instead his mother, Gertrude, drinks it (to the objection of Claudius). Laertes, losing to Hamlet, illegally scratches him with the poisoned sword to ensure Hamlet's death. Hamlet (unknowingly), then switches swords with Laertes, and cuts and poisons him. The queen dies, screaming that she has been poisoned and Laertes, dying, admits of Claudius' treachery. Weakening, Hamlet fatally stabs Claudius, Laertes dies, and Hamlet begins his death speech. Though Horatio wants to commit suicide out of sorrow, Hamlet entreats him to tell the story of King Hamlet's death and Rosencrantz and Guildenstern's deaths to all. Fortinbras, the prince of Norway, arrives from conquest of England, and Hamlet's last dying wish is that Fortinbras becomes the new King of Denmark, as happens.

Hamlet's Soliloquy

1   To be, or not to be: that is the question:
Whether'tis nobler in the mind to suffer
The slings[1] and arrows of outrageous fortune,
Or to take arms against a sea of troubles,
5   And by opposing end them? To die: to sleep;
No more; and by a sleep to say we end
The heart-ache and the thousand natural shocks[2]
That flesh is heir to[3], 'tis a consummation[4]
Devoutly to be wish'd. To die, to sleep;
10   To sleep: perchance[5] to dream: ay[6], there's the rub[7];
For in that sleep of death what dreams may come
When we have shuffled off this mortal coil[8],
Must give us pause: there's the respect[9]
That makes calamity of so long life;
15   For who would bear the whips and scorns of time[10],

---

[1] sling: a device for hurling stone or other missiles
[2] natural shocks: disasters that come from nature or to body
[3] be heir to: be bound to have
[4] consummation: ending
[5] perchance: perhaps
[6] ay: (archaic) ever, always
[7] rub: obstacle, difficulty
[8] mortal coil: troubles and activities of the world
[9] respect: aspect, consideration
[10] whips and scorns of time: the cruelties done by time, e.g. time carves lines on our faces, dies our hair grey, bends our backs and distorts our figures, etc.

Th'^① oppressor's wrong^②, the proud man's contumely^③,
The pangs of despised love^④, the law's delay^⑤,
The insolence of office^⑥ and the spurns^⑦
That patient merit^⑧ of th' unworthy^⑨ takes,
20   When he himself might his quietus make^⑩
With a bare bodkin^⑪? who would fardels^⑫ bear,
To grunt and sweat under a weary life,
But that^⑬ the dread of something after death,
The undiscover'd country from whose bourn^⑭
25   No traveller returns, puzzles the will
And makes us rather bear those ills we have
Than fly to others that we know not of ?
Thus conscience^⑮ does make cowards of us all;
And thus the native hue of resolution
30   Is sicklied o'er with the pale cast of thought^⑯,
And enterprises of great pitch and moment
With this regard their currents turn awry^⑰,
And lose the name of action.

▶▶ STUDY QUESTIONS

Recalling

1. Please point out all the similes and metaphors in the soliloquy and try to find out what the similes and metaphors actually refer to.
2. What is the "calamity of so long life" according to Hamlet? Are there other calamities in life which are not mentioned in the soliloquy?
3. According to the passage, what comfort can sleep bring about? And what puzzles people's will to sleep?
4. What usually makes us "lose the name of action" according to the soliloquy?

① th': the
② wrong: Here means infringing other people's rights.
③ contumely: insult
④ despised love: unrequited love, unreturned love
⑤ the law's delay: the delay of justice
⑥ the insolence of office: disrespectful and insulting attitude of the government officers
⑦ spurn: contemptuous treatment
⑧ the patient merit: virtuous and patient people
⑨ the unworthy: the mean people. The normal order of the sentence: the spurns that patient merit takes of (from) the unworthy.
⑩ his quietus make: to end his life
⑪ bodkin: a dagger
⑫ fardel: (archaic) burden
⑬ but that: if not for
⑭ bourn: realm
⑮ conscience: consciousness, consideration
⑯ line 29 and 30: too much thinking weakens our resolution. A metaphor is used here: the color of thinking (which is pale) makes the original color of resolution sick.
⑰ awry: with a turn or twist to one side. The whole sentence means: because of too much thinking, the original strong will to do sth. becomes weak and changes direction.

Interpreting

5. What is Hamlet's dilemma?

6. What aspect of Hamlet's character does the soliloquy reveal?

 Extending

7. It seems that Hamlet's tragedy is caused by the so-called "flaw" in his character—his irresolution. Is "irresolution" necessarily a "flaw" in the character? Why or why not?

8. Is Hamlet simply thinking about a personal problem? What broader issue is he pondering about?

 ## LITERARY FOCUS

Shakespeare's Tragic Hero

Heroes in Shakespeare's tragedies are not only men of high rank, but also men of certain greatness in character. But together with the greatness in his character, the tragic hero also carries with him a certain fatal flaw or "tragic flaw". This tragic flaw usually displays as excessiveness in some action or emotion, for example it is excessive thinking which results in irresolution for Hamlet and excessive ambition for Macbeth. This flaw, together with other factors such as fate or chance will be responsible for the great tragedy, which usually involves the death of the hero and other main characters. The emotion aroused by the tragedy is pity and awe. Pity because the tragedy usually comes in calamity which is more than the hero deserves. Awe because the tragedy can't be avoided. The "tragic flaw" is not unforgivable viciousness but common errors intensified and it is in human nature. In this sense the audience is watching his or her own fate as a human being.

THINKING ABOUT TRAGIC HERO

What makes Hamlet a tragic hero? Does his flaw make him even nobler? How do you feel about his tragedy? Have you ever experienced "catharsis" (the process of being purified) in watching a tragedy or other genre of literature?

VII. *A Clean, Well-lighted Place* by Ernest Hemingway

 ## ABOUT THE AUTHOR

Ernest Miller Hemingway (1899–1961) was an American novelist, short-story writer, and journalist. His distinctive writing style is characterized by economy and understatement and has a significant influence on the development of twentieth century fiction writing. Hemingway's protagonists are typically stoics, often seen as projections of his own character—men who must show "grace under pressure". Many of his works are considered classics in the canon of American literature, for example *The Sun Also Rises* (1926), *A Farewell to Arms* (1929), *For Whom the Bell Tolls* (1940), *The Old Man and the Sea* (1952).

Hemingway was nicknamed "Papa" and part of the 1920s expatriate community in Paris, as described in his memoir *A Moveable Feast*, and was known as part of "the Lost Generation", a name he popularized. He led a turbulent social life, was married four times, and allegedly had various romantic relationships during his lifetime. Hemingway received the Pulitzer Prize in 1953 for *The Old Man and the Sea*. He received the Nobel Prize in Literature in 1954. In 1961, at age 61, he committed suicide, as his father did before him.

A Clean, Well-lighted Place

1　　It was very late and everyone had left the cafe except an old man who sat in the shadow the leaves of the tree made against the electric light. In the day time the street was dusty, but at night the dew settled the dust and the old man liked to sit late because he was deaf and now at night it was quiet and he felt the difference. The two waiters inside the cafe knew that the old man was a little drunk, and while he was a good client they knew that if he became too drunk he would leave without paying, so they kept watch on him.

2　　"Last week he tried to commit suicide," one waiter said.

3　　"Why?"

4　　"He was in despair."

5　　"What about?"

6　　"Nothing."

7　　"How do you know it was nothing?"

8　　"He has plenty of money."

9　　They sat together at a table that was close against the wall near the door of the cafe and looked at the terrace where the tables were all empty except where the old man sat in the shadow of the leaves of the tree that moved slightly in the wind. A girl and a soldier went by in the street. The street light shone on the brass number on his collar. The girl wore no head covering and hurried beside him.

10　　"The guard will pick him up," one waiter said.

11　　"What does it matter if he gets what he's after?"

12　　"He had better get off the street now. The guard will get him. They went by five minutes ago."

13　　The old man sitting in the shadow rapped on his saucer with his glass. The younger waiter went over to him.

14　　"What do you want?"

15　　The old man looked at him. "Another brandy," he said.

16　　"You'll be drunk," the waiter said. The old man looked at him. The waiter went away.

17　　"He'll stay all night," he said to his colleague. "I'm sleepy now. I never get into bed before three o'clock. He should have killed himself last week."

18 The waiter took the brandy bottle and another saucer from the counter inside the cafe and marched out to the old man's table. He put down the saucer and poured the glass full of brandy.

19 "You should have killed yourself last week," he said to the deaf man. The old man motioned with his finger. "A little more," he said. The waiter poured on into the glass so that the brandy slopped over and ran down the stem into the top saucer of the pile. "Thank you," the old man said. The waiter took the bottle back inside the cafe. He sat down at the table with his colleague again.

20 "He's drunk now," he said.

21 "He's drunk every night."

22 "What did he want to kill himself for?"

23 "How should I know."

24 "How did he do it?"

25 "He hung himself with a rope."

26 "Who cut him down?"

27 "His niece."

28 "Why did they do it?"

29 "Fear for his soul."

30 "How much money has he got?"

31 "He's got plenty."

32 "He must be eighty years old."

33 "Anyway I should say he was eighty."

34 "I wish he would go home. I never get to bed before three o'clock. What kind of hour is that to go to bed?"

35 "He stays up because he likes it."

36 "He's lonely. I'm not lonely. I have a wife waiting in bed for me."

37 "He had a wife once too."

38 "A wife would be no good to him now."

39 "You can't tell. He might be better with a wife."

40 "His niece looks after him. You said she cut him down."

41 "I know."

42 "I wouldn't want to be that old. An old man is a nasty thing."

43   "Not always. This old man is clean. He drinks without spilling. Even now, drunk. Look at him."

44   "I don't want to look at him. I wish he would go home. He has no regard for those who must work."

45   The old man looked from his glass across the square, then over at the waiters.

46   "Another brandy," he said, pointing to his glass. The waiter who was in a hurry came over.

47   "Finished," he said, speaking with that omission of syntax stupid people employ when talking to drunken people or foreigners. "No more tonight. Close now."

48   "Another," said the old man.

49   "No. Finished." The waiter wiped the edge of the table with a towel and shook his head.

50   The old man stood up, slowly counted the saucers①, took a leather coin purse from his pocket and paid for the drinks, leaving half a peseta tip. The waiter watched him go down the street, a very old man walking unsteadily but with dignity.

51   "Why didn't you let him stay and drink?" the unhurried waiter asked. They were putting up the shutters. "It is not half-past two."

52   "I want to go home to bed."

53   "What is an hour?"

54   "More to me than to him."

55   "An hour is the same."

56   "You talk like an old man yourself. He can buy a bottle and drink at home."

57   "It's not the same."

58   "No, it is not," agreed the waiter with a wife. He did not wish to be unjust. He was only in a hurry.

59   "And you? You have no fear of going home before your usual hour?"

60   "Are you trying to insult me?"

61   "No, hombre②, only to make a joke."

62   "No," the waiter who was in a hurry said, rising from pulling down the metal shutters. "I have confidence. I am all confidence."

63   "You have youth, confidence, and a job," the older waiter said. "You have everything."

64   "And what do you lack?"

65   "Everything but work."

---

① count the saucers: the way the waiters keep track of the bill for each table is by giving a new saucer with each drink. Each saucer represents one drink, so to calculate the final bill they count the saucers, as we see the old man doing later in the story, and multiply the number of saucers by the price per drink.
② hombre: Spanish word, man or friend

66　　　"You have everything I have."

67　　　"No. I have never had confidence and I am not young."

68　　　"Come on. Stop talking nonsense and lock up."

69　　　"I am of those who like to stay late at the cafe," the older waiter said.

70　　　"With all those who do not want to go to bed. With all those who need a light for the night."

71　　　"I want to go home and into bed."

72　　　"We are of two different kinds," the older waiter said. He was now dressed to go home. "It is not only a question of youth and confidence although those things are very beautiful. Each night I am reluctant to close up because there may be some one who needs the cafe."

73　　　"Hombre, there are bodegas① open all night long."

74　　　"You do not understand. This is a clean and pleasant cafe. It is well lighted. The light is very good and also, now, there are shadows of the leaves."

75　　　"Good night," said the younger waiter.

76　　　"Good night," the other said. Turning off the electric light he continued the conversation with himself. It was the light of course but it is necessary that the place be clean and pleasant. You do not want music. Certainly you do not want music. Nor can you stand before a bar with dignity although that is all that is provided for these hours. What did he fear? It was not a fear or dread, it was a nothing that he knew too well. It was all a nothing and a man was a nothing too. It was only that and light was all it needed and a certain cleanness and order. Some lived in it and never felt it but he knew it all was nada y pues nada y nada y pues nada②. Our nada who art in nada③, nada be thy name thy kingdom nada thy will be nada in nada as it is in nada. Give us this nada our daily nada and nada us our nada as we nada our nadas and nada us not into nada but deliver us from nada; pues nada. Hail nothing full of nothing, nothing is with thee. He smiled and stood before a bar with a shining steam pressure coffee machine.

77　　　"What's yours?" asked the barman.

78　　　"Nada."

79　　　"Otro loco mas④," said the barman and turned away.

80　　　"A little cup," said the waiter.

81　　　The barman poured it for him.

82　　　"The light is very bright and pleasant but the bar is unpolished," the waiter said.

83　　　The barman looked at him but did not answer. It was too late at night for conversation.

---

① bodega: A bodega is a cellar or shop selling wine and food, especially in a Spanish-speaking country.

② nada y pues nada y nada y pues nada: Literally means *nothing and then nothing and nothing and then nothing.*

③ our nada who art in nada: the beginning of the Lord's prayer with significant words replaced by "nada" or nothing. The Lord's prayer begins: "Our Father who art in Heaven, hallowed be thy name, thy kingdom come, thy will be done." After this the waiter does the same for "Hail Mary full of grace...".

④ otro loco mas: These words mean another lunatic.

84 "You want another copita①?" the barman asked.

85 "No, thank you," said the waiter and went out. He disliked bars and bodegas. A clean, well-lighted cafe was a very different thing. Now, without thinking further, he would go home to his room. He would lie in the bed and finally, with daylight, he would go to sleep. After all, he said to himself, it's probably only insomnia. Many must have it.

▶ STUDY QUESTIONS

Recalling

1. Please find out images of light and darkness in the text.
2. What kind of person is the old man?
3. What is the old waiter's attitude towards life? And the young waiters attitude?

Interpreting

4. Why does the old man attempt suicide?
5. Why does the old man love drinking in the cafe instead of at home? What is the significance of "a clean, well-lighted place" to the old man?
6. What does the old waiter's long conversation with himself suggest?
7. What is the meaning of life to the old man, the old waiter, and the young waiter?

Extending

8. What is the style of language in this story? Do you think the style of language is related with the theme of the story? If it is, how?
9. The two songs by John Lennon and Paul McCartney, "Hamlet's Soliloquy" and *A Clean, Well-lighted Place* all talk about the meaning of life. Is it hard for you to find the meaning of life? What gives meaning to your life?

▶ LITERARY FOCUS

Existentialism and Hemingway

  Existentialism is a twentieth-century philosophy arguing that ethical human beings are in a sense cursed with absolute free will in a purposeless universe. Therefore, individuals must fashion their own sense of meaning in life instead of relying thoughtlessly on religious, political, and social conventions. These merely provide a facade of meaning according to existential philosophy. Those who rely on such conventions without thinking through them deny their own ethical responsibilities. The basic principles of existentialism are (1) a concern with man's essential being and nature, (2) an idea that existential "angst" or "anguish" is the common lot of all thinking humans who see the essential meaninglessness of transitory human life, (3) the belief that thought and logic are insufficient to cope with existence, and (4) the conviction that a true sense of morality can only come from honestly facing the dilemma of existential freedom and participating in life actively and positively. The ethical idea is that, if the universe is essentially meaningless, and human existence does not matter in the long run,

---

① copita: A copita can mean a glass of brandy. It also can be translated as "a little cup".

then the only thing that can provide a moral backdrop is humanity itself, and neglecting to do this is neglecting our duty to ourselves and to each other.

Existentialism is a major component of Hemingway's fiction. We see the focus on the strength and perseverance of the individual, the underlying theme that we create ourselves, existence before essence. It's the responsibility of Hemingway's characters to create their essence, to make their choices, to realize that if the world is meaningless, if it doesn't mean anything to be good or bad, if there are no heavenly rewards, if all is permitted, you can curl up (usually in a drunken stupor) and do nothing, let Nature take it's obvious course, let yourself succumb to your biological trap, or you can act as if something does have meaning and create a type of moral code. Many of Hemingway's so-called heroes attempt to create such a code, one which must be practiced and upheld with intense self-discipline, the legendary "grace under pressure".

▶ THINKING ABOUT EXISTENTIALISM IN *A CLEAN, WELL-LIGHTED PLACE*

How does the story *A Clean, Well-lighted Place* reflect Hemingway's existentialist idea? What is the old man's code of living? Do you like the existentialist ideas? Why or why not?

VIII. *A Hunger Artist* by Franz Kafka

▶ ABOUT THE AUTHOR

Franz Kafka (1883–1924), an Austrian writer whose stories, such as *The Metamorphosis*, and novels, including *The Trial* and *The Castle*, concern troubled individuals in a nightmarishly impersonal world—a major theme of Existentialism and reality.

Kafka was born into a Jewish middle-class family in Prague, Bohemia (now in the Czech Republic), on July 3, 1883. Kafka was the object of scorn because of his religion, ethnicity, and position and led a very unhappy childhood. He earned a degree in law and worked as a bureaucrat for 14 years, a position he absolutely loathed. Dogged by poor health, Kafka died of tuberculosis at the age of 41.

The following things said by Kafka may best summarize his works: "I think we ought to read only the kind of books that wound and stab us...We need the kind of books that affect us like a disaster, that grieve us deeply, like the death of someone we loved more than ourselves, like being banished into forests far from everyone, like a suicide. A book must be the axe for the frozen sea inside us."

A Hunger Artist

Translated by Ian Johnston of Malaspina University-College, Nanaimo, BC

1   In the last decades interest in hunger artists has declined considerably. Whereas in earlier days there was good money to be earned putting on major productions of this sort under one's own management, nowadays that is totally impossible. Those were different times. Back then the hunger artist captured the attention of the entire city. From day to day while the fasting lasted, participation

increased. Everyone wanted to see the hunger artist at least once a day. During the later days there were people with subscription tickets who sat all day in front of the small barred cage①. And there were even viewing hours at night, their impact heightened by torchlight. On fine days the cage was dragged out into the open air, and then the hunger artist was put on display particularly for the children. While for grown-ups the hunger artist was often merely a joke, something they participated in because it was fashionable, the children looked on amazed, their mouths open, holding each other's hands for safety, as he sat there on scattered straw—spurning② a chair—in black tights, looking pale, with his ribs sticking out prominently, sometimes nodding politely, answering questions with a forced smile, even sticking his arm out through the bars to let people feel how emaciated③ he was, but then completely sinking back into himself, so that he paid no attention to anything, not even to what was so important to him, the striking of the clock, which was the single furnishing in the cage, but merely looking out in front of him with his eyes almost shut and now and then sipping from a tiny glass of water to moisten his lips.

2   Apart from the changing groups of spectators there were also constant observers chosen by the public—strangely enough they were usually butchers④ —who, always three at a time, were given the task of observing the hunger artist day and night, so that he didn't get anything to eat in some secret manner. It was, however, merely a formality, introduced to reassure the masses, for those who understood knew well enough that during the period of fasting the hunger artist would never, under any circumstances, have eaten the slightest thing, not even if compelled by force. The honour of his art forbade it. Naturally, none of the watchers understood that. Sometimes there were nightly groups of watchers who carried out their vigil⑤ very laxly⑥, deliberately sitting together in a distant corner and putting all their attention into playing cards there, clearly intending to allow the hunger artist a small refreshment, which, according to their way of thinking, he could get from some secret supplies. Nothing was more excruciating⑦ to the hunger artist than such watchers. They depressed him. They made his fasting terribly difficult. Sometimes he overcame his weakness and sang during the time they were observing, for as long as he could keep it up, to show people how unjust their suspicions about him were. But that was little help. For then they just wondered among themselves about his skill at being able to eat even while singing. He much preferred the observers who sat down right against the bars and, not satisfied with the dim backlighting of the room, illuminated him with electric flashlights, which the impresario⑧ made available to them. The glaring⑨ light didn't bother him in the slightest. Generally he couldn't sleep at all, and he could always doze off⑩ a little under any lighting and at any hour, even in an overcrowded, noisy auditorium. With such observers, he was very happily prepared to spend the entire night without sleeping. He was ready to joke with them, to recount stories from his nomadic⑪ life and then, in turn, to listen to their stories—

---

① barred cage: cage equipped with bars
② spurn: to reject with scorn
③ emaciated: very thin, wasted, haggard
④ butcher: a person who slaughter certain animals, or a retail or wholesale dealer in meat
⑤ vigil: watch
⑥ laxly: not strictly or severely
⑦ excruciating: extremely painful, unbearably distressing
⑧ impresario: a person who organizes or manages public entertainment
⑨ glaring: excessively bright
⑩ doze off: to sleep lightly or for a short time
⑪ nomadic: wandering around

doing everything just to keep them awake, so that he could keep showing them once again that he had nothing to eat in his cage and that he was fasting as none of them could.

3   He was happiest, however, when morning came and a lavish① breakfast was brought for them at his own expense, on which they hurled② themselves with the appetite of healthy men after a hard night's work without sleep. True, there were still people who wanted to see in this breakfast an unfair means of influencing the observers, but that was going too far, and if they were asked whether they wanted to undertake the observers' night shift for its own sake, without the breakfast, they excused themselves. But nonetheless they stood by their suspicions.

4   However, it was, in general, part of fasting that these doubts were inextricably③ associated with it. For, in fact, no one was in a position to spend time watching the hunger artist every day and night without interruption, so no one could know, on the basis of his own observation, whether this was a case of truly continuous, flawless fasting. The hunger artist himself was the only one who could know that and, at the same time, the only spectator capable of being completely satisfied with his own fasting. But the reason he was never satisfied was something different. Perhaps it was not fasting at all which made him so very emaciated that many people, to their own regret, had to stay away from his performance, because they couldn't bear to look at him. For he was also so skeletal④ out of dissatisfaction with himself, because he alone knew something that even initiates didn't know—how easy it was to fast. It was the easiest thing in the world. About this he did not remain silent, but people did not believe him. At best they thought he was being modest. Most of them, however, believed he was a publicity seeker or a total swindler⑤, for whom, at all events, fasting was easy, because he understood how to make it easy, and then still had the nerve to half admit it. He had to accept all that. Over the years he had become accustomed to it. But this dissatisfaction kept gnawing⑥ at his insides all the time and never yet—and this one had to say to his credit—had he left the cage of his own free will after any period of fasting.

5   The impresario had set the maximum length of time for the fast at forty days—he would never allow the fasting go on beyond that point, not even in the cosmopolitan⑦ cities. And, in fact, he had a good reason. Experience had shown that for about forty days one could increasingly whip up⑧ a city's interest by gradually increasing advertising, but that then the public turned away—one could demonstrate a significant decline in popularity. In this respect, there were, of course, small differences among different towns and among different countries, but as a rule it was true that forty days was the maximum length of time.

6   So then on the fortieth day the door of the cage—which was covered with flowers—was opened, an enthusiastic audience filled the amphitheatre⑨, a military band played, two doctors

① lavish: in great amount
② hurl: to throw with vigor
③ inextricably: incapable of being disconnected
④ skeletal: like a skeleton
⑤ swindler: a person who cheats
⑥ gnaw: to bite, or chew on, esp. insistently
⑦ cosmopolitan: not local, with international atmosphere
⑧ whip up: to incite, arouse, stir
⑨ amphitheatre: an oval or round building with tiers of seats around the central open area, as those used in Ancient Rome for gladiatorial contests

entered the cage, in order to take the necessary measurements of the hunger artist, the results were announced to the auditorium through a megaphone, and finally two young ladies arrived, happy about the fact that they were the ones who had just been selected by lot, and sought to lead the hunger artist down a couple of steps out of the cage, where on a small table a carefully chosen hospital meal was laid out. And at this moment the hunger artist always fought back. Of course, he still freely laid his bony arms in the helpful outstretched hands of the ladies bending over him, but he did not want to stand up. Why stop right now after forty days? He could have kept going for even longer, for an unlimited length of time. Why stop right now, when he was in his best form, indeed, not yet even in his best fasting form? Why did people want to rob him of the fame of fasting longer, not just so that he could become the greatest hunger artist of all time, which, in fact, he probably was already, but also so that he could surpass himself in some unimaginable way, for he felt there were no limits to his capacity for fasting. Why did this crowd, which pretended to admire him so much, have so little patience with him? If he kept going and kept fasting even longer, why would they not tolerate it? Then, too, he was tired and felt good sitting in the straw. Now he was supposed to stand up straight and tall and go to eat, something which, when he merely imagined it, made him feel nauseous[1] right away. With great difficulty he repressed mentioning this only out of consideration for the women. And he looked up into the eyes of these women, apparently so friendly but in reality so cruel, and shook his excessively heavy head on his feeble neck.

7　　　But then happened what always happened. The impresario came forward without a word—the music made talking impossible—raised his arms over the hunger artist, as if inviting heaven to look upon its work here on the straw, this unfortunate martyr[2], something the hunger artist certainly was, only in a completely different sense, grabbed the hunger artist around his thin waist, in the process wanting with his exaggerated caution to make people believe that here he had to deal with something fragile, and handed him over—not without secretly shaking him a little, so that the hunger artist's legs and upper body swung back and forth uncontrollably—to the women, who had in the meantime turned as pale as death. At this point, the hunger artist endured everything. His head lay on his chest—it was as if it had inexplicably rolled around and just stopped there—his body was arched back, his legs, in an impulse of self-preservation, pressed themselves together at the knees, but scraped the ground, as if they were not really on the floor but were looking for the real ground, and the entire weight of his body, admittedly very small, lay against one of the women, who appealed for help with flustered breath, for she had not imagined her post of honour would be like this, and then stretched her neck as far as possible, to keep her face from the least contact with the hunger artist, but then, when she couldn't manage this and her more fortunate companion didn't come to her assistance but trembled and remained content to hold in front of her the hunger artist's hand, that small bundle of knuckles, she broke into tears, to the delighted laughter of the auditorium, and had to be relieved by an attendant who had been standing ready for some time. Then came the meal. The impresario put a little food into the mouth of the hunger artist, now dozing as if he were fainting, and kept up a cheerful patter[3] designed to divert attention away from the hunger artist's condition. Then

---

① nauseous: sick

② martyr: a person who is put to death or great suffering because of some belief

③ patter: a rapid succession of light taps

a toast was proposed to the public, which was supposedly whispered to the impresario by the hunger artist, the orchestra confirmed everything with a great fanfare[1], people dispersed, and no one had the right to be dissatisfied with the event, no one except the hunger artist—he was always the only one.

8   He lived this way, taking small regular breaks, for many years, apparently in the spotlight, honoured by the world, but for all that, his mood was usually gloomy, and it kept growing gloomier all the time, because no one understood how to take it seriously. But how was he to find consolation? What was there left for him to wish for? And if a good-natured man who felt sorry for him ever wanted to explain to him that his sadness probably came from his fasting, then it could happen, especially at an advanced stage of the fasting, that the hunger artist responded with an outburst of rage and began to shake the cage like an animal, frightening everyone. But the impresario had a way of punishing moments like this, something he was happy to use. He would make an apology for the hunger artist to the assembled public, conceding that the irritability had been provoked only by his fasting, which well-fed people did not readily understand and which was capable of excusing the behaviour of the hunger artist. From there he would move on to speak about the equally hard to understand claim of the hunger artist that he could go on fasting for much longer than he was doing. He would praise the lofty striving, the good will, and the great self-denial no doubt contained in this claim, but then would try to contradict it simply by producing photographs, which were also on sale, for in the pictures one could see the hunger artist on the fortieth day of his fast, in bed, almost dead from exhaustion. Although the hunger artist was very familiar with this perversion[2] of the truth, it always strained his nerves again and was too much for him. What was a result of the premature ending of the fast people were now proposing as its cause! It was impossible to fight against this lack of understanding, against this world of misunderstanding. In good faith he always still listened eagerly to the impresario at the bars of his cage, but each time, once the photographs came out, he would let go of the bars and, with a sigh, sink back into the straw, and a reassured public could come up again and view him.

9   When those who had witnessed such scenes thought back on them a few years later, often they were unable to understand themselves. For in the meantime that change mentioned above had set it. It happened almost immediately. There may have been more profound reasons for it, but who bothered to discover what they were? At any rate, one day the pampered[3] hunger artist saw himself abandoned by the crowd of pleasure seekers, who preferred to stream to other attractions. The impresario chased around half of Europe one more time with him, to see whether he could still re-discover the old interest here and there. It was all futile. It was as if a secret agreement against the fasting performances had really developed everywhere. Naturally, the truth is that it could not have happened so quickly, and people later remembered some things which in the days of intoxicating[4] success they had not paid sufficient attention to, some inadequately suppressed indications, but now it was too late to do anything to counter them.

---

[1] fanfare: a fanciful or short sound played on trumpets or the like
[2] perversion: a change to abnormal
[3] pampered: spoiled
[4] intoxicating: too exciting that one is beside himself

Of course, it was certain that the popularity of fasting would return once more someday, but for those now alive that was no consolation. What was the hunger artist to do now? The man whom thousands of people had cheered on could not display himself in show booths at small fun fairs, and the hunger artist was not only too old to take up a different profession, but was fanatically devoted to fasting more than anything else. So he said farewell to the impresario, an incomparable companion on his life's road, and let himself be hired by a large circus. In order to spare his own feelings, he didn't even look at the terms of his contract at all.

10   A large circus with its huge number of men, animals, and gimmicks①, which are constantly being let go and replenished②, can use anyone at any time, even a hunger artist, provided, of course, his demands are modest. Moreover, in this particular case it was not only the hunger artist himself who was engaged, but also his old and famous name. In fact, given the characteristic nature of his art, which was not diminished by his advancing age, one could never claim that a worn-out artist, who no longer stood at the pinnacle of his ability, wanted to escape to a quiet position in the circus. On the contrary, the hunger artist declared that he could fast just as well as in earlier times—something that was entirely credible. Indeed, he even affirmed that if people would let him do what he wanted—and he was promised this without further ado③—he would really now legitimately amaze the world for the first time, an assertion which, however, given the mood of the time, something the hunger artist in his enthusiasm easily overlooked, only brought smiles from the experts.

11   However, basically the hunger artist had also not forgotten his sense of the way things really were, and he took it as self-evident that people would not set him and his cage up as some star attraction in the middle of the arena, but would move him outside in some other readily accessible spot near the animal stalls. Huge brightly painted signs surrounded the cage and announced what there was to look at there. During the intervals in the main performance, when the general public pushed out towards the menagerie④ in order to see the animals, they could hardly avoid moving past the hunger artist and stopping there a moment. They would perhaps have remained with him longer, if those pushing up behind them in the narrow passageway, who did not understand this pause on the way to the animal stalls they wanted to see, had not made a longer peaceful observation impossible. This was also the reason why the hunger artist began to tremble before these visiting hours, which he naturally used to long for as the main purpose of his life. In the early days he could hardly wait for the pauses in the performances. He had looked forward with delight to the crowd pouring around him, until he became convinced only too quickly—and even the most stubborn, almost deliberate self-deception could not hold out against the experience—that, judging by their intentions, most of these people were, time and again without exception, only visiting the menagerie. And this view from a distance still remained his most beautiful moment. For when they had come right up to him, he immediately got an earful from the shouting and cursing of the two steadily increasing groups, the ones who wanted to take their time looking at the hunger artist, not with any understanding but on a whim

---

① gimmick: a clever device used to trick the audience or to gain their attention
② replenished: refilled or renewed
③ ado: fuss, confusion
④ menagerie: a collection of wild or unusual animals, esp. for exhibition

or from mere defiance—for him these ones were soon the more painful—and a second group of people whose only demand was to go straight to the animal stalls.

12   Once the large crowds had passed, the late-comers would arrive, and although there was nothing preventing these people any more from sticking around for as long as they wanted, they rushed past with long strides, almost without a sideways glance, to get to the animals in time. And it was an all-too-rare stroke of luck when the father of a family came by with his children, pointed his finger at the hunger artist, gave a detailed explanation about what was going on here, and talked of earlier years, when he had been present at similar but incomparably more magnificent performances, and then the children, because they had been inadequately prepared at school and in life, always stood around still uncomprehendingly. What was fasting to them? But nonetheless the brightness of the look in their searching eyes revealed something of new and more gracious times coming. Perhaps, the hunger artist said to himself sometimes, everything would be a little better if his location were not quite so near the animal stalls. That way it would be easy for people to make their choice, to say nothing of the fact that he was very upset and constantly depressed by the stink from the stalls, the animals' commotion at night, the pieces of raw meat dragged past him for the carnivorous[①] beasts, and the roars at feeding time. But he did not dare to approach the administration about it. In any case, he had the animals to thank for the crowds of visitors among whom, now and then, there could also be one destined for him. And who knew where they would hide him if he wished to remind them of his existence and, along with that, of the fact that, strictly speaking, he was only an obstacle on the way to the menagerie.

13   A small obstacle, at any rate, a constantly diminishing obstacle. People became accustomed to thinking it strange that in these times they would want to pay attention to a hunger artist, and with this habitual awareness the judgment on him was pronounced. He might fast as well as he could—and he did—but nothing could save him any more. People went straight past him. Try to explain the art of fasting to anyone! If someone doesn't feel it, then he cannot be made to understand it. The beautiful signs became dirty and illegible[②]. People tore them down, and no one thought of replacing them. The small table with the number of days the fasting had lasted, which early on had been carefully renewed every day, remained unchanged for a long time, for after the first weeks the staff grew tired of even this small task. And so the hunger artist kept fasting on and on, as he once had dreamed about in earlier times, and he had no difficulty at all managing to achieve what he had predicted back then, but no one was counting the days—no one, not even the hunger artist himself, knew how great his achievement was by this point, and his heart grew heavy. And when once in a while a person strolling past stood there making fun of the old number and talking of a swindle, that was in a sense the stupidest lie which indifference and innate[③] maliciousness could invent, for the hunger artist was not being deceptive—he was working honestly—but the world was cheating him of his reward.

14   Many days went by once more, and this, too, came to an end. Finally the cage caught the attention of a supervisor, and he asked the attendant why they had left this perfectly useful cage

---

① carnivorous: flesh-eating
② illegible: hard to read
③ innate: existing in one from birth

standing here unused with rotting straw inside. Nobody knew, until one man, with the help of the table with the number on it, remembered the hunger artist. They pushed the straw around with poles and found the hunger artist in there. "Are you still fasting?" the supervisor asked. "When are you finally going to stop?" "Forgive me everything," whispered the hunger artist. Only the supervisor, who was pressing his ear up against the cage, understood him. "Certainly," said the supervisor, tapping his forehead with his finger in order to indicate to the staff the state the hunger artist was in, "we forgive you." "I always wanted you to admire my fasting," said the hunger artist. "But we do admire it," said the supervisor obligingly. "But you shouldn't admire it," said the hunger artist. "Well then, we don't admire it," said the supervisor, "but why shouldn't we admire it?" "Because I had to fast. I can't do anything else," said the hunger artist. "Just look at you," said the supervisor, "why can't you do anything else?" "Because," said the hunger artist, lifting his head a little and, with his lips pursed as if for a kiss, speaking right into the supervisor's ear so that he wouldn't miss anything, "because I couldn't find a food which tasted good to me. If had found that, believe me, I would not have made a spectacle of myself and would have eaten to my heart's content, like you and everyone else." Those were his last words, but in his failing eyes there was still the firm, if no longer proud, conviction that he was continuing to fast.

15   "All right, tidy this up now," said the supervisor. And they buried the hunger artist along with the straw. But in his cage they put a young panther. Even for a person with the dullest mind it was clearly refreshing to see this wild animal prowling^① around in this cage, which had been dreary for such a long time. It lacked nothing. Without thinking about it for any length of time, the guards brought the animal food whose taste it enjoyed. It never seemed once to miss its freedom. This noble body, equipped with everything necessary, almost to the point of bursting, even appeared to carry freedom around with it. That seem to be located somewhere or other in its teeth, and its joy in living came with such strong passion from its throat that it was not easy for spectators to keep watching. But they controlled themselves, kept pressing around the cage, and had no desire at all to move on.

> ## ▶▶ STUDY QUESTIONS

 ### Recalling

1. How does the hunger artist look like?
2. How does the audience look at the fasting of the hunger artist?
3. Is the fasting in later years different from the earlier ones? If so, in what way?

B ▷ Interpreting

4. Why does the impresario set the days of fasting to about forty days?
5. Why is the hunger artist not satisfied with his fasting?
6. What is the meaning of fasting to the audience? What is the meaning of fasting to the artist?
7. What does the contrast between the young panther and the hunger artist suggest?

---

① prowl: to go around stealthily, as in search of prey

Extending

8. Does the story sound absurd to you? Why or why not?

9. What does Franz Kafka want to express through the story?

IX. *Rice* by Mary Loh Chieu Kwuan

▶ ABOUT THE AUTHOR

Mary Loh Chieu Kwuan (1959–) obtained her master's degree in literature from the National University of Singapore (NUS). In 1989, she collaborated with two other local Singapore writers, Desmond Sim and Ovidia Yu, to produce the anthology *Mistress and Other Creative Take-Offs* and in the same year won the Shell Short Play Competition. Her play *Fast Cars and Fancy Women* was first staged by Theatre Works in 1991. Currently, she works as an arts' marketing consultant and occasionally conducts writing workshops for young people.

Rice

1   Fluffy[①] white flakes in a porcelain bowl. Steam rises and with it, the particular fragrance. Like a kind of incense, it wafts[②] and weaves so many, many memories.

2   "Rice is served...Come and eat," Ma calls to no one in particular. With the regularity of clockwork, dinner at our house is always served at 7:30 p.m., and we are gathered at the table for dinner. The meal is eaten in reverent[③] silence, slowly and with meaningful silence. The plates are emptied and quietly we collect the dishes for washing. This gradually changed, bit by bit as each of us grew busy with work that kept us back at the office. But this I long remember of a family ritual; we've always had rice for dinner. Rice was served even when we had turkey at Christmas. Pa would always have his ubiquitous[④] bowl of rice and Ma would always serve it.

3   Ma taught me how to cook rice at the age of ten.

4   "Okay, one milk tin full for four people. Empty the tin of rice into this pot. Now, pick out all the sand and unhusked[⑤] rice and if you see any little black crawling weevils[⑥], pick them out and squeeze them to kill them.

5   "Now fill the pot with water. You put both hands in the pot and rub the grains of rice gently between your hands. Now pour out the water and be careful that not a single grain of rice spills with the water. Rice is precious, remember that.

6   "Fill your pot once again and rinse the rice one more time. This time the water should be almost clear.

7   "Put your hand there, flat on the top of the rice—now fill the water up to the level of the knuckle of your finger. Too much water and you'll be eating porridge. Too little, you'll be eating uncooked grains which taste like sand.

---

① fluffy: light or airy
② waft: to carry lightly or smoothly through the air
③ reverent: deeply respectful
④ ubiquitous: existing or being everywhere
⑤ unhusked: not removed from the cover
⑥ weevil: a kind of rice worm

8   "Let the rice boil for five minutes. Stir and lower the flame.

9   "Stir to make sure that the rice does not stick to the bottom of the pot. Cover and let it cook over a slow flame until the water dries up. Turn off the fire. The rice is now ready to be served..."

10   Thereafter twice a week, until I went to university, I had the duty of cooking rice for the family.

11   "Ma, please come home..."

12   "I c...can't...I d...don't want to..."

13   We stood in the middle of the road in the pouring rain, tears streaming down our faces. The cars roared past us and before us, their headlights blinding us. There had been a big fight at home, over what I forget now, but Pa had said something, something about duty and responsibility. Ma answered back. Pa raised his voice. Soon there was shouting and more shouting. A plate was thrown, the crashing resounding through the house. More crashing sounds, more shouting. We covered our ears, trying in vain to block out the noise and confusion. Even then, I heard Pa say, "Go. See if I care—the clothes you wear, the roof over your head and the food you eat, everything you have you owe to me and you bloody well dare to answer back..."

14   Suddenly, there was a silence.

15   Ma ran out of the house into the rainy night.

16   "Come home, please, Ma...please, Ma."

17   "Go home, you go home. Your Ma wants to die here."

18   "Please, Ma, I don't want you to die."

19   "Go home. The others have to eat. Go home and serve your Pa his rice."

20   "No, Ma, I won't go home...I won't go home without you..."

21   "Go home, I tell you, go home and serve your Pa his rice."

22   We stood there for the longest time, the cars hooting us to warn us from standing too close to the edge of the pavement. I did not dare to let go of her hand. My hands hurt from holding her hand so tightly. Slowly, bit by bit, I could feel the slack, the tension easing. Both of us sobbed in silence. Ma's shoulders drooped and slowly I was allowed to lead her home. We left the main road and slowly made our way through the quiet suburban lanes, the winding alleys and finally reached home.

23   Pa sat stone-faced before the television, his face grim, his lips set in a straight line. He refused to say a word. I led Ma into her bedroom, closed the door and went into the kitchen. Lifting up the cover of the pot, I spooned the thick white flakes into Pa's bowl and set the bowl on the table.

24   "Pa, time to eat."

25   Silence.

26   "Pa, eat rice."

27   "Don't want to eat."

28   The bowl of rice sat on the end of the table, getting colder and colder.

29   After that, without fail, day after day, for as many days as there were in a year, Ma would place a steaming hot bowl of rice before Pa. Even if she had to go out for her mahjong games in the afternoon, she would return in time to serve the bowl of rice. If she was going out in the evening, she would wait till Pa had finished his bowl of rice and had laid aside his chopsticks. Only then would she pick up her bag and leave on her occasional outings.

30   I hate eating white rice. White rice is bland① and boring. It has to be made more interesting

---

① bland: not highly flavored, mild, tasteless

with a variety of other dishes. One hardly eats rice on its own, to savour[1] its full-bodied flavour, simply because it has none. It is a staple[2], a stomach filler, little else. I make concessions for brown rice, which I eat sparingly, more as a health lad rather than as real food. I am, my Ma says, "western-educated" and prefer hong-mo sek. Pasta is a definite favourite, all kinds of it, from capellini[3] to lettucine[4] to lasagna[5], smothered with thick creamy sauces, and yes, I love cheese—the Bleus with their coloured blue green ridges and sharp-smelling Bries which turn Ma green with disgust. Parmesan toasts had me turned out of the house because no one could bear the smell of the cheese I was eating—which is a continual joke to my neighbours who see me sitting in the garden in the evenings, chewing on foul-smelling toasted bread. Of course, I like breads, French, Danish, Manoucher deli-style sandwiches with pickles[6] and relishes[7], sandwiches which are so large that two hands are required to grip the bread together while large mouthfuls are chewed vigorously and then swallowed. Yes, don't forget salads. I am the resident rabbit in the office—please pass the greens over. Healthy crunchy[8] lettuces with loads of lovely dressings make my day. But rice ... I cannot take rice two meals in a row. I'd rather go hungry.

31   I remember that Ma was very particular that we never wasted any rice. Not a single grain was to be left on the plate or else, every single grain left would appear as ugly marks on the face of our eventual intended[9]. Certainly not wanting to marry any man with a scarred or marred complexion, we faithfully cleaned out plates and through our dating years, every close encounter with men with chronic acne resulted in real guilt that perhaps, just perhaps, this might be retribution[10] for that one plate of rice we had not finished.

32   When I went to University and did Philosophy, the logic of this underwent severe examination. Did some, say, scientists in China, gather up two separate groups of women as a test case for this hypothesis? Did they force one group to finish their plates of rice clean? And the other, not? Did they then observe and track the progress of both groups through life till marriage and deduce conclusively, based upon empirical findings, that girls who did not finish their rice would marry pock-marked husbands? Why did this rule never apply to men? Or did it?

33   I hate that bowl of rice. I hate what that bowl of rice means.

34   I remember my grandmother's favourite rice-bowl, the one from which each noonday and each evening she would lift to her face and shovel the white rice into her open mouth. It was a creamy white bowl with a swirl of blue outside. It was grandmother's special rice-bowl, one with which she associated fond memories, memories which she did not share with any of us. I remember gingerly[11] handling it when we held it over the basin of soapy water. My older sister would carefully rinse it, wipe it dry and put it into the great wooden cupboard, only to take it out again, at the next mealtime, to scoop the soft white grains gently into the bowl.

35   It was an accident! We didn't mean for it to break, Grandmother's precious bowl. It was

① savour: to taste
② staple: a basic, necessary item of food
③ capellini: pasta in very long, fine strand
④ lettucine: a kind of pasta
⑤ lasagna: large, flat, rectangular strips of pasta
⑥ pickles: vegetables preserved with salt or vinegar
⑦ relish: something flavored or appetizing added to a meal
⑧ crunchy: to bite or chew with a cracking sound
⑨ eventual intended: future husband
⑩ retribution: punishment for wrongdoings
⑪ gingerly: with great caution

an accident, the bowl slipped. We clutched desperately, our fingers barely missing the rim and finding only empty air. The silence in the kitchen reverberated with the crash as the bowl shattered into a thousand pieces. We looked shamefaced at each other, before Grandmother came bursting in.

36   We left the house that day, Pa, Ma, my sisters and my brother. In silence, we gathered up our belongings and stepped through the old gate of the family home without a backward glance. I remember the last word my grandmother said, a word which I had heard her mutter under breath for so long: fan-thong.

37   In Cantonese, a fan-thong or vessel for rice is used as an epithet[①]. It implies that a person is of no more use than a receptacle of rice, that all the rice that has been consumed is wasted and therefore such a person is useless.

38   We never saw my grandmother after that, not even when she passed away.

39   So I married Brian Worth, an Englishman whose idea of great cuisine[②] was bangers[③] and beans and whose face was as smooth as a baby's bottom, though he swore he had chronic acne during his teenage years. Aside from his wit, his love for the same kind of music and writers drew us closer, making us more than good friends. When he proposed, I thought, what a relief, I can handle bangers and beans and the occasional steak and potatoes. Heck, I could even do a turkey at Christmas, complete with cranberry sauce and pudding. I won't have to serve his rice every day, seven days a week, every week of the year.

40   There was rice sprinkled[④] at our wedding, instead of confetti[⑤]. As we ran down the aisle, the rice was scattered like rain. Afterwards, like monkeys, Brian and I picked the rice from each other's hair. The sprinkling of rice was symbolic of fertility, just as in Singapore they had forced us to drive around with a pair of chickens, one male and one female. In the heat, one poor chicken expired[⑥], leaving the other one alone to weather[⑦] the storms of marital pomp[⑧] and ceremony. This, I hoped, was not a bad omen.

41   "You are marrying a *kwei-lo*[⑨]! Why do you want to bring more *chap-cheng kia*[⑩] into the world?" Pa snorted in disgust.

42   "Pa, Brian is not a kwei-lo. Brian is Brian. I'm not marrying a race. I'm marrying a man."

43   "I tell you, they are all the same. Your Pa has seen how they always behave, so smelly and dirty, always getting drunk. You think they are getting serious with you. So many Chinese girls have been fooled. They are all alike, these kwei-los. All the same.

44   "And I tell you, your Pa drives the school bus around for so many years, I know the chap-cheng kia are the worst. All like monkeys, climbing here and there and always fighting. They never respect their parents. Your children will be exactly the same."

45   "Pa, I think you're wrong. Brian respects you and he respects Ma. Look, he is always

---

① epithet: a word or phrase used to show contempt or abuse
② cuisine: cooking
③ banger: a kind of sausage
④ sprinkle: to scatter in drops
⑤ confetti: some piece of paper, usu. colored, thrown from a height to enhance the gaiety of a festive event
⑥ expire: to die
⑦ weather: to bear
⑧ pomp: splendid display
⑨ kwei-lo: Cantonese, meaning foreigner
⑩ chap-cheny kia: Cantonese, meaniny hybrid

helpful and kind to Ma. He is not a tourist or a sailor and even if he were, not all sailors or tourists are the same.

46　　"Pa, he cares about me. You dislike him because of the colour of his skin but Pa, underneath we are all the same. I am marrying a man and not a race. He loves me and he will look after me and he doesn't treat me as if I was an inferior. Nothing you say will change my mind about marrying him."

47　　"Do what you like. Your Pa has nothing more to say. I am an old man. I have eaten more salt than you have eaten rice. You wait and see..."

48　　Fan-thong. My father called me fan-thong and said he regretted the day I was born.

49　　Italy was wonderful. We dined on sunkissed green terraces, on the best pastas, cheeses and wines. Along old cobbled streets, we wandered, the strong smell of spiced breads baking. We picnicked in the old squares, the misty spray from the ancient fountains rising up to refresh us. As the sun went down on the city, we sat on open rooftops and drank wine from each other's lips.

50　　"Darling...?" I murmured into his ear.

51　　"Hmmm...what?" His strong suntanned arms snaked around me. The dull light of a dying day filtered through the drawn curtains, casting dim shadows around the bedroom of our new flat.

52　　"What would you like for our first meal home?"

53　　"I'd like you for dinner." His teeth sank playfully into my shoulder.

54　　"Ouch, stop it, Brian, that's ticklish① ...Stop, don't bite!" I squealed in protest. "Stop, I'm serious ..."

55　　He sobered② and looked into my eyes. "Well, after that long flight and that nap, I am hungry..." He paused. "Actually, darling, I miss your mum's cooking. It would really be nice if you learnt to cook like she did. Do you think you could rustle up③ one or two Chinese dishes...and a bowl of rice? Please?"

▶▶ STUDY QUESTIONS

A▷ Recalling

1. In paragraph 1 the writer describes the steam from rice as "incense" and in paragraph 2 eating rice is described as a "family ritual". What is the significance of the word choice here?

2. From paragraph 3 to 10, Mary Loh Chieu Kwuan goes at great length to elaborate on what the ceremony of eating is like and how rice-cooking is taught by her mother. What is the significance of the detailed description?

3. What might be the cause of the quarrel between mother and father? What does the quarrel tell us about the mother? Has she gained any power after the quarrel?

4. On what basis does the father reject the speaker's marriage with a foreigner? What does that tell of the father?

B▷ Interpreting

5. Why is the grandmother so angry after the speaker and her sister have broken the rice bowl? What

___

① ticklish: to be sensitive to tickle
② sober: to get serious
③ rustle up: to prepare

is the significance of that?

6. What is the significance of sprinkling rice at the wedding ceremony?

7. Please compare the speaker, the mother and the grandmother. Do they have the same fate as women? Do they have the same attitude towards their fate?

8. What does the ending of the story suggest?

9. What is the story about?

C ▷ *Extending*

10. Does this story sound similar with the story of your grandma, or your mother, your sister? Or do you have a different story to tell?

▶ LITERARY FOCUS

▷ *Symbol*

Symbols are a part of our everyday lives. The dragon is a symbol of China; the eagle is a symbol of America; the skull and crossbones on a bottle is a symbol of poison; and the dove is a symbol of peace. The literary symbol shares something similar. Generally speaking, a symbol is a sign which suggests more than its literal meaning. A symbol is an image but an image is not necessarily a symbol.

Literary symbols are of two broad types: the conventional ones and the occasionally-coined ones. Certain symbols occur again and again in literature, thus becoming conventional and possessing almost settled symbolic meanings. For instance, roses symbolize love; spring symbolizes life, and the winter death; a journey on the road often symbolizes the journey through life. These conventional symbols are easy to recognize and identify. However, in order to convey particular meanings, writers often create their own symbols in their writing. This type of symbols acquires its suggestiveness not only from qualities inherent in itself but also from the way in which it is used in a given work or context.

▶ THINKING ABOUT SYMBOL

What does "rice" symbolize in the story? Does "rice" have the same symbolic meaning in every culture? Does "rice" have a special symbolic meaning for you or your family?

X. *Luck* by Mark Twain

▶ ABOUT THE AUTHOR

Samuel Langhorne Clemens (1835–1910), better known by his pen name **Mark Twain**, was an American author and humorist. He wrote *The Adventures of Tom Sawyer* (1876) and its sequel, *Adventures of Huckleberry Finn* (1885), the latter often called "the Great American Novel". He was lauded as the "greatest American humorist of his age", and William Faulkner called Twain "the father of American literature".

Luck

[NOTE.—This is not a fancy sketch. I got it from a clergyman who was an instructor at Woolwich forty years ago, and who vouched for its truth.—M.T.]

1   It was at a banquet in London in honour of one of the two or three conspicuously illustrious[1] English military names of this generation. For reasons which will presently appear, I will withhold his real name and titles, and call him Lieutenant-General Lord Arthur Scoresby, V.C., K.C.B., etc., etc., etc. What a fascination there is in a renowned name! There sat the man, in actual flesh, whom I had heard of so many thousands of times since that day, thirty years before, when his name shot suddenly to the zenith from a Crimean[2] battle-field, to remain for ever celebrated. It was food and drink to me to look, and look, and look at that demigod; scanning, searching, noting: the quietness, the reserve, the noble gravity of his countenance; the simple honesty that expressed itself all over him; the sweet unconsciousness of his greatness—unconsciousness of the hundreds of admiring eyes fastened upon him, unconsciousness of the deep, loving, sincere worship welling out of the breasts of those people and flowing toward him.

2   The clergyman at my left was an old acquaintance of mine—clergyman now, but had spent the first half of his life in the camp and field, and as an instructor in the military school at Woolwich. Just at the moment I have been talking about, a veiled and singular light glimmered in his eyes, and he leaned down and muttered confidentially[3] to me—indicating the hero of the banquet with a gesture, — "Privately—his glory is an accident—just a product of incredible luck."

3   This verdict was a great surprise to me. If its subject had been Napoleon, or Socrates, or Solomon, my astonishment could not have been greater.

4   Some days later came the explanation of this strange remark, and this is what the Reverend[4] told me.

5   About forty years ago I was an instructor in the military academy at Woolwich. I was present in one of the sections when young Scoresby underwent his preliminary examination. I was touched to the quick with pity; for the rest of the class answered up brightly and handsomely, while he—why, dear me, he didn't know anything, so to speak. He was evidently good, and sweet, and lovable, and guileless[5] ; and so it was exceedingly painful to see him stand there, as serene as a graven image, and deliver himself of answers which were veritably[6] miraculous for stupidity and ignorance. All the compassion in me was aroused on his behalf. I said to myself, when he comes to be examined again, he will be flung over[7] , of course; so it will be simple a harmless act of charity to ease his fall as much as I can.

6   I took him aside, and found that he knew a little of Caesar's history; and as he didn't know anything else, I went to work and drilled[8] him like a galley-slave[9] on a certain line of stock

---

[1] illustrious: highly distinguished, renown
[2] Crimean: a peninsula in southeast Ukraine
[3] confidential: spoken, written or acted on, etc, in strict privacy and secrecy
[4] the Reverend: used as a title of respect to the name of a member of the clergy
[5] guileless: sincere, honest
[6] veritable: very much
[7] be flung over: be cast away
[8] drill: to teach through strict discipline and repetition
[9] galley-slave: the person condemned to work at an oar on galley

questions concerning Caesar which I knew would be used. If you'll believe me, he went through with flying colours① on examination day! He went through on that purely superficial "cram", and got compliments, too, while others, who knew a thousand times more than he, got plucked②. By some strangely lucky accident—an accident not likely to happen twice in a century—he was asked no question outside of the narrow limits of his drill.

7　　It was stupefying. Well, although through his course I stood by him, with something of the sentiment which a mother feels for a crippled child; and he always saved himself—just by miracle, apparently.

8　　Now of course the thing that would expose him and kill him at last was mathematics. I resolved to make his death as easy as I could; so I drilled him and crammed③ him, and crammed him and drilled him, just on the line of questions which the examiner would be most likely to use, and then launched him on his fate. Well, sir, try to conceive of the result: to my consternation④, he took the first prize! And with it he got a perfect ovation⑤ in the way of compliments.

9　　Sleep! There was no more sleep for me for a week. My conscience tortured me day and night. What I had done I had done purely through charity, and only to ease the poor youth's fall—I never had dreamed of any such preposterous⑥ result as the thing that had happened. I felt as guilty and miserable as the creator of Frankenstein⑦. Here was a wooden-head whom I had put in the way of glittering⑧ promotions and prodigious⑨ responsibilities, and but one thing could happen: he and his responsibilities would all go to ruin together at the first opportunity.

10　　The Crimean war had just broken out. Of course there had to be a war, I said to myself: we couldn't have peace and give this donkey a chance to die before he is found out. I waited for the earthquake. It came. And it made me reel⑩ when it did come. He was actually gazetted⑪ to a captaincy in a marching regiment! Better men grow old and gray in the service before they climb to a sublimity like that. And who could ever have foreseen that they would go and put such a load of responsibility on such green and inadequate shoulders? I could just barely have stood it if they had made him a cornet⑫; but a captain—think of it! I thought my hair would turn white.

11　　Consider what I did—I who so loved repose and inaction. I said to myself, I am responsible to the country for this, and I must go along with him and protect the country against him as far as I can. So I took my poor little capital that I had saved up through years of work and grinding economy, and went with a sigh and bought a cornetcy in his regiment, and away we went to the field.

---

① with flying colours: with complete success
② be plucked: be cast away
③ cram: to fill by force with more than one can easily hold
④ consternation: a sudden, alarming amazement
⑤ ovation: an enthusiastic public reception of somebody
⑥ preposterous: completely contrary to reason, absurd
⑦ Frankenstein: the person who creates a monster that can't be controlled or brings himself to ruin
⑧ glittering: brilliant
⑨ prodigious: very big
⑩ to reel: to have a sensation of whirling
⑪ to be gazetted: to be announced officially
⑫ cornet: the lowest rank of commissioned cavalry officer in the British army

12   And there—oh dear, it was awful. Blunders? why, he never did anything but blunder. But, you see, nobody was in the fellow's secret—everybody had him focused wrong, and necessarily misinterpreted his performance every time—consequently they took his idiotic blunders for inspirations of genius; they did honestly! His mildest blunders were enough to make a man in his right mind cry; and they did make me cry—and rage and rave too, privately. And the thing that kept me always in a sweat of apprehension was the fact that every fresh blunder he made increased the lustre① of his reputation! I kept saying to myself, he'll get so high that when discovery does finally come it will be like the sun falling out of the sky.

13   He went right along up, from grade to grade, over the dead bodies of his superiors, until at last, in the hottest moment of the battle of...down went our colonel, and my heart jumped into my mouth, for Scoresby was next in rank! Now for it, said I; we'll all land in Sheol② in ten minutes, sure.

14   The battle was awfully hot; the allies were steadily giving way all over the field. Our regiment occupied a position that was vital; a blunder now must be destruction. At this critical moment, what does this immortal fool do but detach the regiment from its place and order a charge over a neighbouring hill where there wasn't a suggestion of an enemy! "There you go!" I said to myself; "this is the end at last."

15   And away we did go, and were over the shoulder of the hill before the insane movement could be discovered and stopped. And what did we find? An entire and unsuspected Russian army in reserve! And what happened? We were eaten up? That is necessarily what would have happened in ninety-nine cases out of a hundred. But no; those Russians argued that no single regiment would come browsing around there at such a time. It must be the entire English army, and that the sly Russian game was detected and blocked; so they turned tail③ , and away they went, pell-mell④ , over the hill and down into the field, in wild confusion, and we after them; they themselves broke the solid Russia centre in the field, and tore through, and in no time there was the most tremendous rout you ever saw, and the defeat of the allies was turned into a sweeping and splendid victory! Marshal Canrobert looked on, dizzy with astonishment, admiration, and delight; and sent right off for Scoresby, and hugged him, and decorated him on the field in presence of all the armies!

16   And what was Scoresby's blunder that time? Merely the mistaking his right hand for his left—that was all. An order had come to him to fall back and support our right; and instead he fell forward and went over the hill to the left. But the name he won that day as a marvellous military genius filled the world with his glory, and that glory will never fade while history books last.

17   He is just as good and sweet and lovable and unpretending as a man can be, but he doesn't know enough to come in when it rains. He has been pursued, day by day and year by year, by a most phenomenal and astonishing luckiness. He has been a shining soldier in all our wars for

---

① lustre: brilliance
② Sheol: (in Hebrew theology) the place of the dead
③ to turn tail: to run away, to flee
④ pell-mell: in a confused and hurried manner

half a generation; he has littered his military life with blunders, and yet has never committed one that didn't make him a knight or a baronet or a lord or something. Look at his breast; why, he is just clothed in domestic and foreign decorations. Well, sir, every one of them is a record of some shouting stupidity or other; and, taken together, they are proof that the very best thing in all this world that can befall a man is to be born lucky.

▶▶ STUDY QUESTIONS

A> *Recalling*

1. What is Scoresby like in the eyes of the public?
2. What kind of fellow is Scoresby in the eyes of the instructor (the priest)?
3. What makes the instructor help him at the very beginning?
4. How is Scoresby saved by luck each time?
5. How does the attitude of the instructor change as Scoresby climbs in rank and fame?

B> *Interpreting*

6. What do you think Scoresby thinks of his own success?
7. In what tone does the priest narrate the story? What does the tone reveal?
8. What will the story about Scoresby told by a fellow soldier be like?
9. What does the story tell us about knowing a person? About life?

C> *Extending*

10. What role does luck play in life?
11. What kind of person does luck favor? When does luck favor a person?

▶▶ FURTHER READING

William Shakespeare, *Hamlet*
Franz Kafka, *The Metamorphosis*
Richard Wright, *The Man Who Was Almost a Man*
Toni Morrison, *The Bluest Eye*
余华,《活着》《我没有名字》

▶▶ MOVIES RECOMMENDED

Boys Don't Cry (1999), directed by Kimberly Pierce
The Joy Luck Club (1993), directed by Wayne Wang
Mean Girls (2004), directed by Mark Waters
Mulan (1998), directed by Tony Bancroft, Barry Cook

Unit Two   Spiritual Growth

I. *I Wandered Lonely as a Cloud* by William Wordsworth

▶ ABOUT THE POET

William Wordsworth (1770-1850), British poet who spent his life in the Lake District of Northern England. Along with Samuel Taylor Coleridge, he can be said to have started the English Romantic movement with their collection *Lyrical Ballads* in 1798. When many poets still wrote about ancient heroes in grandiloquent style, Wordsworth focused on nature, children, the poor, common people, and used ordinary words to express his personal feelings. His definition of poetry as "the spontaneous overflow of powerful feelings arising from emotion recollected in tranquility" was shared by a number of his followers. In 1843 he succeeded Robert Southey (1774-1843) as England's poet laureate. Wordsworth died on April 23, 1850.

I Wandered Lonely as a Cloud

1   I wandered lonely as a cloud
      That floats on high o'er vales① and hills,
      When all at once I saw a crowd,
      A host, of golden daffodils②;
5   Beside the lake, beneath the trees,
      Fluttering and dancing in the breeze.

      Continuous as the stars that shine
      And twinkle on the milky way,
      They stretched in never-ending line
10   Along the margin of a bay:
      Ten thousand saw I at a glance,
      Tossing their heads in sprightly③ dance.

      The waves beside them danced; but they
      Out-did the sparkling waves in glee④:
15   A poet could not but be gay,
      In such a jocund⑤ company:
      I gazed and gazed but little thought

---

① o'er vales: (poetic), over valleys
② daffodils: 水仙花
③ sprightly: cheerful, lively
④ glee: great delight
⑤ jocund: cheerful and full of good humor

What wealth the show to me had brought:

For oft①, when on my couch I lie
20　In vacant or in pensive② mood,
They flash upon that inward eye
Which is the bliss③ of solitude;
And then my heart with pleasure fills,
And dances with the daffodils.

▶ STUDY QUESTIONS

A > *Recalling*

1. What kind of scenery does the poet come across?
2. How do "I" feel before "I" saw the daffodils?
3. How do "I" feel when "I" saw the daffodils?
4. How does the sight of daffodils affect "me" afterwards?
5. What is the rhyming scheme of the poem?

B > *Interpreting*

6. How would you describe the influence of nature on human beings as revealed by this poem?
7. Is nature simply nature according to this poem? If it is not, what other force does it represent?

C > *Extending*

8. Read the poem aloud and pay attention to the music of the poem.
9. Please compare the poem with the following poem by Tao Yuanming (陶渊明).

饮　酒

结庐在人境，而无车马喧。
问君何能尔？心远地自偏。
采菊东篱下，悠然见南山。
山气日夕佳，飞鸟相与还。
此中有真意，欲辨已忘言。

　　What is the relationship between nature and the poet as revealed in this poem? Is the relationship the same as that revealed in poem *I Wandered Lonely as a Cloud* ? Which view of nature do you feel closer to?

▶ LITERARY FOCUS

A > *The Music of Poetry (I)*

　　The poet chooses words for sound as well as for meaning. Verbal music is one of the important

---

① oft: (poetic) often
② pensive: deeply thoughtful
③ bliss: spiritual joy

resources that enable the poet to do something more than communicating mere information. Essential elements in all music are repetition and variation. The repetition of initial consonant sounds, as in "tried and true", "safe and sound", "fish and fowl", "rime and reason", is **alliteration**. The repetition of vowel sounds, as in "mad as a hatter", "free and easy", "slapdash", is **assonance**. The repetition of final consonant sounds, as in "first and last", "odds and ends", "short and sweet", "a stroke of luck", is **consonance**. The combination of assonance and consonance is **rhyme**. Rhyme is the repetition of the accented vowel sound and all succeeding sounds. **Rhyme scheme** is the exact correspondence of rhyming sounds at the end of each line of poetry, identified by the first end rhyme represented by a lower case "a", the next variation by a "b", "c" and so on.

Stopping by Woods on a Snowy Evening

By Robert Frost

1 Whose woods these are I think I *know*. a
   His house is in the village *though*; a
   He will not see me stopping *here* b
   To watch his woods fill up with *snow*. a

5 My little horse must think it *queer* b
   To stop without a farmhouse *near* b
   Between the woods and frozen *lake* c
   The darkest evening of the *year*. b
   He gives his harness bells a *shake* c

10 To ask if there is some *mistake*. c
   The only other sound's the *sweep* d
   Of easy wind and downy *flake*. c

   The woods are lovely, dark and *deep*, d
   But I have promises to *keep*, d

15 And miles to go before I *sleep*. d
   And miles to go before I *sleep*. d

Hence, the rhyme scheme is: aaba bbcb ccdc dddd.

▶ THINKING ABOUT THE MUSIC OF POETRY

Please read the poem *I Wandered Lonely as a Cloud* again to find out the musical elements in it. What is the rhyming scheme? Is there any use of alliteration? The use of assonance? Or consonance? How do the musical elements affect the poem?

II. *Anecdote of the Jar* by Wallace Stevens

▶ ABOUT THE POET

Wallace Stevens (1879–1955) was an American Modernist poet. He was born in Reading, Pennsylvania, educated at Harvard and then New York Law School, and he spent most of his life

working as an executive for an insurance company in Hartford, Connecticut. He won the Pulitzer Prize for Poetry for his Collected Poems in 1955. More than any other modern poet, Stevens was concerned with the transformative power of the imagination. His major works include *Ideas of Order* (1935), *The Man with the Blue Guitar* (1937), *Notes Towards a Supreme Fiction* (1942), *Thirteen Ways of Looking at a Blackbird* (1917), and a collection of essays on poetry, *The Necessary Angel* (1951).

Anecdote of the Jar

1   I placed a jar in Tennessee,
    And round it was, upon a hill.
    It made the slovenly① wilderness
    Surround that hill.

5   The wilderness rose up to it,
    And sprawled② around, no longer wild.
    The jar was round upon the ground
    And tall and of a port in air.

    It took dominion③ every where.
10   The jar was gray and bare.
    It did not give of④ bird or bush,
    Like nothing else in Tennessee.

▶▶ STUDY QUESTIONS

A▷ Recalling

1. What is the wilderness like before the jar is placed on the hill?
2. What change does the jar bring to the hill?
3. What is the jar like?

B▷ Interpreting

4. What magic power does the jar possess?
5. Where does the magic power come from?
6. What is the symbolic meaning of the jar?

C▷ Extending

7. What is your feeling with a piece of art (painting, music, sculpture, architecture, etc.)? Please describe that feeling. Can you write a poem to convey that feeling?
8. Please compare this poem with *I Wandered Lonely as a Cloud*. What does each poem pay tribute to?

---

① slovenly: untidy, unclean
② sprawl: to spread out, extend
③ dominion: governing or controlling
④ give of: to produce

III. *Incident* by Countee Cullen

ABOUT THE POET

Countee Cullen (1903–1946), American poet, novelist, playwright, and educator. Cullen was one of the best-known black poets of the first half of the 20th century and an important figure in the Harlem Renaissance. He wrote lyric poetry about the black American experience but avoided stereotyping his characters. Cullen published several volumes of poetry including *Color* (1925) and *Copper Sun* (1927).

Incident

1   Once riding in old Baltimore①,
     Heart–filled, head-filled with glee,
     I saw a Baltimorean
     Keep looking straight at me.

5   Now I was eight and very small,
     And he was no whit② bigger,
     And so I smiled, but he poked out③
     His tongue, and called me, "Nigger④."

     I saw the whole of Baltimore
10   From May until December;
     Of all the things that happened there
     That's all that I remember.

▶ STUDY QUESTIONS

A> *Recalling*

1. How did the little boy feel at first?
2. What happened to him then?

B> *Interpreting*

3. What is the effect of the incident on the boy?
4. What would be a black reader's response to this poem?
5. What would be a white reader's response to this poem?
6. How do you feel after reading the poem?

---

① Baltimore: a city of northern Maryland in the US
② no whit: not a bit
③ poke out: to stretch out
④ nigger: an extremely offensive way to call black people

C > *Extending*

7. In your growing-up process is there any incident that suddenly wakens you up to the realization of something? If there is, in what way has the incident affected you?

IV. *When I Was One-and-Twenty* by A . E. Housman

▶ ABOUT THE POET

Alfred Edward Housman (1859–1936), usually known as A. E. Housman, was an English classical scholar and poet, best known to the general public for his cycle of poems *A Shropshire Lad*. Lyrical and almost epigrammatic in form, the poems' wistful evocation of doomed youth in the English countryside, in spare language and distinctive imagery, appealed strongly to late Victorian and Edwardian taste, and to many early 20th-century English composers (beginning with Arthur Somervell) both before and after the First World War. Housman was counted one of the foremost classicists of his age, and has been ranked as one of the greatest scholars of all time.

When I Was One-and-Twenty

1   When I was one-and-twenty
    I heard a wise man say,
    "Give crowns and pounds and guineas①
    But not your heart away;
5   Give pearls away and rubies②
    But keep your fancy free."
    But I was one-and-twenty,
    No use to talk to me.

    When I was one-and-twenty
10   I heard him say again,
    "The heart out of the bosom
    Was never given in vain;
    'Tis paid with sighs a plenty
    And sold for endless rue③."
15   And I am two-and-twenty,
    And oh, 'tis true, 'tis true.

---

① guinea: a gold coin issued by Great Britain from 1663–1813
② ruby: 红宝石
③ rue: sorrow, regret

▶ STUDY QUESTIONS

A ▷ Recalling

1. What does "give your heart away" mean?
2. What does "keep your fancy free" mean?

B ▷ Interpreting

3. What is the expense of giving away the heart?
4. What do you think makes "I" admit at two-and-twenty that "'tis true, 'tis true"?
5. What do you think is the theme of the poem?
6. This poem was set to music by some composer. Find out what is musical about the poem.

C ▷ Extending

7. Think about the life you have lived. Is there anything or event in the past you can understand better now or wish you had undone it?
8. What is wisdom? How is wisdom gained?

V. *Araby* by James Joyce

▶ ABOUT THE AUTHOR

James Joyce (1882–1941), Irish author, whose writings feature revolutionary innovations in prose techniques. He was one of the foremost literary figures of the 20th century. Joyce is best known for his epic novel *Ulysses* (1922), which uses stream of consciousness, a literary technique that attempts to portray the natural and sometimes irrational flow of thoughts and sensations in a person's mind. Among his other important works, there are *Finnegans Wake* (1939), *Dubliners* (1914), *Portrait of the Artist as a Young Man* (1916).

Araby

1   North Richmond Street, being blind, was a quiet street except at the hour when the Christian Brothers' School set the boys free. An uninhabited house of two storeys stood at the blind end, detached from its neighbours in a square ground. The other houses of the street, conscious of decent lives within them, gazed at one another with brown imperturbable[①] faces.

2   The former tenant of our house, a priest, had died in the back drawing-room. Air, musty from having been long enclosed, hung in all the rooms, and the waste room behind the kitchen was littered with old useless papers. Among these I found a few paper-covered books, the pages

---

① imperturbable: not easily excited, calm

of which were curled and damp: *The Abbot*[①], by Walter Scott, *The Devout Communicant*[②], and *The Memoirs of Vidocq*[③].I liked the last best because its leaves were yellow. The wild garden behind the house contained a central apple-tree and a few straggling[④] bushes, under one of which I found the late tenant's rusty bicycle-pump. He had been a very charitable priest; in his will he had left all his money to institutions and the furniture of his house to his sister.

3   When the short days of winter came, dusk fell before we had well eaten our dinners. When we met in the street the houses had grown sombre. The space of sky above us was the colour of ever-changing violet and towards it the lamps of the street lifted their feeble lanterns. The cold air stung us and we played till our bodies glowed. Our shouts echoed in the silent street. The career of our play brought us through the dark muddy lanes behind the houses, where we ran the gauntlet of the rough tribes from the cottages[⑤], to the back doors of the dark dripping gardens where odours arose from the ashpits, to the dark odorous stables where a coachman smoothed and combed the horse or shook music from the buckled harness. When we returned to the street, light from the kitchen windows had filled the areas. If my uncle was seen turning the corner, we hid in the shadow until we had seen him safely housed. Or if Mangan's sister came out on the doorstep to call her brother in to his tea, we watched her from our shadow peer up and down the street. We waited to see whether she would remain or go in and, if she remained, we left our shadow and walked up to Mangan's steps resignedly[⑥]. She was waiting for us, her figure defined by the light from the half-opened door. Her brother always teased her before he obeyed, and I stood by the railings looking at her. Her dress swung as she moved her body, and the soft rope of her hair tossed from side to side.

4   Every morning I lay on the floor in the front parlour watching her door. The blind was pulled down to within an inch of the sash[⑦] so that I could not be seen. When she came out on the doorstep my heart leaped. I ran to the hall, seized my books and followed her. I kept her brown figure always in my eye and, when we came near the point at which our ways diverged, I quickened my pace and passed her. This happened morning after morning. I had never spoken to her, except for a few casual words, and yet her name was like a summons[⑧] to all my foolish blood.

5   Her image accompanied me even in places the most hostile to romance[⑨]. On Saturday evenings when my aunt went marketing I had to go to carry some of the parcels. We walked through the flaring streets, jostled by drunken men and bargaining women, amid the curses of labourers, the shrill litanies[⑩] of shop-boys who stood on guard by the barrels of pigs'cheeks,

---

① *The Abbot* is a historical story by Walter Scott, the word Abbot, meaning father, is a title given to the head of the monastery in various traditions, including Christianity.

② *The Devout Communicant* can refer to two books of the same title. No matter which book it refers to, the title suggests a religious significance.

③ *The Memoirs of Vidocq* is a popular 19th century novel about a police thief.

④ straggle: to spread irregularly

⑤ Here mentions a kind of game played by the children, in which they imagine they are attacked by rows of savages from the cottages when they run through the dark muddy lanes behind the houses.

⑥ resignedly: willingly, without resistance

⑦ sash: the framework of the window

⑧ summons: an authoritative command, such as the summons of God

⑨ The sentence means her image appears in places most unsuitable for romantic ideas.

⑩ litany: It originally means a form of long pray in the Christian church which the priest calls and the people reply, here refers to the shop boys' callings.

the nasal chanting of street-singers, who sang a *come-all-you* about O'Donovan Rossa, or a ballad about the troubles in our native land. These noises converged in a single sensation of life for me[1]: I imagined that I bore my chalice[2] safely through a throng of foes. Her name sprang to my lips at moments in strange prayers and praises which I myself did not understand. My eyes were often full of tears (I could not tell why) and at times a flood from my heart seemed to pour itself out into my bosom. I thought little of the future. I did not know whether I would ever speak to her or not or, if I spoke to her, how I could tell her of my confused adoration. But my body was like a harp and her words and gestures were like fingers running upon the wires.

6   One evening I went into the back drawing-room in which the priest had died. It was a dark rainy evening and there was no sound in the house. Through one of the broken panes I heard the rain impinge[3] upon the earth, the fine incessant needles of water playing in the sodden[4] beds. Some distant lamp or lighted window gleamed below me. I was thankful that I could see so little. All my senses seemed to desire to veil themselves and, feeling that I was about to slip from them, I pressed the palms of my hands together until they trembled, murmuring: "*O love! O love*" many times.

7   At last she spoke to me. When she addressed the first words to me I was so confused that I did not know what to answer. She asked me was I going to *Araby*. I forgot whether I answered yes or no. It would be a splendid bazaar; she said she would love to go.

8   "And why can't you?" I asked.

9   While she spoke she turned a silver bracelet round and round her wrist. She could not go, she said, because there would be a retreat[5] that week in her convent[6]. Her brother and two other boys were fighting for their caps, and I was alone at the railings. She held one of the spikes, bowing her head towards me. The light from the lamp opposite our door caught the white curve of her neck, lit up her hair that rested there and, falling, lit up the hand upon the railing. It fell over one side of her dress and caught the white border of a petticoat, just visible as she stood at ease.

10   "It's well for you," she said.

11   "If I go," I said, "I will bring you something."

12   What innumerable follies laid waste my waking and sleeping thoughts after that evening! I wished to annihilate[7] the tedious intervening days. I chafed[8] against the work of school. At night in my bedroom and by day in the classroom her image came between me and the page I strove to read. The syllables of the word *Araby* were called to me through the silence in which

---

① The sentence means these noises combined make me feel the excitedness of life.
② chalice: a cup for the wine of the religious ritual of Mass where wine is drunk and bread is eaten symbolically as the blood and body of Jesus
③ impinge: strike
④ sodden: soaked with water
⑤ retreat: a retirement or a period retirement for religious exercise or meditation
⑥ convent: here refers to the school run by nuns.
⑦ annihilate: to cancel
⑧ chafe: to get irritated by

my soul luxuriated[①] and cast an Eastern enchantment over me[②]. I asked for leave to go to the bazaar on Saturday night. My aunt was surprised, and hoped it was not some Freemason[③] affair. I answered few questions in class. I watched my master's face pass from amiability to sternness; he hoped I was not beginning to idle. I could not call my wandering thoughts together. I had hardly any patience with the serious work of life which, now that it stood between me and my desire, seemed to me child's play, ugly monotonous child's play.

13   On Saturday morning I reminded my uncle that I wished to go to the bazaar in the evening. He was fussing at[④] the hallstand, looking for the hat-brush, and answered me curtly[⑤]:

14   "Yes, boy, I know."

15   As he was in the hall I could not go into the front parlour and lie at the window. I felt the house in bad humour and walked slowly towards the school. The air was pitilessly raw and already my heart misgave[⑥] me.

16   When I came home to dinner my uncle had not yet been home. Still it was early. I sat staring at the clock for some time and, when its ticking began to irritate me, I left the room. I mounted the staircase and gained the upper part of the house. The high, cold, empty, gloomy rooms liberated me and I went from room to room singing. From the front window I saw my companions playing below in the street. Their cries reached me weakened and indistinct and, leaning my forehead against the cool glass, I looked over at the dark house where she lived. I may have stood there for an hour, seeing nothing but the brown-clad[⑦] figure cast by my imagination, touched discreetly[⑧] by the lamplight at the curved neck, at the hand upon the railings and at the border below the dress.

17   When I came downstairs again I found Mrs Mercer sitting at the fire. She was an old, garrulous[⑨] woman, a pawnbroker's widow, who collected used stamps for some pious purpose. I had to endure the gossip of the tea-table. The meal was prolonged beyond an hour and still my uncle did not come. Mrs Mercer stood up to go: she was sorry she couldn't wait any longer, but it was after eight o'clock and she did not like to be out late, as the night air was bad for her. When she had gone I began to walk up and down the room, clenching my fists. My aunt said:

18   "I'm afraid you may put off your bazaar for this night of Our Lord."

19   At nine o'clock I heard my uncle's latchkey in the hall door. I heard him talking to himself and heard the hallstand rocking when it had received the weight of his overcoat. I could interpret these signs. When he was midway through his dinner I asked him to give me the money to go to the bazaar. He had forgotten.

20   "The people are in bed and after their first sleep now," he said.

① luxuriate: to enjoy and thrive on
② cast an Eastern enchantment over me: put me under a magic spell. The East is usually regarded as a place of mystery.
③ Freemason: some secret society (with branches in many parts of Europe and America) for mutual help and fellowship
④ fuss at: to do sth. in a careless and casual way
⑤ curtly: briefly
⑥ misgive: to make one feel uneasy, restless
⑦ brown-clad: dressed in brown. *Clad* is the simple past tense and past participle of clothe.
⑧ discreetly: with care
⑨ garrulous: excessively talkative

21   I did not smile. My aunt said to him energetically:

22   "Can't you give him the money and let him go? You've kept him late enough as it is."

23   My uncle said he was very sorry he had forgotten. He said he believed in the old saying: "All work and no play makes Jack a dull boy." He asked me where I was going and, when I told him a second time, he asked me did I know *The Arab's Farewell to His Steed.* When I left the kitchen he was about to recite the opening lines of the piece to my aunt.

24   I held a florin① tightly in my hand as I strode down Buckingham Street towards the station. The sight of the streets thronged with buyers and glaring with gas recalled to me the purpose of my journey. I took my seat in a third-class carriage of a deserted train. After an intolerable delay the train moved out of the station slowly. It crept onward among ruinous houses and over the twinkling river. At Westland Row Station a crowd of people pressed to the carriage doors; but the porters moved them back, saying that it was a special train for the bazaar. I remained alone in the bare carriage. In a few minutes the train drew up beside an improvised② wooden platform. I passed out on to the road and saw by the lighted dial of a clock that it was ten minutes to ten. In front of me was a large building which displayed the magical name.

25   I could not find any sixpenny entrance and, fearing that the bazaar would be closed, I passed in quickly through a turnstile③, handing a shilling to a weary-looking man. I found myself in a big hall girdled④ at half its height by a gallery. Nearly all the stalls were closed and the greater part of the hall was in darkness. I recognized a silence like that which pervades⑤ a church after a service. I walked into the centre of the bazaar timidly. A few people were gathered about the stalls which were still open. Before a curtain, over which the words *Cafe Chantant* were written in coloured lamps, two men were counting money on a salver. I listened to the fall of the coins.

26   Remembering with difficulty why I had come, I went over to one of the stalls and examined porcelain vases and flowered tea-sets. At the door of the stall a young lady was talking and laughing with two young gentlemen. I remarked their English accents and listened vaguely to their conversation.

27   "O, I never said such a thing!"

28   "O, but you did!"

29   "O, but I didn't!"

30   "Didn't she say that?"

31   "Yes. I heard her."

32   "O, there's a...fib⑥!"

① florin: British coin, worth of two shillings, or the tenth part of a pound; equal to ten new pence after the decimalization in 1971
② improvised: made for temporary use
③ turnstile: a structure set at the entrance to allow the controlled passage of people
④ girdled: surrounded
⑤ pervade: to spread to all parts
⑥ fib: a lie

33 Observing me, the young lady came over and asked me did I wish to buy anything.

34 The tone of her voice was not encouraging; she seemed to have spoken to me out of a sense of duty. I looked humbly at the great jars that stood like eastern guards at either side of the dark entrance to the stall and murmured:

35 "No, thank you."

36 The young lady changed the position of one of the vases and went back to the two young men. They began to talk of the same subject. Once or twice the young lady glanced at me over her shoulder.

37 I lingered before her stall, though I knew my stay was useless, to make my interest in her wares seem the more real. Then I turned away slowly and walked down the middle of the bazaar. I allowed the two pennies to fall against the sixpence in my pocket. I heard a voice call from one end of the gallery that the light was out. The upper part of the hall was now completely dark.

38 Gazing up into the darkness I saw myself as a creature driven and derided① by vanity; and my eyes burned with anguish② and anger.

▶ STUDY QUESTIONS

 Recalling

1. Please work on the first 3 paragraphs and figure out the setting of the story.
2. How old is the boy?
3. What is Mangan's sister like in the boy's eyes?
4. What "symptoms of love" does the boy have? Are they different from those of an adult?
5. Why did the boy want to go to Araby so much?
6. What did the boy realize in the end?

 Interpreting

7. The story plays a lot with the images of darkness and shadow. Please find out those images first and think about the significance of those images.
8. Does the back drawing-room have any special meaning in the story?
9. Why "my eyes burned with anguish and anger" towards the end of the story?
10. What does the journey to Araby symbolize?
11. Who narrated the story? Is it "I" as a boy or "I" as an adult?
12. What role do the adult characters play in the story (aunt and uncle, lady in the stall, etc.)?

 Extending

13. Do you have similar experience? How do you look at it now?

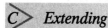

① deride: to mock, scorn, laugh at
② anguish: acute distress or pain

LITERARY FOCUS

> *Setting*

The time and location in which a story takes place is called the setting. For some stories the setting is very important, while for others it is not. There are several aspects of a story's setting to consider when examining how setting contributes to a story (some, or all, may be present in a story):

(1) place—geographical location. Where is the action of the story taking place?

(2) time—When is the story taking place? (historical period, time of day, year, etc.)

(3) weather conditions—Is it rainy, sunny, stormy, etc.?

(4) social conditions—What is the daily life of the characters like? Does the story contain local colour (writing that focuses on the speech, dress, mannerisms, customs, etc. of a particular place)?

(5) mood or atmosphere—What feeling is created at the beginning of the story? Is it bright and cheerful or dark and frightening?

THINKING ABOUT SETTING

What is the setting of the story *Araby*? Is there anything special about the setting? How important is the setting in the story? How does the setting contribute to the story?

The Starry Night [***Nuit étoilée***]
Vincent van Gogh, 1889.
The Museum of Modern Art, New York.

VI. *A Handful of Dates* by Tayeb Salih

►► ABOUT THE AUTHOR

Tayeb Salih was born in Northern Sudan in 1929 and educated at the University of Khartoum. After a brief period working as a teacher, he moved to London to work with the BBC Arabic Service and to pursue his studies. Salih later worked as Director-General of Information in Qatar in the Arabian Gulf; with UNESOC in Paris and as UNESOC's representative in the Arab Gulf States. Tayeb Salih is widely acknowledged to be one of the most important contemporary Arab writers. In 2001 his *Season of Migration to the North* was selected by a panel of Arab writers and critics as the most important Arab novel of the twentieth century.

A Handful of Dates
Translated from the Arabic by Denys Johnson-Davies

1   I must have been very young at the time. While I don't remember exactly how old I was, I do remember that when people saw me with my grandfather they would pat me on the head and give my cheek a pinch[1] —things they didn't do to my grandfather. The strange thing was that I never used to go out with my father, rather it was my grandfather who would take me with him wherever he went, except for the mornings when I would go to the mosque[2] to learn the Koran[3]. The mosque, the river[4] and the fields—these were the landmarks in our life. While most of the children of my age grumbled[5] at having to go to the mosque to learn the Koran, I used to love it. The reason was, no doubt, that I was quick at learning by heart and the Sheikh[6] always asked me to stand up and recite the Chapter of the Merciful[7] whenever we had visitors, who would pat me on my head and cheek just as people did when they saw me with my grandfather.

2   Yes, I used to love the mosque, and I loved the river too. Directly we finished our Koran reading in the morning I would throw down my wooden slate and dart off, quick as a genie[8], to my mother, hurriedly swallow down my breakfast, and run off for a plunge in the river. When tired of swimming about I would sit on the bank and gaze at the strip of water that wound away eastwards and hid behind a thick wood of acacia trees[9]. I loved to give rein to my imagination and picture to myself a tribe of giants living behind that wood, a people tall and thin with white beards and sharp noses, like my grandfather. Before my grandfather ever replied to my many questions he would rub the tip of his nose with his forefinger; as for his beard, it was soft

---

① pinch: to squeeze between the finger and the thumb, here as a sign of affection
② Mosque: Moslem house of worship
③ Koran: the Moslem holy book
④ river: here refers to the Nile.
⑤ grumble: to complain
⑥ Sheikh: tribal and religious leader
⑦ Chapter of the Merciful: selection from Koran
⑧ genie: the spirit that can appear and disappear quickly in Moslem mythology
⑨ acacia tree: tree from which gum is obtained

and luxuriant and as white as cotton-wool—never in my life have I seen anything of a purer whiteness or greater beauty. My grandfather must also have been extremely tall, for I never saw anyone in the whole area address him without having to look up at him, nor did I see him enter a house without having to bend so low that I was put in mind of the way the river wound round behind the wood of acacia trees. I loved him and would imagine myself, when I grew to be a man, tall and slender like him, walking along with great strides.

3   I believe I was his favorite grandchild: no wonder, for my cousins were a stupid bunch and I —so they say—was an intelligent child. I used to know when my grandfather wanted me to laugh, when to be silent; also I would remember the times for his prayers and would bring him his prayer-rug[1] and fill the ewer[2] for his ablutions[3] without his having to ask me. When he had nothing else to do he enjoyed listening to me reciting to him from the Koran in a lilting[4] voice, and I could tell from his face that he was moved.

4   One day I asked him about our neighbor Masood. I said to my grandfather: "I fancy you don't like our neighbor Masood?"

5   To which he answered, having rubbed the tip of his nose: "He's an indolent[5] man and I don't like such people."

6   I said to him: "What's an indolent man?"

7   My grandfather lowered his head for a moment, then looking across at the wide expanse of field, he said: "Do you see it stretching out from the edge of the desert up to the Nile bank? A hundred feddans[6]. Do you see all those date palms? And those trees—*sant*, acacia, and *sayal* ? All this fell into Masood's lap, was inherited by him from his father."

8   Taking advantage of the silence that had descended upon my grandfather, I turned my gaze from him to the vast area defined by his words. "I don't care," I told myself, "who owns those date palms, those trees or this black, cracked earth—all I know is that it's the arena[7] for my dreams and my playground."

9   My grandfather then continued: "Yes, my boy, forty years ago all this belonged to Masood—two-thirds of it is now mine."

10   This was news to me for I had imagined that the land had belonged to my grandfather ever since God's Creation.

11   "I didn't own a single feddan when I first set foot in this village. Masood was then the owner of all these riches. The position has changed now, though, and I think that before Allah[8] calls me to Him I shall have bought the remaining third as well."

12   I do not know why it was I felt fear at my grandfather's words—and pity for our neighbor Masood. How I wished my grandfather wouldn't do what he'd said! I remembered Masood's singing, his beautiful voice and powerful laugh that resembled the gurgling of water. My grandfather never used to laugh.

---

[1] payer-rug: Moslems traditionally kneel on rugs while praying
[2] ewer: large, wide-mouthed jug
[3] ablution: a ritual washing of the body
[4] lilting: rising and falling rhythmically
[5] indolent: not willing to make an effort to do things
[6] feddan: unit of land measurement used in many North African nations. One feddan equals 1.038 acres.
[7] arena: central place for games or fights
[8] Allah: Moslem name for God

13　　I asked my grandfather why Masood had sold his land.

14　　"Women," and from the way my grandfather pronounced the word I felt that "women" was something terrible. "Masood, my boy, was a much-married man. Each time he married he sold me a feddan or two. I made the quick calculation that Masood must have married some ninety women. Then I remembered his three wives, his shabby appearance, his lame donkey and its dilapidated① saddle, his djellaba② with the torn sleeves. I had all but rid my mind of the thoughts that jostled③ in it when I saw the man approaching us, and my grandfather and I exchanged glances.

15　　"We'll be harvesting the dates today," said Masood. "Don't you want to be there?"

16　　I felt, though, that he did not really want my grandfather to attend. My grandfather, however, jumped to his feet and I saw that his eyes sparkled momentarily with an intense brightness. He pulled me by the hand and we went off to the harvesting of Masood's dates.

17　　Someone brought my grandfather a stool covered with an ox-hide④, while I remained standing. There was a vast number of people there, but though I knew them all, I found myself, for some reason, watching Masood: aloof from that great gathering of people, he stood as though it were no concern of his, despite the fact that the date palms to be harvested were his own. Sometimes his attention would be caught by the sound of a huge clump⑤ of dates crashing down from on high. Once he shouted up at the boy perched on the very summit of the date palm who had begun hacking⑥ at a clump with his long, sharp sickle: "Be careful you don't cut the heart of the palm."

18　　No one paid any attention to what he said and the boy seated at the very summit of the date palm continued, quickly and energetically, to work away at the branch with his sickle till the clump of dates began to drop like something descending from the heavens.

19　　I, however, had begun to think about Masood's phrase "the heart of the palm." I pictured the palm tree as something with feeling, something possessed of a heart that throbbed. I remembered Masood's remark to me when he had once seen me playing about with the branch of a young palm tree: "Palm trees, my boy, like humans, experience joy and suffering." And I had felt an inward and unreasoned embarrassment.

20　　When I again looked at the expanse of ground stretching before me I saw my young companions swarming⑦ like ants around the trunks of the palm trees, gathering up dates and eating most of them. The dates were collected into high mounds. I saw people coming along and weighing them into measuring bins⑧ and pouring them into sacks, of which I counted thirty. The crowd of people broke up, except for Hussein the merchant, Mousa the owner of the field next to ours on the east, and two men I'd never seen before.

21　　I heard a low whistling sound and saw that my grandfather had fallen asleep. Then I noticed that Masood had not changed his stance, except that he had placed a stalk in his mouth and

---

① dilapidated: partially ruined, decayed
② djellaba: loose-fitting hooded robe worn by men and women in some North African countries
③ jostle: to push toughly
④ ox-hide: the skin of ox
⑤ clump: a small, close group of, a cluster
⑥ hack: to cut roughly or clumsily
⑦ swarm: to move along in great numbers as bees
⑧ bin: large container

was munching[1] at it like someone surfeited[2] with food who doesn't know what to do with the mouthful he still has.

22   Suddenly my grandfather woke up, jumped to his feet and walked towards the sacks of dates. He was followed by Hussein the merchant, Mousa the owner of the field next to ours, and the two strangers. I glanced at Masood and saw that he was making his way towards us with extreme slowness, like a man who wants to retreat but whose feet insist on going forward. They formed a circle round the sacks of dates and began examining them, some taking a date or two to eat. My grandfather gave me a fistful, which I began munching. I saw Masood filling the palms of both hands with dates and bringing them up close to his nose, then returning them.

23   Then I saw them dividing up the sacks between them. Hussein the merchant took ten; each of the strangers took five. Mousa the owner of the field next to ours on the eastern side took five, and my grandfather took five. Understanding nothing, I looked at Masood and saw that his eyes were darting about[3] to left and right like two mice that have lost their way home.

24   "You're still fifty pounds in debt to me," said my grandfather to Masood. "We'll talk about it later."

25   Hussein called his assistants and they brought along donkeys, the two strangers produced camels, and the sacks of dates were loaded on to them. One of the donkeys let out a braying[4] which set the camels frothing[5] at the mouth and complaining noisily. I felt myself drawing close to Masood, felt my hand stretch out towards him as though I wanted to touch the hem of his garment. I heard him make a noise in his throat like the rasping[6] of a lamb being slaughtered. For some unknown reason, I experienced a sharp sensation of pain in my chest.

26   I ran off into the distance. Hearing my grandfather call after me, I hesitated a little, then continued on my way. I felt at that moment that I hated him. Quickening my pace, it was as though I carried within me a secret I wanted to rid myself of. I reached the river bank near the bend it made behind the wood of acacia trees. Then, without knowing why, I put my finger into my throat and spewed[7] up the dates I'd eaten.

▶ STUDY QUESTIONS

A Recalling

1. According to the story's opening, what four things does the narrator love as a young boy?
2. What does the grandfather explain about the land he now owns and his plans for the future? What does the narrator remember about Masood then?
3. What do the grandfather, Mousa, and Hussein do after Masood's dates are harvested? About what does the grandfather remind Masood?
4. In the last paragraph, what does the narrator do with the dates his grandfather gave him?

---

① munch: to eat with much force and movement of the jaws
② surfeit: to take too much of anything
③ dart about: to move swiftly
④ braying: the loud, harsh cry of a donkey
⑤ froth: to produce bubbles or foam
⑥ rasping: a harsh, grating sound
⑦ spew up: to throw up, to spit, to vomit

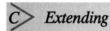

B **Interpreting**

5. Explain the significance of the boy's actions in the final paragraph.

6. What change occurs in the boy's opinion of his grandfather? What causes the change?

7. What qualities make Masood a good person but a bad businessman? In what way might Masood's remarks about the heart of the palm apply to his own experiences in the story?

8. Why is it significant that at the start of the story the boy often recites from the Koran, especially from the Chapter of the Merciful, to his grandfather and others?

9. The grandfather loves to hear "me" recite from the Chapter of the "Merciful" but in reality he seems to show no mercy towards Masood. Why?

10. What do the images "river", "land", "mosque", "palm tree", and "dates" symbolize respectively?

11. Do you think the narrator as an adult has changed his opinion of his grandfather? Please support your opinion with evidence from the text.

12. What is the conflict of the story?

13. What is the theme of the story?

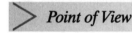

C **Extending**

14. How to carry out one's religious belief in reality? Should people adjust their belief to reality? Or should the belief be carried out to every word?

▶▶ LITERARY FOCUS

> **Point of View**

Point of view is defined as the angle from which the story is narrated. It is also called narration. According to the narrator's position in relation to the story being told, point of view can be classified to:

(1) **First-person View**—The story is told by the protagonist or one of the characters who interacts closely with the protagonist or other characters (using pronouns I, me, we, etc.). The reader sees the story through this person's eyes as he/she experiences it and only knows what he/she knows or feels.

(2) **Second-person View**—It is the rarest mode of narration. By referring the readers as "you" second-person view makes the readers feel that he or she is a character in the story. This view is commonly used in letters.

(3) **Third-person View**—Third-person view is the angle of a non-participant of the story, an outside voice. The narrator always refers to the characters as he, she, it or they. Third-person view includes **omniscient third-person** view and **third-person limited**. In third-person omniscient the narrator knows everything about the story, knows every character's mind. He is omniscient. In third-person limited, the narrator's knowledge is limited to one character. He knows everything about this character but not beyond. Generally, third-person view provides the author greatest flexibility to tell a story thus becomes the commonest way of narration.

To complicate the narration, sometimes, the story is told by several narrators, each presenting a different story, or by a child, a fool or a lunatic, the reader has to think and to judge as to the reliability of the narration. The former is called **multi-narration** and the latter is called the **Innocent Eye**, both techniques are favored by modern writers.

▶ THINKING ABOUT POINT OF VIEW

From whose point of view is the story *A Handful of Dates* told? Is the narrator a boy or a man? How does the point of view affect the story?

VII. *The Story of an Hour* by Kate Chopin

▶ ABOUT THE AUTHOR

Kate Chopin, born Katherine O'Flaherty (1850–1904), was an American author of short stories and novels. She is now considered by some to have been a forerunner of feminist authors of the 20th century. Her important short stories included *Desiree's Baby*, a tale of miscegenation in antebellum Louisiana (published in 1893), *The Story of an Hour* (1894), and *The Storm* (1898). *The Storm* is a sequel to *At the'Cadian Ball*, which appeared in her first collection of short stories, *Bayou Folk*. Chopin also wrote two novels: *At Fault* (1890) and *The Awakening* (1899). She acknowledged her debt to the contemporary French naturalists Emile Zola and Guy de Maupassant.

The Story of an Hour

1   Knowing that Mrs. Mallard was afflicted[①] with a heart trouble, great care was taken to break to her as gently as possible the news of her husband's death.

2   It was her sister Josephine who told her, in broken sentences; veiled hints that revealed in half concealing. Her husband's friend Richards was there, too, near her. It was he who had been in the newspaper office when intelligence of the railroad disaster was received, with Brently Mallard's name leading the list of "killed". He had only taken the time to assure himself of its truth by a second telegram, and had hastened to forestall any less careful, less tender friend in bearing the sad message.

3   She did not hear the story as many women have heard the same, with a paralyzed[②] inability to accept its significance. She wept at once, with sudden, wild abandonment, in her sister's arms. When the storm of grief had spent itself she went away to her room alone. She would have no one follow her.

4   There stood, facing the open window, a comfortable, roomy armchair. Into this she sank, pressed down by a physical exhaustion that haunted her body and seemed to reach into her soul.

5   She could see in the open square before her house the tops of trees that were all aquiver[③] with the new spring life. The delicious breath of rain was in the air. In the street below a peddler[④] was crying his wares. The notes of a distant song which some one was singing reached her faintly, and countless sparrows were twittering in the leaves.

---

① afflict: to cause severe mental or physical distress
② paralyzed: unable to move
③ aquiver: shaking with excitement
④ peddler: somebody travelling from place to place to sell goods

6   There were patches of blue sky showing here and there through the clouds that had met and piled one above the other in the west facing her window.

7   She sat with her head thrown back upon the cushion of the chair, quite motionless, except when a sob came up into her throat and shook her, as a child who has cried itself to sleep continues to sob in its dreams.

8   She was young, with a fair, calm face, whose lines bespoke repression and even a certain strength. But now there was a dull stare in her eyes, whose gaze was fixed away off yonder[①] on one of those patches of blue sky. It was not a glance of reflection, but rather indicated a suspension of intelligent thought.

9   There was something coming to her and she was waiting for it, fearfully. What was it? She did not know; it was too subtle and elusive[②] to name. But she felt it, creeping out of the sky, reaching toward her through the sounds, the scents, the color that filled the air.

10   Now her bosom rose and fell tumultuously[③]. She was beginning to recognize this thing that was approaching to possess her, and she was striving to beat it back with her will—as powerless as her two white slender hands would have been.

11   When she abandoned herself a little whispered word escaped her slightly parted lips. She said it over and over under her breath: "free, free, free!" The vacant stare and the look of terror that had followed it went from her eyes. They stayed keen and bright. Her pulses beat fast, and the coursing blood warmed and relaxed every inch of her body.

12   She did not stop to ask if it were or were not a monstrous joy that held her. A clear and exalted[④] perception enabled her to dismiss the suggestion as trivial.

13   She knew that she would weep again when she saw the kind, tender hands folded in death; the face that had never looked save with love upon her, fixed and gray and dead. But she saw beyond that bitter moment a long procession of years to come that would belong to her absolutely. And she opened and spread her arms out to them in welcome.

14   There would be no one to live for during those coming years; she would live for herself. There would be no powerful will bending hers in that blind persistence with which men and women believe they have a right to impose a private will upon a fellow-creature. A kind intention or a cruel intention made the act seem no less a crime as she looked upon it in that brief moment of illumination.

15   And yet she had loved him—sometimes. Often she had not. What did it matter! What could love, the unsolved mystery, count for in face of this possession of self-assertion which she suddenly recognized as the strongest impulse of her being!

16   "Free! Body and soul free!" she kept whispering.

---

① yonder: over there
② elusive: difficult to find, catch, understand, define or identify
③ tumultuously: involving great excitement, confusion, and emotional agitation
④ exalted: excited

17   Josephine was kneeling before the closed door with her lips to the keyhole, imploring for admission. "Louise, open the door! I beg, open the door—you will make yourself ill. What are you doing Louise? For heaven's sake open the door."

18   "Go away. I am not making myself ill." No; she was drinking in a very elixir^① of life through that open window.

19   Her fancy was running riot along those days ahead of her. Spring days, and summer days, and all sorts of days that would be her own. She breathed a quick prayer that life might be long. It was only yesterday she had thought with a shudder that life might be long.

20   She arose at length and opened the door to her sister's importunities. There was a feverish triumph in her eyes, and she carried herself unwittingly like a goddess of Victory. She clasped her sister's waist, and together they descended the stairs. Richards stood waiting for them at the bottom.

21   Some one was opening the front door with a latchkey. It was Brently Mallard who entered, a little travel-stained, composedly carrying his grip-sack and umbrella. He had been far from the scene of accident, and did not even know there had been one. He stood amazed at Josephine's piercing cry; at Richards' quick motion to screen him from the view of his wife.

22   But Richards was too late.

23   When the doctors came they said she had died of heart disease   of joy that kills.

▶ STUDY QUESTIONS

Recalling

1. What is Mrs. Mallard's initial reaction at the news of her husband's death?
2. What does Mrs. Mallard notice outside the window when she shuts herself in the room? What does that suggest?
3. What is the marriage of the Mallards like?
4. Does Mrs. Mallard try to hide her sense of relief when she comes out of her room?
5. What is the spiritual experience of Mrs. Mallard during this one hour?

B⟩ Interpreting

6. What is the real cause of Mrs. Mallard's death?
7. What does Mrs. Mallard's death tell us?

Extending

8. Does the psychological ambivalence dramatized in *The Story of an Hour* ring true or uncomfortably real when we consider honestly our own feelings?

---

① elixir: a panacea or drink or magical cure

▶ LITERARY FOCUS

> ### *Plot*

It is a term to indicate how the events are arranged to affect the reader. It is an artificial rather than a natural ordering of events. It is composed of two basic aspects of narration: (a) the sequence, i.e. the story told in chronological order, or with a lot of flashback, or in psychic order; (b) the development, i.e. whether in the traditional linear pattern (set-up/exposition → rising action/ complications → climax → resolution/ falling action/consequence → denouement, unravelling) or modernist way (little action, inner world depiction, dialogues, no development). A work may have just one plot, or double plots, or multiple plots.

▶ THINKING ABOUT PLOT

How does *The Story of an Hour* develop? Does the story develop in the traditional linear pattern or in the modernist way? What is the climax of the story? How does the story end? Do you like the way it ends? Why or why not?

VIII. *Three Days to See* by Helen Keller

▶ ABOUT THE AUTHOR

Helen Adams Keller (1880–1968) was an American author, political activist, and lecturer. She was the first deaf-blind person to earn a Bachelor of Arts degree. After graduation, Helen Keller began her life's work of helping blind and deaf-blind people. She appeared before state and national legislatures and international forums, travelled around the world to lecture and to visit areas with a high incidence of blindness, and wrote numerous books and articles. Books she has written include *The Story of My Life, The World I Live in, Out of the Dark, Light in My Darkness*. She met every U.S. president from Grover Cleveland to Lyndon Johnson, and played a major role in focusing the world's attention on the problems of the blind and the need for preventive measures.

Three Days to See

I

1   All of us have read thrilling stories in which the hero had only a limited and specified time to live. Sometimes it was as long as a year; sometimes as short as twenty-four hours. But always we were interested in discovering just how the doomed man chose to spend his last days or his last hours. I speak, of course, of free men who have a choice, not condemned criminals whose sphere of activities is strictly delimited.

2   Such stories set us thinking, wondering what we should do under similar circumstances. What events, what experiences, what associations, should we crowd into those last hours as mortal beings? What happiness should we find in reviewing the past, what regrets?

3   Sometimes I have thought it would be an excellent rule to live each day as if we should

die tomorrow. Such an attitude would emphasize sharply the values of life. We should live each day with a gentleness, a vigor, and a keenness of appreciation which are often lost when time stretches before us in the constant panorama① of more days and months and years to come. There are those, of course, who would adopt the epicurean② motto of "Eat, drink, and be merry", but most people would be chastened③ by the certainty of impending④ death.

4   In stories, the doomed hero is usually saved at the last minute by some stroke of fortune, but almost always his sense of values is changed. He becomes more appreciative of the meaning of life and its permanent spiritual values. It has often been noted that those who live, or have lived, in the shadow of death bring a mellow⑤ sweetness to everything they do.

5   Most of us, however, take life for granted. We know that one day we must die, but usually we picture that day as far in the future. When we are in buoyant⑥ health, death is all but unimaginable. We seldom think of it. The days stretch out in an endless vista. So we go about our petty tasks, hardly aware of our listless⑦ attitude toward life.

6   The same lethargy⑧, I am afraid, characterizes the use of all our faculties and senses. Only the deaf appreciate hearing, only the blind realize the manifold blessings that lie in sight. Particularly does this observation apply to those who have lost sight and hearing in adult life. But those who have never suffered impairment of sight or hearing seldom make the fullest use of these blessed faculties. Their eyes and ears take in all sights and sounds hazily, without concentration and with little appreciation. It is the same old story of not being grateful for what we have until we lose it, of not being conscious of health until we are ill.

7   I have often thought it would be a blessing if each human being were stricken blind and deaf for a few days at some time during his early adult life. Darkness would make him more appreciative of sight; silence would teach him the joys of sound.

8   Now and then I have tested my seeing friends to discover what they see. Recently I was visited by a very good friend who had just returned from a long walk in the woods, and I asked her what she had observed. "Nothing in particular," she replied. I might have been incredulous had I not been accustomed to such responses, for long ago I became convinced that the seeing see little.

9   How was it possible, I asked myself, to walk for an hour through the woods and see nothing worthy of note? I who cannot see find hundreds of things to interest me through mere touch. I feel the delicate symmetry of a leaf. I pass my hands lovingly about the smooth skin of a silver birch, or the rough, shaggy⑨ bark of a pine. In spring I touch the branches of trees hopefully in search of a bud, the first sign of awakening Nature after her winter's sleep. I feel the delightful, velvety texture of a flower, and discover its remarkable convolutions⑩; and something of the

① panorama: a continuous passing or changing thing, or unfolding events
② epicurean: indulging in sensual pleasure
③ chasten: improve through suffering
④ impending: about to happen
⑤ mellow: soft, sweet and rich
⑥ buoyant: cheerful or energetic
⑦ listless: indifferent, spiritless
⑧ lethargy: indifference, dullness, laziness
⑨ shaggy: rough
⑩ convolution: a rolled up or coiled condition

miracle of Nature is revealed to me. Occasionally, if I am very fortunate, I place my hand gently on a small tree and feel the happy quiver of a bird in full song. I am delighted to have the cool waters of a brook rush through my open fingers. To me a lush carpet of pine needles or spongy grass is more welcome than the most luxurious Persian rug. To me the pageant① of seasons is a thrilling and unending drama, the action of which streams through my finger tips.

10　　At times my heart cries out with longing to see all these things. If I can get so much pleasure from mere touch, how much more beauty must be revealed by sight. Yet, those who have eyes apparently see little. The panorama of color and action which fills the world is taken for granted. It is human, perhaps, to appreciate little that which we have and to long for that which we have not, but it is a great pity that in the world of light the gift of sight is used only as a mere convenience rather than as a means of adding fullness to life.

11　　If I were the president of a university I should establish a compulsory course in "How to Use Your Eyes". The professor would try to show his pupils how they could add joy to their lives by really seeing what passes unnoticed before them. He would try to awake their dormant② and sluggish faculties.

II

12　　Perhaps I can best illustrate by imagining what I should most like to see if I were given the use of my eyes, say, for just three days. And while I am imagining, suppose you, too, set your mind to work on the problem of how you would use your own eyes if you had only three more days to see. If with the oncoming darkness of the third night you knew that the sun would never rise for you again, how would you spend those three precious intervening days? What would you most want to let your gaze rest upon?

13　　I, naturally, should want most to see the things which have become dear to me through my years of darkness. You, too, would want to let your eyes rest long on the things that have become dear to you so that you could take the memory of them with you into the night that loomed before you.

14　　If, by some miracle, I were granted three seeing days, to be followed by a relapse③ into darkness, I should divide the period into three parts.

15　　On the first day, I should want to see the people whose kindness and gentleness and companionship have made my life worth living. First I should like to gaze long upon the face of my dear teacher, Mrs. Anne Sullivan Macy, who came to me when I was a child and opened the outer world to me. I should want not merely to see the outline of her face, so that I could cherish it in my memory, but to study that face and find in it the living evidence of the sympathetic tenderness and patience with which she accomplished the difficult task of my education. I should like to see in her eyes that strength of character which has enabled her to stand firm in the face of difficulties, and that compassion for all humanity which she has revealed to me so often.

16　　I do not know what it is to see into the heart of a friend through that "window of the soul",

---

① pageant: a colorful, splendid exhibition
② dormant: lying asleep, inactive
③ relapse: to fall back into former state, or illness, or wrongdoing, etc.

the eye. I can only "see" through my finger tips the outline of a face. I can detect laughter, sorrow, and many other obvious emotions. I know my friends from the feel of their faces. But I cannot really picture their personalities by touch. I know their personalities, of course, through other means, through the thoughts they express to me, through whatever of their actions are revealed to me. But I am denied that deeper understanding of them which I am sure would come through sight of them, through watching their reactions to various expressed thoughts and circumstances, through noting the immediate and fleeting reactions of their eyes and countenance.

17   Friends who are near to me I know well, because through the months and years they reveal themselves to me in all their phases; but of casual friends I have only an incomplete impression, an impression gained from a handclasp, from spoken words which I take from their lips with my finger tips, or which they tap into the palm of my hand.

18   How much easier, how much more satisfying it is for you who can see to grasp quickly the essential qualities of another person by watching the subtleties of expression, the quiver of a muscle, the flutter of a hand. But does it ever occur to you to use your sight to see into the inner nature of a friend or acquaintance? Do not most of you seeing people grasp casually the outward features of a face and let it go at that?

19   For instance, can you describe accurately the faces of five good friends? Some of you can, but many cannot. As an experiment, I have questioned husbands of long standing about the color of their wives' eyes, and often they express embarrassed confusion and admit that they do not know. And, incidentally, it is a chronic① complaint of wives that their husbands do not notice new dresses, new hats, and changes in household arrangements.

20   The eyes of seeing persons soon become accustomed to the routine of their surroundings, and they actually see only the startling and spectacular. But even in viewing the most spectacular sights the eyes are lazy. Court records reveal every day how inaccurately "eyewitnesses" see. A given event will be "seen" in several different ways by as many witnesses. Some see more than others, but few see everything that is within the range of their vision.

21   Oh, the things that I should see if I had the power of sight for just three days!

22   The first day would be a busy one. I should call to me all my dear friends and look long into their faces, imprinting upon my mind the outward evidences of the beauty that is within them. I should let my eyes rest, too, on the face of a baby, so that I could catch a vision of the eager, innocent beauty which precedes the individual's consciousness of the conflicts which life develops.

23   And I should like to look into the loyal, trusting eyes of my dogs—the grave, canny little Scottie, Darkie, and the stalwart, understanding Great Dane, Helga, whose warm, tender, and playful friendships are so comforting to me.

24   On that busy first day I should also view the small simple things of my home. I want to see the warm colors in the rugs under my feet, the pictures on the walls, the intimate trifles② that transform a house into home. My eyes would rest respectfully on the books in raised type which

---

① chronic: constant, habitual, recurring frequently
② trifle: an article or thing of very little value

I have read, but they would be more eagerly interested in the printed books which seeing people can read, for during the long night of my life the books I have read and those which have been read to me have built themselves into a great shining lighthouse, revealing to me the deepest channels of human life and the human spirit.

25   In the afternoon of that first seeing day, I should take a long walk in the woods and intoxicate① my eyes on the beauties of the world of Nature, trying desperately to absorb in a few hours the vast splendor which is constantly unfolding itself to those who can see. On the way home from my woodland jaunt② my path would lie near a farm so that I might see the patient horses ploughing in the field (perhaps I should see only a tractor!) and the serene③ content of men living close to the soil. And I should pray for the glory of a colorful sunset.

26   When dusk had fallen, I should experience the double delight of being able to see by artificial light, which the genius of man has created to extend the power of his sight when Nature decrees④ darkness.

27   In the night of that first day of sight, I should not be able to sleep, so full would be my mind of the memories of the day.

III

28   The next day—the second day of sight—I should arise with the dawn and see the thrilling miracle by which night is transformed into day. I should behold with awe the magnificent panorama of light with which the sun awakens the sleeping earth.

29   This day I should devote to a hasty glimpse of the world, past and present. I should want to see the pageant of man's progress, the kaleidoscope⑤ of the ages. How can so much be compressed into one day? Through the museums, of course. Often I have visited the New York Museum of Natural History to touch with my hands many of the objects there exhibited, but I have longed to see with my eyes the condensed history of the earth and its inhabitants displayed there—animals and the races of men pictured in their native environment; gigantic carcasses of dinosaurs and mastodons⑥ which roamed the earth long before man appeared, with his tiny stature and powerful brain, to conquer the animal kingdom; realistic presentations of the processes of evolution in animals, in man, and in the implements which man has used to fashion for himself a secure home on this planet; and a thousand and one other aspects of natural history.

30   I wonder how many readers of this article have viewed this panorama of the face of living things as pictured in that inspiring museum. Many, of course, have not had the opportunity, but I am sure that many who have had the opportunity have not made use of it. There, indeed, is a place to use your eyes. You who see can spend many fruitful days there, but I, with my imaginary three days of sight, could only take a hasty glimpse, and pass on.

31   My next stop would be the Metropolitan Museum of Art, for just as the Museum of

---

① intoxicate: to indulge
② jaunt: a short journey, esp. one taken for pleasure
③ serene: peaceful, tranquil
④ decree: to order in a formal and authoritative way
⑤ kaleidoscope: a continually changing pattern of shapes and colors
⑥ mastodon: 乳齿象（已绝种）

Natural History reveals the material aspects of the world, so does the Metropolitan show the myriad[1] facets of the human spirit. Throughout the history of humanity the urge to artistic expression has been almost as powerful as the urge for food, shelter, and procreation. And here, in the vast chambers of the Metropolitan Museum, is unfolded before me the spirit of Egypt, Greece, and Rome, as expressed in their art. I know well through my hands the sculptured gods and goddesses of the ancient Nile land. I have felt copies of Parthenon[2] friezes[3], and I have sensed the rhythmic beauty of charging Athenian warriors. Apollos and Venuses and the Winged Victory of Samothrace[4] are friends of my finger tips. The gnarled[5], bearded features of Homer are dear to me, for he, too, knew blindness.

32   My hands have lingered upon the living marble of Roman sculpture as well as that of later generations. I have passed my hands over a plaster cast of Michelangelo's[6] inspiring and heroic Moses[7]; I have sensed the power of Rodin[8]; I have been awed by the devoted spirit of Gothic wood carving. These arts which can be touched have meaning for me, but even they were meant to be seen rather than felt, and I can only guess at the beauty which remains hidden from me. I can admire the simple lines of a Greek vase, but its figured decorations are lost to me.

33   So on this, my second day of sight, I should try to probe into the soul of man through his art. The things I knew through touch I should now see. More splendid still, the whole magnificent world of painting would be opened to me, from the Italian Primitives, with their serene religious devotion, to the Moderns, with their feverish visions. I should look deep into the canvases of Raphael[9], Leonardo da Vinci, Titian[10], Rembrandt[11]. I should want to feast my eyes upon the warm colors of Veronese[12], study the mysteries of El Greco[13], catch a new vision of Nature from Corot[14]. Oh, there is so much rich meaning and beauty in the art of the ages for you who have eyes to see!

34   Upon my short visit to this temple of art I should not be able to review a fraction of that great world of art which is open to you. I should be able to get only a superficial impression. Artists tell me that for a deep and true appreciation of art one must educate the eye. One must learn through experience to weigh the merits of line, of composition, of form and color. If I had eyes, how happily would I embark upon so fascinating a study! Yet I am told that, to many of you who have eyes to see, the world of art is a dark night, unexplored and unilluminated.

---

(1) myriad: infinitely great number of
(2) Parthenon: temple of Athena at Athens, regarded the finest Doric temple
(3) frieze: the border along the top of the wall of a building, usu. decorated with pictures, patterns, etc.
(4) Samothrace: a Greek island in the North East of Aegean
(5) gnarled: rough and twisted
(6) Michelangelo: Florentine sculptor, painter, architect and poet, one of the outstanding figures of Renaissance
(7) Moses: the Hebrew prophet who led the Israelites out of Egypt and delivered the law
(8) Rodin: French sculptor, noted for his portrayal of human shape, his works include *The Kiss*, *The Burghers of Calais* and *The Thinker*.
(9) Raphael: Italian painter and architect, one of the greatest artists of the High Renaissance
(10) Titian: an Italian 16th century painter known for his portraits and for his innovative use of colors
(11) Rembrandt: a 17th century Dutch painter, one of the greatest painters in history, unique for his handling of shade and light. *The Night Watch* is one of his best-known paintings.
(12) Veronese: Italian painter of the Venetian school
(13) EL Greco: the Spanish painter during the Renaissance
(14) Corot: a 19th century French landscape and portrait painter

35　　It would be with extreme reluctance that I should leave the Metropolitan Museum, which contains the key to beauty—a beauty so neglected. Seeing persons, however, do not need a Metropolitan to find this key to beauty. The same key lies waiting in smaller museums, and in books on the shelves of even small libraries. But naturally, in my limited time of imaginary sight, I should choose the place where the key unlocks the greatest treasures in the shortest time.

36　　The evening of my second day of sight I should spend at a theatre or at the movies. Even now I often attend theatrical performances of all sorts, but the action of the play must be spelled into my hand by a companion. But how I should like to see with my own eyes the fascinating figure of Hamlet, or the gusty① Falstaff② amid colorful Elizabethan trappings! How I should like to follow each movement of the graceful Hamlet, each strut of the hearty Falstaff! And since I could see only one play, I should be confronted by a many-horned dilemma, for there are scores of plays I should want to see. You who have eyes can see any you like. How many of you, I wonder, when you gaze at a play, a movie, or any spectacle, realize and give thanks for the miracle of sight which enables you to enjoy its color, grace, and movement?

37　　I cannot enjoy the beauty of rhythmic movement except in a sphere restricted to the touch of my hands. I can vision only dimly the grace of a Pavlowa③, although I know something of the delight of rhythm, for often I can sense the beat of music as it vibrates through the floor. I can well imagine that cadenced motion must be one of the most pleasing sights in the world. I have been able to gather something of this by tracing with my fingers the lines in sculptured marble; if this static grace can be so lovely, how much more acute must be the thrill of seeing grace in motion.

38　　One of my dearest memories is of the time when Joseph Jefferson allowed me to touch his face and hands as he went through some of the gestures and speeches of his beloved Rip Van Winkle④. I was able to catch thus a meagre⑤ glimpse of the world of drama, and I shall never forget the delight of that moment. But, oh, how much I must miss, and how much pleasure you seeing ones can derive from watching and hearing the interplay of speech and movement in the unfolding of a dramatic performance! If I could see only one play, I should know how to picture in my mind the action of a hundred plays which I have read or had transferred to me through the medium of the manual alphabet.

39　　So, through the evening of my second imaginary day of sight, the great figures of dramatic literature would crowd sleep from my eyes.

IV

40　　The following morning, I should again greet the dawn, anxious to discover new delights, for I am sure that, for those who have eyes which really see, the dawn of each day must be a perpetually new revelation of beauty.

41　　This, according to the terms of my imagined miracle, is to be my third and last day of

---

① gusty: (here) full of pretentious talk
② Falstaff: a jovial, fat knight in Shakespeare's *Henry IV*
③ Pavlowa: great Russian ballerina
④ Rip Van Winkle: the main character in Washington Irving's novel *Rip Van Winkle* who has slept away twenty years
⑤ meager: inadequate, deficient

sight. I shall have no time to waste in regrets or longings; there is too much to see. The first day I devoted to my friends, animate and inanimate. The second revealed to me the history of man and Nature. Today I shall spend in the workaday world of the present, amid the haunts of men going about the business of life. And where can one find so many activities and conditions of men as in New York? So the city becomes my destination.

42   I start from my home in the quiet little suburb of Forest Hills, Long Island. Here, surrounded by green lawns, trees, and flowers, are neat little houses, happy with the voices and movements of wives and children, havens① of peaceful rest for men who toil in the city. I drive across the lacy structure of steel which spans the East River, and I get a new and startling vision of the power and ingenuity of the mind of man. Busy boats chug② and scurry③ about the river—racy speed boats, stolid④, snorting tugs. If I had long days of sight ahead, I should spend many of them watching the delightful activity upon the river.

43   I look ahead, and before me rise the fantastic towers of New York, a city that seems to have stepped from the pages of a fairy story. What an awe-inspiring sight, these glittering spires, these vast banks of stone and steel—structures such as the gods might build for themselves! This animated picture is a part of the lives of millions of people every day. How many, I wonder, give it so much as a second glance? Very few, I fear. Their eyes are blind to this magnificent sight because it is so familiar to them.

44   I hurry to the top of one of those gigantic structures, the Empire State Building, for there, a short time ago, I "saw" the city below through the eyes of my secretary. I am anxious to compare my fancy with reality. I am sure I should not be disappointed in the panorama spread out before me, for to me it would be a vision of another world.

45   Now I begin my rounds of the city. First, I stand at a busy corner, merely looking at people, trying by sight of them to understand something of their lives. I see smiles, and I am happy. I see serious determination, and I am proud. I see suffering, and I am compassionate.

46   I stroll down Fifth Avenue. I throw my eyes out of focus, so that I see no particular object but only a seething⑤ kaleidoscope of color. I am certain that the colors of women's dresses moving in a throng must be a gorgeous spectacle of which I should never tire. But perhaps if I had sight I should be like most other women—too interested in styles and the cut of individual dresses to give much attention to the splendor of color in the mass. And I am convinced, too, that I should become an inveterate⑥ window shopper, for it must be a delight to the eye to view the myriad articles of beauty on display.

47   From Fifth Avenue I make a tour of the city—to Park Avenue, to the slums, to factories, to parks where children play. I take a stay-at-home trip abroad by visiting the foreign quarters. Always my eyes are open wide to all the sights of both happiness and misery so that I may probe deep and add to my understanding of how people work and live. My heart is full of the images

① haven: place of safety
② chug: a short, dull, explosive sound
③ scurry: to go or move quickly
④ stolid: impassive, unemotional
⑤ seething: to be in a state of agitation or excitement
⑥ inveterate: habitual

of people and things. My eye passes lightly over no single trifle; it strives to touch and hold closely each thing its gaze rests upon. Some sights are pleasant, filling the heart with happiness; but some are miserably pathetic. To these latter I do not shut my eyes, for they, too, are part of life. To close the eye on them is to close the heart and mind.

48   My third day of sight is drawing to an end. Perhaps there are many serious pursuits to which I should devote the few remaining hours, but I am afraid that on the evening of that last day I should again run away to the theatre, to a hilariously funny play, so that I might appreciate the overtones of comedy in the human spirit.

49   At midnight my temporary respite① from blindness would cease, and permanent night would close in on me again. Naturally in those three short days I should not have seen all I wanted to see. Only when darkness had again descended upon me should I realize how much I had left unseen. But my mind would be so crowded with glorious memories that I should have little time for regrets. Thereafter the touch of every object would bring a glowing memory of how that object looked.

50   Perhaps this short outline of how I should spend three days of sight does not agree with the programme you would set for yourself if you knew that you were about to be stricken blind. I am, however, sure that if you actually faced that fate your eyes would open to things you had never seen before, storing up memories for the long night ahead. You would use your eyes as never before. Everything you saw would become dear to you. Your eyes would touch and embrace every object that came within your range of vision. Then, at last, you would really see, and a new world of beauty would open itself before you.

51   I who am blind can give one hint to those who see—one admonition② to those who would make full use of the gift of sight: Use your eyes as if tomorrow you would be stricken blind. And the same method can be applied to the other senses. Hear the music of voices, the song of a bird, the mighty strains of an orchestra, as if you would be stricken deaf tomorrow. Touch each object you want to touch as if tomorrow your tactile sense would fail. Smell the perfume of flowers, taste with relish③ each morsel, as if tomorrow you could never smell and taste again. Make the most of every sense; glory in all the facets of pleasure and beauty which the world reveals to you through the several means of contact which Nature provides. But of all the senses, I am sure that sight must be the most delightful.

▶▶ STUDY QUESTIONS

 Recalling

1. Why does Helen think it is a blessing if each human being were stricken blind and deaf for a few days?
2. How does Helen get to know the world?
3. What does Helen want to see for the first day of her sight? The second day? The third day?

---

① respite: temporary suspension
② admonition: advice or caution
③ relish: liking, appreciation

B⟩ *Interpreting*

4. Why do people usually look without seeing and listen without hearing?

5. Do you think the blind sees more? Why or why not?

C⟩ *Extending*

6. If you have only three days to see, what things are you going to let your gaze upon long?

7. In addition to what is proposed by Helen, is there other means that can pull people out of their lethargy?

8. How are you going to live your life if you are blind or deaf?

▶ FURTHER READING

Dante Alighirie, *The Divine Comedy*

Jean Jacques Rousseau, *The Confessions*

Khaled Hosseini, *The Kite Runner*

Sherwood Anderson, *I Want to Know Why*

Nathaniel Hawthorne, *My Kinsman, Major Molineux*

Raymond Carver, *Cathedral*

▶ MOVIES RECOMMENDED

The Beautiful Mind (2001), directed by Ron Howard

Gandhi (1982), directed by Richard Attenborough

Jerry Maguire (1996), directed by Cameron Crowe

Little Miss Sunshine (2006), directed by Jonathan Dayton and Valerie Faris

《十七岁的单车》（2001），导演王小帅

Unit Three   Love

I. "Guan Ju" from *Shijing* (*Book of Verse*)

▶▶ ABOUT *SHIJING*

Chinese literature begins with *Shijing* (*Book of Verse*), an anthology of songs, poems, and hymns. It consists of 311 poems (6 without text) dating from the Zhou Dynasty (1027 BC–771 BC) to the Spring and Autumn Period (770 BC–476 BC). The collection is divided into four main sections:

1. *Guofeng (Lessons from the States)*: poems or folk songs from ordinary people.
2. *Xiaoya (Minor Odes of the Kingdom)*: poems or songs concerning life of the nobility.
3. *Daya (Greater Odes of the Kingdom)*: poems or songs of praise of the rulers and their life.
4. *Song (Odes of the Temple and the Altar)*: hymns written for religious ceremonies of the court.

Shijing has been translated into English by a number of prominent scholars since 18th century. The translation we use here is by James Legge (1814–1897) and has substituted his transliteration of Chinese names with Pinyin. The following poem is the first poem in *Book of Verse*, collected in *Guofeng: Zhounan*.

<table>
<tr><td colspan="2">关　雎</td><td colspan="2" align="center">Guan Ju</td></tr>
<tr><td>1</td><td>关关雎鸠①，在河之洲②。
窈窕淑女，君子好逑。</td><td>1</td><td>Guan-guan go the ospreys,
On the islet in the river.
The modest, retiring, virtuous, young lady —
For our prince a good mate she.</td></tr>
<tr><td></td><td>参差荇菜③，左右流之。
窈窕淑女，寤寐求之④。</td><td></td><td></td></tr>
<tr><td>5</td><td>求之不得，寤寐思服。
悠哉悠哉⑤，辗转反侧。</td><td>5</td><td>Here long, there short, is the duckweed,
To the left, to the right, borne about by the current.
The modest, retiring, virtuous, young lady
Waking and sleeping, he sought her.</td></tr>
<tr><td></td><td>参差荇菜，左右采之。
窈窕淑女，琴瑟友之。</td><td></td><td>He sought her and found her not,</td></tr>
<tr><td></td><td>参差荇菜，左右芼之⑥。</td><td>10</td><td>And waking and sleeping he thought about her.
Long he thought; oh! long and anxiously;
On his side, on his back, he turned, and back again.</td></tr>
<tr><td>10</td><td>窈窕淑女，钟鼓乐之。</td><td></td><td>Here long, there short, is the duckweed;
On the left, on the right, we gather it.</td></tr>
</table>

---

①关关：水鸟鸣叫的声音；雎（jū）鸠：一种水鸟
②洲：水中的陆地
③逑：配偶
④参差：(cēn cī)：长短不齐的样子；荇（xìng）菜：一种多年生的水草，叶子可以食用
⑤寤（wù）：睡醒；寐（mèi）：睡着
⑦悠哉：忧思的样子
⑧芼（mào）：采摘

15   The modest, retiring, virtuous, young lady
        With lutes, small and large, let us give her friendly welcome.

        Here long, there short, is the duckweed;
        On the left, on the right, we cook and present it.
        The modest, retiring, virtuous, young lady
20   With bells and drums let us show our delight in her.

 ## STUDY QUESTIONS

 ### *A* > *Recalling*

1. What images are used in the poem?
2. What is the story?

B > *Interpreting*

3. What are the specific functions of the images " 关关雎鸠 " and "参差荇菜 "?
4. Are the images "琴瑟 " and "钟鼓 " s imply visual images? Besides visual effect, what other effects do they produce?
5. What kind of mood has the poem created?

 ### *C* > *Extending*

6. Do the Chinese poem and the English translation create the same or different effect? If the effects are different, in what way are they different? Which one do you like better?
7. Please read the poem aloud and pay attention to the music of it.
8. What is falling in love like for you? Please write a poem about it.

II. *La Belle Dame sans Merci: A Ballad* by John Keats

 ## ABOUT THE POET

John Keats (1795–1821), English Romantic poet, one of the main figures of the second generation Romantic poets along with Lord Byron, Percy Bysshe Shelley. Keats' poetry is characterized by sensual imagery, mostly notably in the series of odes, which include *Ode to a Nightingale, Ode on a Grecian Urn,* etc.

La Belle Dame sans Merci①: A Ballad

1

O what can ail② thee, knight at arms,
Alone and palely loitering③?
The sedge④ has wither'd from the lake,
And no birds sing.

2

O what can ail thee,knight at arms,
So haggard⑤ and so woe-begone⑥?
The squirrel's granary⑦ is full,
And the harvest's done.

3

I see a lily on thy brow
With anguish moist and fever dew,
And on thy cheek a fading rose
Fast withereth too.

4

I met a lady in the meads⑧
Full beautiful'a faery's child;
Her hair was long, her foot was light,
And her eyes were wild.

5

I made a garland⑨ for her head,
And bracelets too, and fragrant zone⑩,
She looked at me as she did love,
And made sweet moan.

6

I set her on my pacing steed,
And nothing else saw all day long,

---

① La Belle Dame sans Merci: the lovely lady without pity
② ail: to cause pain
③ loiter: to linger aimlessly
④ sedge: rushlike or grasslike plant
⑤ haggard: having a wasted or exhausted appearance, as from suffering or anxiety
⑥ woe-begone: gloomy, suffering from pain
⑦ granary: storehouse
⑧ mead: (archaic or poetic) meadow
⑨ garland: wreath of flowers or leaves
⑩ zone: (poetic) girdle or belt

For sideways would she bend, and sing
A faery's song.

7

She found me roots of relish[1] sweet,
And honey wild,and manna[2] dew,
And sure in language strange she said—
I love thee true.

8

She took me to her elfin grot[3],
And there she wept and sigh'd full sore,
And there I shut her wild wild eyes—
With kisses four.

9

And there she lulled me asleep,
And there I dream'd,—Ah! Woe betide[4]!
The latest dream I ever dream'd
On the cold hill's side.

10

I saw pale kings, and princes too,
Pale warriors,death-pale were they all,
Who cried — "La belle Dame sans Merci
Hath thee in thrall[5]!"

11

I saw their starv'd lips in the gloam[6]
With horrid warning gaped[7] wide,
And I awoke and found me here
On the cold hill's side.

12

And this is why I sojourn[8] here
Alone and palely loitering,
Though the sedge is wither'd from the lake,
And no birds sing.

[1] relish: appetizing food
[2] manna: divine food
[3] elfin grot: the cave that is the residence of an elf, or fairy
[4] woe-betide: exclamation, pain befalls
[5] hath thee in thrall: has enslaved you
[6] gloam: twilight
[7] gape: to open the mouth involuntarily
[8] sojourn: to stay temporary

▶ STUDY QUESTIONS

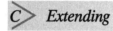 Recalling

1. What does the knight at arms look like?
2. What is the surrounding like when the knight loiters around?
3. What is the lady like?
4. How does the lady show her love?
5. What does the knight see in his dream?

B Interpreting

6. How do the images in the poem impress you? What effects have they created?
7. Why does the poet describe the lips of the kings, princes and warriors as "starv'd"? What implication does the knight get from the images of the kings, princes and warriors?
8. Please point out the contrasts in the poem. What do the contrasts suggest?
9. The poem has shown a dream of the knight in which he sees the starved kings, etc. Can you detect any other dream in the poem?
10. Compare this poem with "Guan Ju" (《关雎》) and *The Lorelei* and share your findings.

C Extending

11. What elements in the poem have contributed to the ballad quality of it?

III. *The Lorelei* by Heinrich Heine

▶ ABOUT THE POET

Heinrich Heine (1797–1856) was one of Germany's greatest poets. Born in the city of Dusseldorf, Heine was encouraged by his family to study law, but he was always more interested in history and literature. His best-known poems, including *The Lorelei*, were set to music and travelled all over the world as songs. According to German legend, the Lorelei was a siren, or beautiful female spirit, who sat on a cliff overlooking Germany's Rhine River and sang an enticing song that lured sailors to their deaths in the rocky waters nearby.

The Lorelei
Translated from the German by Aaron Kramer

1   I cannot explain the sadness
     That's fallen on my breast.
     An old, old fable haunts me,
     And will not let me rest.

5   The air grows cool in the twilight,
     And softly the Rhine flows on;
     The peak of a mountain sparkles
     Beneath the setting sun.

     More lovely than a vision,
10   A girl sits high up there;
     Her golden jewellery glistens,
     She combs her golden hair.

     With a comb of gold she combs it,
     And sings an evensong[①];
15   The wonderful melody reaches
     A boat, as it sails along.

     The boatman hears, with an anguish
     More wild than was ever known;
     He's blind to the rocks around him;
20   His eyes are for her alone.

     —At last the waves devoured
     The boat, and the boatman's cry;
     And this she did with her singing,
     The golden Lorelei.

STUDY QUESTIONS

 ## Recalling

1. In the opening stanza, what does the narrator say about the effects the fable of the Lorelei has had on him?
2. What details of time and place are provided in the second stanza?
3. Please briefly describe the girl and her actions in the third and fourth stanzas.
4. According to the last two stanzas, what happens to the boatman when he hears the girl's song?
5. What images are used in this poem?

 ## Interpreting

6. In what sense is the ending of the poem ironic?
7. What details contribute to the fairy-tale qualities of the poem?
8. What view of beauty does the poem provide?

 ## Extending

9. What aspects of human experience might the Lorelei represent? Do you have similar experience?

---

① evensong: evening song

▶ LITERARY FOCUS

▷ *Types of Poetry*

Poetry is often divided into three categories. Narrative poems tell stories in verse. Some narrative poems concentrate on relating the main events of the plot; others provide extensive details of plot, setting, and character. Lyric poems express a speaker's personal thoughts and feelings. Most lyric poems are short and are marked by intense emotion and musical language. Dramatic poems, like plays, present characters speaking to themselves, to each other, or to the reader.

The three categories of poetry sometimes overlap, so identifying a particular poem by category will depend on what you feel is the poet's main purpose. When classifying a poem, ask yourself if the main purpose is to tell a story (narrative), to express private feelings (lyric), or to reveal character through speech (dramatic).

▶ THINKING ABOUT TYPES OF POETRY

Into which category will you put "Guan Ju*", La Belle Dame sans Merci* and *The Lorelei*?

IV. *A Red, Red Rose* by Robert Burns

▶ ABOUT THE POET

Robert Burns (1759–1796) (also known as Scotland's favourite son, the Ploughman Poet, the Bard of Ayrshire and in Scotland as The Bard) was a Scottish poet and lyricist. He is widely regarded as the national poet of Scotland and is celebrated worldwide. He is one of the best known of the poets who have written in the Scots language, although much of his writing is also in English and a light Scots dialect, accessible to audience beyond Scotland. He is regarded as a pioneer of the Romantic movement. As well as making original compositions, Burns also collected folk songs from across Scotland, often revising or adapting them. His poem (and song) *Auld Lang Syne* is often sung at Hogmanay (the last day of the year), and *Scots Wha Hae* served for a long time as an unofficial national anthem of the country. Other poems and songs of Burns that remain well-known across the world today include *A Red, Red Rose, A Man's A Man for A' That, To a Louse, To a Mouse, The Battle of Sherramuir, Tam o' Shanter*, and *Ae Fond Kiss*.

A Red, Red Rose

1   O MY Luve's① like a red, red rose,
      That's newly sprung in June;
      O my Luve's like the melodie
      That's sweetly play'd in tune!

---

① luve: (Scottish) love

5   As fair art① thou②, my bonnie lass③,
    So deep in luve am I;
    And I will luve thee still, my dear,
    Till a' the④ seas gang dry.

    Till a' the seas gang dry, my dear,
10   And the rocks melt wi' the sun⑤;
    I will luve thee still, my dear,
    While the sands o' life⑥ shall run.

    And fare thee weel⑦, my only Luve,
    And fare thee weel a while!
15   And I will come again, my Luve,
    Tho' it⑧ were ten thousand mile.

STUDY QUESTIONS

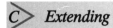 A Recalling

1. Please point out the images in the poem.
2. What does the speaker compare his love to?

B Interpreting

3. In what ways is "love" comparable with "rose" and "melody"?
4. What figure of speech is used in the line "Till a' the seas gang dry, my dear/And the rocks melt wi' the sun"? And what figure of speech is used in "sands of life"?
5. Besides the use of images, what other poetical devices make this poem beautiful and memorable?

C Extending

6. If "rose" is the conventional symbol of "love" in western culture, what flower is the symbol of "love" in traditional Chinese culture?
7. What would you like to compare your love to?
8. Read the poem aloud and feel the music of it.

LITERARY FOCUS

The Music of Poetry (II)

The term **rhythm** refers to any wave-like recurrence of motion or sound. **Meter** is the kind of

① art: (archaic) are
② thou: (archaic) you
③ bonnie lass: pretty girl
④ a' the: all the
⑤ wi' the sun: with the sun
⑥ sands o' life: sands of life
⑦ fare thee weel: farewell to you
⑧ tho' it: thought it

rhythm we can tap our foot to. Metrical language is called verse; non-metrical language is prose.

The **foot** is the metrical unit by which a line of poetry is measured; it usually consists of one **stressed** or accented (') and one or two **unstressed** or unaccented syllables (-).

Name of Foot	Name of Meter	Measure
Iamb	Iambic	-'
Trochee	Trochaic	'-
Anapest	Anapestic	--'
Dactyl	Dactylic	'--
Spondee	Spondaic	' '
Pyrrhus	Pyrrhic	--

The secondary unit of measurement, the **line**, is measured by naming the number of feet in it. A line that ends with a stressed syllable is said to have a **masculine ending** and a line that ends with an extra syllable is said to have a **feminine ending**. A pause within a line is called a **caesura** and is identified by a double vertical line (II). A line with a pause at its end is called **end-stopped line**, whereas a line that continues without a pause is called **run-on line** or **enjambment**. The following **metrical names** are used to identify the lengths of lines:

Length	Name
one foot	Monometer
two feet	Dimeter
three feet	Trimeter
four feet	Tetrameter
five feet	Pentameter
six feet	Hexameter
seven feet	Heptameter
eight feet	Octameter

The third unit, the **stanza**, consists of a group of lines whose metrical pattern is repeated throughout the poem.

The process of measuring verse is referred to as **scansion**. To scan a poem we do these three things: (a) we identify the prevailing **meter**; (b) we give a **metrical name** to the number of feet in a line; and (c) we describe the stanza pattern or **rhyme-scheme**.

Cattleya Orchid and Three Brazilian Hummingbirds
Martin Johnson Heade, 1871.
Gift of The Morris and Gwendolyn Cafritz Foundation.

V. *SONNET 130* by William Shakespeare

SONNET 130

1   My mistress' eyes are nothing like the sun;
     Coral is far more red than her lips' red;
     If snow be white, why then her breasts are dun;
     If hairs be wires[1], black wires grow on her head.
5   I have seen roses damask'd[2], red and white,
     But no such roses see I in her cheeks;
     And in some perfumes is there more delight
     Than in the breath that from my mistress reeks[3].
     I love to hear her speak, yet well I know
10   That music hath a far more pleasing sound;
     I grant I never saw a goddess go;
     My mistress, when she walks, treads on the ground:
     And yet, by heaven, I think my love as rare
     As any she belied with false compare.

[1] If hairs be wires: woman's hairs is often compared to golden wires.
[2] roses damask'd: roses that are like designs on silk or linen material with reflection of light
[3] reeks: breathes

▶ STUDY QUESTIONS

A▷ Recalling

1. Please point out the images in the poem.
2. What does the speaker's lover look like according to the poem?
3. What does a traditional beauty look like?

B▷ Interpreting

4. Why do you think Shakespeare praises his love in this rather unconventional way?
5. Do you think the lady to whom the poem presents will be pleased by the poem? Why or why not?
6. Please point out the rhyming scheme of the poem.

C▷ Extending

7. Compare Shakespeare's sonnet with Robert Burns'*A Red, Red Rose*, which one is truer to a person in love? Why?

▶ LITERARY FOCUS

▷ Shakespeare's Sonnet

In the late 1500s it was fashionable for English gentleman authors to write sonnets—lyric poems composed of 14 lines. The sonnet is composed with a formal rhyme scheme, denoting different thoughts, moods, or emotions, sometimes summed up in the last lines of the poem. The two main forms of the sonnet are the Petrarchan (Italian) and the Shakespearean (English).

Shakespearean sonnet is in iambic pentameter and the rhyme scheme is *abab, cdcd, efef, gg*. Each quatrain takes a different appearance of the idea or develops a different image to express the theme while the last two lines (the couplet) summarizes or presents some change of view or tone or surprise. William Shakespeare composed 154 sonnets in his lifetime. All of his sonnets were in this form except for the poems he wrote earlier in life. The 154 sonnets can be formed three groups:

(1) Twenty-six sonnets written mostly to a young man, seventeen of them urging marriage.

(2) One hundred and one sonnets, also written to a young man (probably the same young nobleman as in the first twenty-six). These have a variety of themes, such as the beauty of the loved one; destruction of beauty; competition with a Rival Poet; despair about the absence of a loved one; and reaction toward the young man's coldness.

(3) The remaining twenty-seven sonnets written mainly to a woman, popularly known as "the Dark Lady". Many students of Shakespeare's work believe that he had a love affair with this woman.

Most Elizabethan sonnets were written about joys and sorrows of love. Some of Shakespeare's sonnet arrangements are thought to be autobiographical. This is why scholars have tried to learn about William Shakespeare's life from his sonnets.

▶ THINKING ABOUT SONNET

1. Where does the change of tone occur in *Sonnet 130*?

2. Sonnet is still popular as the form of a love poem. Do you think "love" is better presented in free verse or in a strict form such as sonnet?

VI. *When You Are Old* by William Butler Yeats

▶ ABOUT THE POET

William Butler Yeats (1865–1939), who is regarded as Ireland's greatest poet, was born near Dublin when Ireland was still part of Great Britain. A supporter of Irish cultural independence, Yeats revived interest in ancient Irish myths and legends and helped found Dublin's Abbey Theatre. He was also Ireland's first writer to win the Nobel Prize.

When You Are Old

1   When you are old and grey and full of sleep,
And nodding by the fire, take down this book,
And slowly read, and dream of the soft look
Your eyes had once, and of their shadows deep;

5   How many loved your moments of glad grace,
And loved your beauty with love false or true,
But one man loved the pilgrim soul in you,
And loved the sorrows of your changing face;

And bending down beside the glowing bars[①],
10   Murmur, a little sadly, how Love fled
And paced upon the mountains overhead
And hid his face amid a crowd of stars.

▶ STUDY QUESTIONS

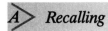 *Recalling*

1. According to the poem, what is the lover like when she is young? And what is she like when she is old?

2. What does the speaker love about his lover?

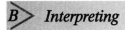 *Interpreting*

3. Why does the speaker "loved the sorrows of your changing face"?

① bar: wood

4. What is the lover sorrowful and sad about?

5. Why is the last "Love" in the poem capitalized? What is the image of Love presented in the last three stanzas? What does the image suggest?

6. Think about the form of the poem. How does the form contribute to what is being said?

C> *Extending*

7. Please compare this poem with the previous love poems in this unit. What is similar and what is different?

VII. *How Do I Love Thee* by Elizabeth Barrett Browning

▶ ABOUT THE POETESS

Elizabeth Barrett Browning (1806–1861) was one of the most prominent poets of the Victorian era. Her fame rests not only on her literary achievements but also on the love between her and Robert Browning, the writer with equal eminence. Their love has given birth to Elizabeth Browning's most influential work *Sonnets from the Portuguese*. Her poetry was widely popular in both England and the United States during her lifetime.

From *Sonnets from the Portuguese*
XLIII

1   How do I love thee? Let me count the ways.
    I love thee to the depth and breadth and height
    My soul can reach, when feeling out of sight
    For the ends of Being and ideal Grace.
5   I love thee to the level of everyday's
    Most quiet need, by sun and candlelight.
    I love thee freely, as men strive for Right;
    I love thee purely, as they turn from Praise.
    I love thee with the passion put to use
10   In my old griefs, and with my childhood's faith.
    I love thee with a love I seemed to lose
    With my lost saints, —I love thee with the breath,
    Smiles, tears, of all my life! —and, if God choose,
    I shall but love thee better after death.

▶ STUDY QUESTIONS

A> *Recalling*

1. How many ways of love have been counted?

2. What do "Being" and "ideal Grace" refer to?

 Interpreting

3. What makes "the passion put to use in my old griefs" comparable with the passion put to love?
4. Why love with "my childhood's faith"? What is special about "childhood's faith"?
5. What does "lost saints" suggest? And what does "love thee with a love I seemed to lose/ With my lost saints" suggest?
6. The poem is full of religious images. How are religion and love related in this poem?

C Extending

7. Compare the structure and rhyme of this sonnet with Shakespeare's sonnet. What have you found out?

VIII. *Variations on the Word Love* by Margaret Atwood

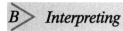 **ABOUT THE POETESS**

 **Margaret (Eleanor) Atwood** (1939–   ) Canadian poet, novelist, and critic, noted for her feminism and mythological themes. Atwood's work has been regarded as a barometer of feminist thought. Her protagonists are often a kind of "everywoman" characters, or weaker members of society. Several of Atwood's novels can be classified as science fiction, although her writing is above the normal formula of the genre.

Variations on the Word Love

1   This is a word we use to plug
    holes with. It's the right size for those warm
    blanks in speech, for those red heart-
    shaped vacancies on the page that look nothing
5   like real hearts. Add lace
    and you can sell
    it. We insert it also in the one empty
    space on the printed form
    that comes with no instructions. There are whole
10   magazines with not much in them
    but the word love, you can
    rub it all over your body and you
    can cook with it too. How do we know
    it isn't what goes on at the cool
15   debaucheries① of slugs② under damp

---

① debauchery: excessive indulgence in sexual pleasure
② slug: any of the snaillike worms without a shell

pieces of cardboard? As for the weed-
seedlings① nosing their tough snouts② up
among the lettuces, they shout it.
Love! Love! sing the soldiers, raising
20   their glittering knives in salute.

Then there's the two
of us. This word
is far too short for us, it has only
four letters, too sparse
25   to fill those deep bare
vacuums between the stars
that press on us with their deafness.
It's not love we don't wish
to fall into, but that fear.
30   this word is not enough but it will
have to do. It's a single
vowel in this metallic
silence, a mouth that says
O again and again in wonder
35   and pain, a breath, a finger
grip on a cliffside. You can
hold on or let go.

▶▶ STUDY QUESTIONS

 Recalling

1. According to the poem, on what occasions do people use the word "love"?
2. Please single out words that suggest "empty" in the first stanza.
3. What emotion is the word "love" usually associated with?

B ▷ Interpreting

4. What is ironical in the first stanza?
5. According to the second stanza, why do "we" have "fear"?
6. Why does the speaker say "This word /is far too short for us"?
7. Can you give examples to show "This word is not enough but it will/have to do"?
8. Read the letter "love" again and again and see if you can feel "a single/vowel in this metallic/ silence" and "a mouth that says/O again and again in wonder/and pain".
9. What does the image "a finger grip on a cliffside" suggest?
10. How are the two parts of the poem related with each other? What is the poet's attitude towards love? Compared with the previous love poems, what is special about this poem?

---

① weed-seedling: the young unwanted plant
② snout: the part of an animal's head projecting forward and containing the nose and jaws

C▷ *Extending*

11. How do you feel about the four-letter word "l-o-v-e" or the Chinese character "爱"? Please write a poem about it.

IX. *Under the Willow Tree* by Hans Christian Andersen

▶ ABOUT THE AUTHOR

Hans Christian Andersen (1805–1875) was a Danish author and poet. Although a prolific writer of plays, travelogues, novels, and poems, Andersen is best remembered for his fairy tales, a literary genre he so mastered that his works have been immortalized in children's world literature. Andersen's popularity was not limited to children, as his fairy tales express universal themes that transcend age and nationality.

Under the Willow Tree

Translated by H. P. Paull

1　　　The region round the little town of Kjøge is very bleak and cold. The town lies on the sea shore, which is always beautiful; but here it might be more beautiful than it is, for on every side the fields are flat, and it is a long way to the forest. But when persons reside in a place and get used to it, they can always find something beautiful in it,—something for which they long, even in the most charming spot in the world which is not home. It must be owned that there are in the outskirts of the town some humble gardens on the banks of a little stream that runs on towards the sea, and in summer these gardens look very pretty. Such indeed was the opinion of two little children, whose parents were neighbors, and who played in these gardens, and forced their way from one garden to the other through the gooseberry-bushes that divided them.

2　　　In one of the gardens grew an elder tree, and in the other an old willow, under which the children were very fond of playing. They had permission to do so, although the tree stood close by the stream, and they might easily have fallen into the water; but the eye of God watches over the little ones, otherwise they would never be safe. At the same time, these children were very careful not to go too near the water; indeed, the boy was so afraid of it, that in the summer, while the other children were splashing about in the sea, nothing could entice① him to join them. They jeered and laughed at him, and he was obliged to bear it all as patiently as he could. Once the neighbor's little girl, Joanna, dreamed that she was sailing in a boat, and the boy—Knud was his name—waded② out in the water to join her, and the water came up to his neck, and at last closed over his head, and in a moment he had disappeared. When little Knud heard this dream, it seemed as if he could not bear the mocking and jeering again; how could he dare to go into the water now, after Joanna's dream! He never would do it, for this dream always satisfied him.

3　　　The parents of these children, who were poor, often sat together while Knud and Joanna played in the gardens or in the road. Along this road—a row of willow-trees had been planted

---

① entice: to lead on by exciting hope or desire
② wade: to walk in water

to separate it from a ditch on one side of it. They were not very handsome trees, for the tops had been cut off; however, they were intended for use, and not for show. The old willow-tree in the garden was much handsomer, and therefore the children were very fond of sitting under it.

4 The town had a large market-place; and at the fair-time there would be whole rows, like streets, of tents and booths containing silks and ribbons, and toys and cakes, and everything that could be wished for. There were crowds of people, and sometimes the weather would be rainy, and splash with moisture the woollen jackets of the peasants; but it did not destroy the beautiful fragrance of the honey-cakes and gingerbread with which one booth was filled; and the best of it was, that the man who sold these cakes always lodged during the fair-time with little Knud's parents. So every now and then he had a present of gingerbread, and of course Joanna always had a share. And, more delightful still, the gingerbread seller knew all sorts of things to tell and could even relate stories about his own gingerbread. So one evening he told them a story that made such a deep impression on the children that they never forgot it; and therefore I think we may as well hear it too, for it is not very long.

5 "Once upon a time," said he, "there lay on my counter two gingerbread cakes, one in the shape of a man wearing a hat, the other of a maiden without a bonnet. Their faces were on the side that was uppermost, for on the other side they looked very different. Most people have a best side to their characters, which they take care to show to the world. On the left, just where the heart is, the gingerbread man had an almond stuck in to represent it, but the maiden was honey cake all over. They were placed on the counter as samples, and after lying there a long time they at last fell in love with each other; but neither of them spoke of it to the other, as they should have done if they expected anything to follow. 'He is a man, he ought to speak the first word,' thought the gingerbread maiden; but she felt quite happy—she was sure that her love was returned. But his thoughts were far more ambitious, as the thoughts of a man often are. He dreamed that he was a real street boy, that he possessed four real pennies, and that he had bought the gingerbread lady, and ate her up. And so they lay on the counter for days and weeks, till they grew hard and dry; but the thoughts of the maiden became ever more tender and womanly. 'Ah well, it is enough for me that I have been able to live on the same counter with him,' said she one day; when suddenly, 'crack,' and she broke in two. 'Ah,' said the gingerbread man to himself, 'if she had only known of my love, she would have kept together a little longer.' And here they both are, and that is their history," said the cake man. "You think the history of their lives and their silent love, which never came to anything, very remarkable; and there they are for you." So saying, he gave Joanna the gingerbread man, who was still quite whole—and to Knud the broken maiden; but the children had been so much impressed by the story, that they had not the heart to eat the lovers up.

6 The next day they went into the churchyard, and took the two cake figures with them, and sat down under the church wall, which was covered with luxuriant ivy in summer and winter, and looked as if hung with rich tapestry. They stuck up the two gingerbread figures in the sunshine among the green leaves, and then told the story, and all about the silent love which came to nothing, to a group of children. They called it, "love," because the story was so lovely, and the other children had the same opinion. But when they turned to look at the gingerbread pair, the broken maiden was gone! A great boy, out of wickedness, had eaten her up. At first the children cried about it; but afterwards, thinking very probably that the poor lover ought not to be

left alone in the world, they ate him up too: but they never forgot the story.

7   The two children still continued to play together by the elder-tree, and under the willow; and the little maiden sang beautiful songs, with a voice that was as clear as a bell. Knud, on the contrary, had not a note of music in him, but knew the words of the songs, and that of course is something. The people of Kjøge, and even the rich wife of the man who kept the fancy shop, would stand and listen while Joanna was singing, and say, "She has really a very sweet voice."

8   Those were happy days; but they could not last forever. The neighbors were separated, the mother of the little girl was dead, and her father had thoughts of marrying again and of residing in the capital, where he had been promised a very lucrative appointment as messenger. The neighbors parted with tears, the children wept sadly; but their parents promised that they should write to each other at least once a year.

9   After this, Knud was bound apprentice to a shoemaker; he was growing a great boy, and could not be allowed to run wild any longer. Besides, he was going to be confirmed①. Ah, how happy he would have been on that festal day in Copenhagen with little Joanna; but he still remained at Kjøge, and had never seen the great city, though the town is not five miles from it. But far across the bay, when the sky was clear, the towers of Copenhagen could be seen; and on the day of his confirmation he saw distinctly the golden cross on the principal church glittering in the sun. How often his thoughts were with Joanna! But did she think of him? Yes. About Christmas came a letter from her father to Knud's parents, which stated that they were going on very well in Copenhagen, and mentioning particularly that Joanna's beautiful voice was likely to bring her a brilliant fortune in the future. She was engaged to sing at a concert, and she had already earned money by singing, out of which she sent her dear neighbors at Kjøge a whole dollar, for them to make merry on Christmas eve, and they were to drink her health. She had herself added this in a postscript, and in the same postscript she wrote, "Kind regards to Knud."

10   The good neighbors wept, although the news was so pleasant; but they wept tears of joy. Knud's thoughts had been daily with Joanna, and now he knew that she also had thought of him; and the nearer the time came for his apprenticeship to end, the clearer did it appear to him that he loved Joanna, and that she must be his wife; and a smile came on his lips at the thought, and at one time he drew the thread so fast as he worked, and pressed his foot so hard against the knee strap, that he ran the awl② into his finger; but what did he care for that? He was determined not to play the dumb lover as both the gingerbread cakes had done; the story was a good lesson to him.

11   At length he became a journeyman; and then, for the first time, he prepared for a journey to Copenhagen, with his knapsack packed and ready. A master was expecting him there, and he thought of Joanna, and how glad she would be to see him. She was now seventeen, and he nineteen years old. He wanted to buy a gold ring for her in Kjøge, but then he recollected how far more beautiful such things would be in Copenhagen. So he took leave of his parents, and on a rainy day, late in the autumn, wandered forth on foot from the town of his birth. The leaves were falling from the trees; and, by the time he arrived at his new master's in the great metropolis③, he was wet through. On the following Sunday he intended to pay his first visit to Joanna's father. When the day came, the new journeyman's clothes were brought out, and a new

---

① confirm: to perform some rite to the baptized person to make him firmer in his belief
② awl: a pointed instrument for piercing small holes in leather, wood, etc.
③ metropolis: any large, busy city

hat, which he had brought in Kjøge. The hat became him very well, for hitherto he had only worn a cap. He found the house that he sought easily, but had to mount so many stairs that he became quite giddy; it surprised him to find how people lived over one another in this dreadful town.

12　　On entering a room in which everything denoted prosperity, Joanna's father received him very kindly. The new wife was a stranger to him, but she shook hands with him, and offered him coffee.

13　　"Joanna will be very glad to see you," said her father. "You have grown quite a nice young man, you shall see her presently; she is a good child, and is the joy of my heart, and, please God, she will continue to be so; she has her own room now, and pays us rent for it." And the father knocked quite politely at a door, as if he were a stranger, and then they both went in. How pretty everything was in that room! A more beautiful apartment could not be found in the whole town of Kjøge; the queen herself could scarcely be better accommodated. There were carpets, and rugs, and window curtains hanging to the ground. Pictures and flowers were scattered about. There was a velvet chair, and a looking-glass against the wall, into which a person might be in danger of stepping, for it was as large as a door.

14　　All this Knud saw at a glance, and yet, in truth, he saw nothing but Joanna. She was quite grown up, and very different from what Knud had fancied her, and a great deal more beautiful. In all Kjøge there was not a girl like her; and how graceful she looked, although her glance at first was odd, and not familiar; but for a moment only, then she rushed towards him as if she would have kissed him; she did not, however, although she was very near it. Yes, she really was joyful at seeing the friend of her childhood once more, and the tears even stood in her eyes. Then she asked so many questions about Knud's parents, and everything, even to the elder-tree and the willow, which she called "elder-mother and willow-father," as if they had been human beings; and so, indeed, they might be, quite as much as the gingerbread cakes. Then she talked about them, and the story of their silent love, and how they lay on the counter together and split in two; and then she laughed heartily; but the blood rushed into Knud's cheeks, and his heart beat quickly. Joanna was not proud at all; he noticed that through her he was invited by her parents to remain the whole evening with them, and she poured out the tea and gave him a cup herself; and afterwards she took a book and read aloud to them, and it seemed to Knud as if the story was all about himself and his love, for it agreed so well with his own thoughts. And then she sang a simple song, which, through her singing, became a true story, and as if she poured forth the feelings of her own heart.

15　　"Oh," he thought, "she knows I am fond of her." The tears he could not restrain rolled down his cheeks, and he was unable to utter a single word; it seemed as if he had been struck dumb.

16　　When he left, she pressed his hand, and said, "You have a kind heart, Knud: remain always as you are now." What an evening of happiness this had been; to sleep after it was impossible, and Knud did not sleep.

17　　At parting, Joanna's father had said, "Now, you won't quite forget us; you must not let the whole winter go by without paying us another visit;" so that Knud felt himself free to go again the following Sunday evening, and so he did. But every evening after working hours—and they worked by candle-light then—he walked out into the town, and through the street in which Joanna lived, to look up at her window. It was almost always lighted up; and one evening he saw the shadow of her face quite plainly on the window blind; that was a glorious evening for him. His master's wife did not like his always going out in the evening, idling, wasting time, as she called it, and she shook her head.

18 But his master only smiled, and said, "He is a young man, my dear, you know."

19 "On Sunday I shall see her," said Knud to himself, "and I will tell her that I love her with my whole heart and soul, and that she must be my little wife. I know I am now only a poor journeyman shoemaker, but I will work and strive, and become a master in time. Yes, I will speak to her; nothing comes from silent love. I learnt that from the gingerbread-cake story."

20 Sunday came, but when Knud arrived, they were all unfortunately invited out to spend the evening, and were obliged to tell him so.

21 Joanna pressed his hand, and said, "Have you ever been to the theatre? you must go once; I sing there on Wednesday, and if you have time on that day, I will send you a ticket; my father knows where your master lives." How kind this was of her! And on Wednesday, about noon, Knud received a sealed packet with no address, but the ticket was inside; and in the evening Knud went, for the first time in his life, to a theatre. And what did he see? He saw Joanna, and how beautiful and charming she looked! He certainly saw her being married to a stranger, but that was all in the play, and only a pretence; Knud well knew that. She could never have the heart, he thought, to send him a ticket to go and see it, if it had been real. So he looked on, and when all the people applauded and clapped their hands, he shouted "hurrah." He could see that even the king smiled at Joanna, and seemed delighted with her singing. How small Knud felt; but then he loved her so dearly, and thought she loved him, and the man must speak the first word, as the gingerbread maiden had thought. Ah, how much there was for him in that childish story. As soon as Sunday arrived, he went again, and felt as if he were about to enter on holy ground. Joanna was alone to welcome him, nothing could be more fortunate.

22 "I am so glad you are come," she said. "I was thinking of sending my father for you, but I had a presentiment① that you would be here this evening. The fact is, I wanted to tell you that I am going to France. I shall start on Friday. It is necessary for me to go there, if I wish to become a first-rate performer."

23 Poor Knud! it seemed to him as if the whole room was whirling round with him. His courage failed, and he felt as if his heart would burst. He kept down the tears, but it was easy to see how sorrowful he was.

24 "You honest, faithful soul," she exclaimed; and the words loosened Knud's tongue, and he told her how truly he had loved her, and that she must be his wife; and as he said this, he saw Joanna change color, and turn pale. She let his hand fall, and said, earnestly and mournfully, "Knud, do not make yourself and me unhappy. I will always be a good sister to you, one in whom you can trust; but I can never be anything more." And she drew her white hand over his burning forehead, and said, "God gives strength to bear a great deal, if we only strive ourselves to endure."

25 At this moment her stepmother came into the room, and Joanna said quickly, "Knud is so unhappy, because I am going away;" and it appeared as if they had only been talking of her journey. "Come, be a man" she added, placing her hand on his shoulder; "you are still a child,

---

① presentiment: a feeling or impression that something is about to happen

and you must be good and reasonable, as you were when we were both children, and played together under the willow-tree."

26   Knud listened, but he felt as if the world had slid out of its course. His thoughts were like a loose thread fluttering to and fro in the wind. He stayed, although he could not tell whether she had asked him to do so. But she was kind and gentle to him; she poured out his tea, and sang to him; but the song had not the old tone in it, although it was wonderfully beautiful, and made his heart feel ready to burst. And then he rose to go. He did not offer his hand, but she seized it, and said—

27   "Will you not shake hands with your sister at parting, my old playfellow?" and she smiled through the tears that were rolling down her cheeks. Again she repeated the word "brother," which was a great consolation certainly; and thus they parted.

28   She sailed to France, and Knud wandered about the muddy streets of Copenhagen. The other journeymen in the shop asked him why he looked so gloomy, and wanted him to go and amuse himself with them, as he was still a young man. So he went with them to a dancing-room. He saw many handsome girls there, but none like Joanna; and here, where he thought to forget her, she was more life-like before his mind than ever. "God gives us strength to bear much, if we try to do our best," she had said; and as he thought of this, a devout feeling came into his mind, and he folded his hands. Then, as the violins played and the girls danced round the room, he started; for it seemed to him as if he were in a place where he ought not to have brought Joanna, for she was here with him in his heart; and so he went out at once. As he went through the streets at a quick pace, he passed the house where she used to live; it was all dark, empty, and lonely. But the world went on its course, and Knud was obliged to go on too.

29   Winter came; the water was frozen, and everything seemed buried in a cold grave. But when spring returned, and the first steamer prepared to sail, Knud was seized with a longing to wander forth into the world, but not to France. So he packed his knapsack, and travelled through Germany, going from town to town, but finding neither rest or peace. It was not till he arrived at the glorious old town of Nuremberg that he gained the mastery over himself, and rested his weary feet; and here he remained.

30   Nuremberg is a wonderful old city, and looks as if it had been cut out of an old picture-book. The streets seem to have arranged themselves according to their own fancy, and as if the houses objected to stand in rows or rank and file. Gables, with little towers, ornamented columns, and statues, can be seen even to the city gate; and from the singular-shaped roofs, waterspouts, formed like dragons, or long lean dogs, extend far across to the middle of the street. Here, in the market-place, stood Knud, with his knapsack on his back, close to one of the old fountains which are so beautifully adorned with figures, scriptural and historical, and which spring up between the sparkling jets of water. A pretty servant-maid was just filling her pails, and she gave Knud a refreshing draught[①]; she had a handful of roses, and she gave him one, which appeared to him like a good omen for the future. From a neighboring church came the sounds of music, and the familiar tones reminded him of the organ at home at Kjøge; so he passed into the great cathedral. The sunshine streamed through the painted glass windows, and between two lofty slender pillars. His thoughts became prayerful, and calm peace rested on his soul. He next sought and found a good master in Nuremberg, with whom he stayed and

---

① draught: here refers to a portion of water.

learnt the German language.

31　　The old moat round the town had been converted into a number of little kitchen gardens; but the high walls, with their heavy-looking towers, are still standing. Inside these walls the ropemaker twisted his ropes along a walk built like a gallery, and in the cracks and crevices[1] of the walls elder bushes grow and stretch their green boughs over the small houses which stand below. In one of these houses lived the master for whom Knud worked; and over the little garret[2] window where he sat, the elder-tree waved its branches. Here he dwelt through one summer and winter, but when spring came again, he could endure it no longer. The elder was in blossom, and its fragrance was so homelike, that he fancied himself back again in the gardens of Kjøge. So Knud left his master, and went to work for another who lived farther in the town, where no elder grew. His workshop was quite close to one of the old stone bridges, near to a water-mill, round which the roaring stream rushed and foamed always, yet restrained by the neighboring houses, whose old, decayed balconies hung over, and seemed ready to fall into the water. Here grew no elder; here was not even a flower-pot, with its little green plant; but just opposite the workshop stood a great willow-tree, which seemed to hold fast to the house for fear of being carried away by the water. It stretched its branches over the stream just as those of the willow-tree in the garden at Kjøge had spread over the river. Yes, he had indeed gone from elder-mother to willow-father. There was something about the tree here, especially in the moonlight nights, that went direct to his heart; yet it was not in reality the moonlight, but the old tree itself. However, he could not endure it: and why? Ask the willow, ask the blossoming elder! At all events, he bade farewell to Nuremberg and journeyed onwards. He never spoke of Joanna to any one; his sorrow was hidden in his heart. The old childish story of the two cakes had a deep meaning for him. He understood now why the gingerbread man had a bitter almond in his left side; his was the feeling of bitterness, and Joanna, so mild and friendly, was represented by the honeycake maiden. As he thought upon all this, the strap of his knapsack pressed across his chest so that he could hardly breathe; he loosened it, but gained no relief. He saw but half the world around him; the other half he carried with him in his inward thoughts; and this is the condition in which he left Nuremberg.

32　　Not till he caught sight of the lofty mountains did the world appear more free to him; his thoughts were attracted to outer objects, and tears came into his eyes. The Alps appeared to him like the wings of earth folded together; unfolded, they would display the variegated[3] pictures of dark woods, foaming waters, spreading clouds, and masses of snow. "At the last day," thought he, "the earth will unfold its great wings, and soar upwards to the skies, there to burst like a soap-bubble in the radiant glance of the Deity. Oh," sighed he, "that the last day were come!"

33　　Silently he wandered on through the country of the Alps, which seemed to him like a fruit garden, covered with soft turf. From the wooden balconies of the houses the young lacemakers nodded as he passed. The summits of the mountains glowed in the red evening sunset, and the green lakes beneath the dark trees reflected the glow. Then he thought of the sea coast by the bay Kjøge, with a longing in his heart that was, however, without pain. There, where the Rhine rolls onward like a great billow, and dissolves itself into snowflakes, where glistening clouds are

---

① crevice: a crack
② garret: an attic, usually a small, wretched one
③ variegated: varied, diversified

ever changing as if here was the place of their creation, while the rainbow flutters about them like a many-colored ribbon, there did Knud think of the water-mill at Kjøge, with its rushing, foaming waters. Gladly would he have remained in the quiet Rhenish town, but there were too many elders and willow-trees.

34   So he travelled onwards, over a grand, lofty chain of mountains, over rugged,—rocky precipices[①], and along roads that hung on the mountain's side like a swallow's nest. The waters foamed in the depths below him. The clouds lay beneath him. He wandered on, treading upon Alpine roses, thistles[②], and snow, with the summer sun shining upon him, till at length he bid farewell to the lands of the north. Then he passed on under the shade of blooming chestnut-trees, through vineyards, and fields of Indian corn, till conscious that the mountains were as a wall between him and his early recollections; and he wished it to be so.

35   Before him lay a large and splendid city, called Milan, and here he found a German master who engaged him as a workman. The master and his wife, in whose workshop he was employed, were an old, pious couple; and the two old people became quite fond of the quiet journeyman, who spoke but little, but worked more, and led a pious, Christian life; and even to himself it seemed as if God had removed the heavy burden from his heart. His greatest pleasure was to climb, now and then, to the roof of the noble church, which was built of white marble. The pointed towers, the decorated and open cloisters, the stately columns, the white statues which smiled upon him from every corner and porch and arch,—all, even the church itself, seemed to him to have been formed from the snow of his native land. Above him was the blue sky; below him, the city and the wide-spreading plains of Lombardy; and towards the north, the lofty mountains, covered with perpetual snow. And then he thought of the church of Kjøge, with its red, ivy-clad walls, but he had no longing to go there; here, beyond the mountains, he would die and be buried.

36   Three years had passed away since he left his home; one year of that time he had dwelt at Milan.

37   One day his master took him into the town; not to the circus in which riders performed, but to the opera, a large building, itself a sight well worth seeing. The seven tiers of boxes, which reached from the ground to a dizzy height, near the ceiling, were hung with rich, silken curtains; and in them were seated elegantly-dressed ladies, with bouquets of flowers in their hands. The gentlemen were also in full dress, and many of them wore decorations of gold and silver. The place was so brilliantly lighted that it seemed like sunshine, and glorious music rolled through the building. Everything looked more beautiful than in the theatre at Copenhagen, but then Joanna had been there, and—could it be? Yes—it was like magic,—she was here also: for, when the curtain rose, there stood Joanna, dressed in silk and gold, and with a golden crown upon her head. She sang, he thought, as only an angel could sing; and then she stepped forward to the front and smiled, as only Joanna could smile, and looked directly at Knud. Poor Knud! He seized his master's hand, and cried out loud, "Joanna," but no one heard him, excepting his master, for the music sounded above everything.

38   "Yes, yes, it is Joanna," said his master; and he drew forth a printed bill, and pointed to her name, which was there in full. Then it was not a dream. All the audience applauded her, and threw wreaths of flowers at her; and every time she went away they called for her again,

---

① precipice: a cliff with vertical or nearly vertical face
② thistle: any of prickly plants

so that she was always coming and going. In the street the people crowded round her carriage, and drew it away themselves without the horses. Knud was in the foremost row, and shouted as joyously as the rest; and when the carriage stopped before a brilliantly lighted house, Knud placed himself close to the door of her carriage. It flew open, and she stepped out; the light fell upon her dear face, and he could see that she smiled as she thanked them, and appeared quite overcome. Knud looked straight in her face, and she looked at him, but she did not recognize him. A man, with a glittering star on his breast, gave her his arm, and people said the two were engaged to be married. Then Knud went home and packed up his knapsack; he felt he must return to the home of his childhood, to the elder-tree and the willow. "Ah, under that willow-tree!" A man may live a whole life in one single hour.

39   The old couple begged him to remain, but words were useless. In vain they reminded him that winter was coming, and that the snow had already fallen on the mountains. He said he could easily follow the track of the closely-moving carriages, for which a path must be kept clear, and with nothing but his knapsack on his back, and leaning on his stick, he could step along briskly. So he turned his steps to the mountains, ascended one side and descended the other, still going northward till his strength began to fail, and not a house or village could be seen. The stars shone in the sky above him, and down in the valley lights glittered like stars, as if another sky were beneath him; but his head was dizzy and his feet stumbled, and he felt ill. The lights in the valley grew brighter and brighter, and more numerous, and he could see them moving to and fro, and then he understood that there must be a village in the distance; so he exerted his failing strength to reach it, and at length obtained shelter in a humble lodging. He remained there that night and the whole of the following day, for his body required rest and refreshment, and in the valley there was rain and a thaw. But early in the morning of the third day, a man came with an organ and played one of the melodies of home; and after that Knud could remain there no longer, so he started again on his journey toward the north. He travelled for many days with hasty steps, as if he were trying to reach home before all whom he remembered should die; but he spoke to no one of this longing. No one would have believed or understood this sorrow of his heart, the deepest that can be felt by human nature. Such grief is not for the world; it is not entertaining even to friends, and poor Knud had no friends; he was a stranger, wandering through strange lands to his home in the north.

40   He was walking one evening through the public roads, the country around him was flatter, with fields and meadows, the air had a frosty feeling. A willow-tree grew by the roadside, everything reminded him of home. He felt very tired; so he sat down under the tree, and very soon began to nod, then his eyes closed in sleep. Yet still he seemed conscious that the willow-tree was stretching its branches over him; in his dreaming state the tree appeared like a strong, old man—the "willow-father" himself, who had taken his tired son up in his arms to carry him back to the land of home, to the garden of his childhood, on the bleak open shores of Kjøge. And then he dreamed that it was really the willow-tree itself from Kjøge, which had travelled out in the world to seek him, and now had found him and carried him back into the little garden on the banks of the streamlet; and there stood Joanna, in all her splendor, with the golden crown on her head, as he had last seen her, to welcome him back. And then there appeared before him two remarkable shapes, which looked much more like human beings than when he had seen them in his childhood; they were changed, but he remembered that they were the two gingerbread cakes,

the man and the woman, who had shown their best sides to the world and looked so good.

41　　"We thank you," they said to Knud, "for you have loosened our tongues; we have learnt from you that thoughts should be spoken freely, or nothing will come of them; and now something has come of our thoughts, for we are engaged to be married." Then they walked away, hand-in-hand, through the streets of Kjøge, looking very respectable on the best side, which they were quite right to show. They turned their steps to the church, and Knud and Joanna followed them, also walking hand-in-hand; there stood the church, as of old, with its red walls, on which the green ivy grew.

42　　The great church door flew open wide, and as they walked up the broad aisle, soft tones of music sounded from the organ. "Our master first," said the gingerbread pair, making room for Knud and Joanna. As they knelt at the altar, Joanna bent her head over him, and cold, icy tears fell on his face from her eyes. They were indeed tears of ice, for her heart was melting towards him through his strong love, and as her tears fell on his burning cheeks he awoke. He was still sitting under the willow-tree in a strange land, on a cold winter evening, with snow and hail falling from the clouds, and beating upon his face.

43　　"That was the most delightful hour of my life," said he, "although it was only a dream. Oh, let me dream again." Then he closed his eyes once more, and slept and dreamed.

44　　Towards morning there was a great fall of snow; the wind drifted it over him, but he still slept on. The villagers came forth to go to church; by the roadside they found a workman seated, but he was dead! Frozen to death under a willow-tree.

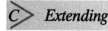

STUDY QUESTIONS

A⟩ *Recalling*

1. What is the garden like?
2. What dream does Joanna have about Knud?
3. Please retell the story about the gingerbread man and gingerbread maiden.
4. What have become of Knud and Joanna respectively when they grow up?
5. What is the first meeting between Knud and Joanna like? And the last?
6. How does Knud react when Joanna tell him they can only be sister and brother?
7. What is Knud's last seeing of Joanna like?

B⟩ *Interpreting*

8. What is the significance of the garden? the willow tree?
9. What role does the gingerbread story play in the whole story?
10. What starts Knud's journey back home?
11. What is beautiful about the story?

C⟩ *Extending*

12. What gives fairy tale quality to the story and what makes it a good reading for the adults?

X. "Balcony Scene" from *Romeo and Juliet* by William Shakespeare

▶ INTRODUCTION TO *ROMEO AND JULIET*

Romeo and Juliet—one of the most popular romantic tragedies in English literature—has entertained readers and spectators for nearly five hundred years. The play is based on Arthur Brooke's poem *The Tragicall Historye of Romeus and Juliet*, published in 1562, which tells the story of two young lovers thwarted by fate and destroyed by their own reckless passion. Although Brooke's poem is the only direct source for *Romeo and Juliet,* the legend of the unfortunate lovers had become a part of European popular tradition by the time Shakespeare wrote his drama. Perhaps what attracted Shakespeare and his predecessors to the tale was its compelling central theme: the story of ill-fated youthful love opposed by a world of violence and hatred. But whereas earlier authors, such as Brooke, emphasized fate or the lovers' headlong passion, Shakespeare created a more complex tragedy in which not only these elements, but also divine will and Romeo and Juliet's innocence play a role in shaping events. Critics continue to debate the relative effectiveness of the tragic design of *Romeo and Juliet* and have yet to achieve a real consensus. Nevertheless, the combination of such diverse elements in this, one of Shakespeare's earliest tragedies, has intrigued generations of students and scholars alike.

The following selection is the famous "Balcony Scene", one of the most renowned in all of Shakespeare.

Romeo and Juliet

SCENE II. Capulet's orchard.

[Enter ROMEO]
ROMEO

1	*He jests at scars that never felt a wound.*	= He jest at scars that has recovered.
	[JULIET appears above at a window]	
	But, *soft*! what light through yonder window breaks?	= short for "go soft", stop
	It is the east, and Juliet is the sun.	
	Arise, fair sun, and *kill the envious moon*,	= Diana, the moon-goddess, who lived a virgin
5	Who is already sick and pale with grief,	all her life and envies Juliet her beauty
	That thou her *maid* art far more fair than she:	= votary, for Diana, who was the patroness of virgins
	Be not her maid, since she is envious;	
	Her *vestal livery* is but sick and green	= virginal dress
	And none but fools do wear it; cast it off.	
10	It is my lady, O, it is my love!	

O, *that she knew she were*!　　　　　　　　　　= if only she knew she were my love

She speaks yet she says nothing: what of that?

Her eye *discourses*; I will answer it.　　　　　　= speaks

I am too bold, 'tis not to me she speaks:

15　Two of the fairest stars in all the heaven,

Having some business, do *entreat* her eyes　　　= earnestly ask

To twinkle in their *spheres* till they return.　　= orbits

What if her eyes were there, they in her head?

The brightness of her cheek would shame those stars,

20　As daylight doth a lamp; her eyes in heaven

Would through the airy region stream so bright　　= Would stream through the airy region so bright

That birds would sing and think it were not night.

See, how she leans her cheek upon her hand!

O, that I were a glove upon that hand,

25　That I might touch that cheek!

JULIET

Ay me!

ROMEO

She speaks:

O, speak again, bright angel! for thou art

As glorious to this night, being o'er my head

30　As is a winged messenger of heaven

Unto the white-upturned wondering eyes

Of mortals that fall back to gaze on him

When he *bestrides* the lazy-pacing clouds　　　= rides on

And sails upon the bosom of the air.

JULIET

35　O Romeo, Romeo! *wherefore* art thou Romeo?　　= why

Deny thy father and refuse thy name;　　　　　= reject, renounce

Or, if thou wilt not, be but sworn my love,

And I'll no longer be a Capulet.

ROMEO

[Aside] Shall I hear more, or shall I speak at this?

JULIET

40 'Tis but thy name that is my enemy;

Thou art thyself, *though not* a Montague.   = even though no longer

What's Montague? it is nor hand, nor foot,

Nor arm, nor face, nor any other part

Belonging to a man. O, be some other name!

45 What's in a name? that which we call a rose

By any other name would smell as sweet;

So Romeo would, *were he not Romeo call'd*,   = even if he were not called Romeo

Retain that dear perfection which he *owes*   = owns

Without that title. Romeo, *doff* thy name,   = give up; put off

50 And *for that name* which is no part of thee   = for the compensation of your name

Take all myself.

ROMEO

I take thee at thy word:

Call me but love, and I'll be *new* baptized;   = anew

Henceforth I never will be Romeo.

JULIET

55 What man art thou that thus *bescreen'd* in night   = covered, hid

So stumblest on my *counsel*?   = private meditation

ROMEO

By a name

I know not how to tell thee who I am:

My name, dear *saint*, is hateful to myself,   = Poets of the Middle Ages often compared lovers

60 Because it is an enemy to thee;   to be saints and courting to be pilgrimage.

Had I it written, I would tear the word.   = Had I written it

JULIET

My ears have not yet drunk a hundred words

Of that tongue's utterance, yet I know the sound:

Art thou not Romeo and a Montague?

ROMEO

65 Neither, fair saint, if either *thee dislike*.   = displease you

JULIET

How camest thou hither, tell me, and wherefore?

The orchard walls are high and hard to climb,

And *the place death*, considering who thou art,   = the place is/means death

If any of my kinsmen find thee here.

ROMEO

70 With love's light wings did I *o'er-perch* these walls;   = fly over

For stony limits cannot *hold love* out,   = keep love out

And *what love can do that dares love attempt*;   = Love dares attempt whatever it can do.

Therefore thy kinsmen are no *let* to me.   = hindrance

JULIET

If they do see thee, they will murder thee.

ROMEO

75 *Alack*, there lies more *peril* in thine eye   = alas // = great danger

Than twenty of their swords: look thou but sweet,

And I am *proof* against their enmity.   = guarded

JULIET

I would not for the world they saw thee here.   = I do not wish

ROMEO

I have night's cloak to hide me from their sight;

80 *And but* thou love me, let them find me here: = if not, unless

My life were better ended by their hate,

Than death *prorogued, wanting of* thy love.   = postponed // = lacking

JULIET

By whose direction found'st thou out this place?

ROMEO

By love, who first did prompt me to inquire;

85 He lent me counsel and I lent him eyes.

I am no pilot; yet, wert thou as far

As that vast shore wash'd with the *farthest sea*,   = the newly found Pacific

I would adventure for such *merchandise*.   = refers to love of Juliet, which, like expensive

JULIET   merchandise, demands courage and risk to obtain

Thou know'st the mask of night is on my face,

90 Else would a maiden blush *bepaint* my cheek   = paint

For that which thou hast heard me speak to-night

Fain would I dwell on *form*, fain, fain deny   = gladly // = etiquette

What I have *spoke*: but farewell *compliment*!   = spoken // = etiquette, polite address

Dost thou love me? I know thou wilt say "Ay,"

95 And I will take thy word: yet if thou swear'st,

Thou mayst prove false; at lovers' *perjuries*   = violations of promises made on oath

Then say, *Jove* laughs. O gentle Romeo,   = Jupiter

If thou dost love, pronounce it faithfully:

Or if thou think'st I am too quickly won,

100 I'll frown and be *perverse* and *say thee nay*,   = contrary to what is wanted // = say no to you

So thou wilt woo; *but else, not for the world*.   = if you do not think I am quickly won, I will not

In truth, fair Montague, I am too *fond*,   for the world frown /// = foolishly loving

And therefore thou mayst think my *'havior light*:   = behavior // = frivolous

But trust me, gentleman, I'll prove more true

105 Than those that have more cunning to be *strange*.   = aloof, distant, reserved

I should have been more strange, I must confess,

But that thou overheard'st, ere I was *ware*,   = if you had not overheard // = before // = aware

My true love's passion: therefore pardon me,

And not *impute* this yielding to light love,   = attribute

110   Which the dark night hath so *discovered*.   = revealed

ROMEO

Lady, by yonder blessed moon I swear

That tips with silver all these fruit-tree tops—

JULIET

O, swear not by the moon, the inconstant moon,

That monthly changes in her circled orb,

115   Lest that thy love prove likewise variable.

ROMEO

What shall I swear by?

JULIET

Do not swear at all;

Or, if thou wilt, swear by thy gracious self,

Which is the god of my *idolatry*,   = worship (of an idol)

120   And I'll believe thee.

ROMEO

If my heart's dear love—

JULIET

Well, do not swear: although I *joy* in thee,   = rejoice

I have no joy of this *contract* to-night: = meeting

It is too rash, too *unadvised*, too sudden;   = thoughtless

125   Too like the lightning, which doth cease to be

Ere one can say "It *lightens*." *Sweet*, good night!   = flashes // = sweetheart

This bud of love, by summer's ripening breath,

May prove a beauteous flower when next we meet.

Good night, good night! as sweet repose and rest

130   Come to thy heart as *that* within my breast!   = the heart

ROMEO

O, wilt thou leave me so unsatisfied?

JULIET

What satisfaction canst thou have to-night?

ROMEO

The exchange of thy love's faithful vow for mine.

JULIET

I gave thee mine before thou didst request it:

135   And yet I *would it were to give again*.   = wish it would be something to be given a second time

ROMEO

Wouldst thou withdraw it? for what purpose, love?

JULIET

But to be *frank*, and give it thee again.   = only // = generous

And yet I wish but for the thing I have:

My *bounty* is as boundless as the sea,   = liberality, generosity

140   My love as deep; the more I give to thee,

The more I have, for both are infinite.

[Nurse calls within]

I hear some noise within; dear love, *adieu*!   = goodbye

Anon, good nurse! Sweet Montague, be true.   = in one (instant)

Stay but a little, I will come again.

[Exit, above]

ROMEO

145   O blessed, blessed night! I am *afeard*.   = afraid, frightened

Being in night, all this is but a dream,

Too flattering-sweet to be substantial.

[Re-enter JULIET, above]

JULIET

Three words, dear Romeo, and good night indeed.

If that thy *bent* of love *be honourable*,   = inclination // = be honorable, here refers to marriage

150   Thy purpose marriage, send me word to-morrow,

By one that I'll *procure* to come to thee,   = get (a person to do something)

Where and what time thou wilt perform *the rite*;   — the wedding ceremony

And all my fortunes at thy foot I'll lay

And follow thee my *lord* throughout the world.   = husband

Nurse

155   [Within] Madam!

JULIET

I come, anon.—But if thou mean'st not well,

I do *beseech* thee—   = ask earnestly

Nurse

[Within] Madam!

JULIET

By and by, I come:—   = immediately

160   To cease thy suit, and leave me to my grief:

To-morrow will I *send*.   = send somebody

ROMEO

So thrive my soul—

JULIET

A thousand times good night!

[Exit, above]

ROMEO

A thousand times the worse, to *want* thy light.   = lack

165   Love goes toward love, as schoolboys from their books,

But love from love, toward school with *heavy* looks.

[Retiring]

[Re-enter JULIET, above]

JULIET

Hist! Romeo, hist! O, for a falconer's voice,   = hush, silence

To lure this *tassel-gentle* back again!   = 易于驯养的雄猎鹰

Bondage is hoarse, and may not speak aloud;   = Juliet is afraid of be discovered by her family, so she can't speak aloud

170 Else would I tear the cave where Echo lies,

And make *her* airy tongue more hoarse than mine,   = Echo's

With repetition of my Romeo's name.

ROMEO

It is my soul that calls upon my name:

How silver-sweet sound lovers' tongues by night,

175 Like softest music to *attending* ears!   = paying attention

JULIET

Romeo!

ROMEO

My dear?

JULIET

At what o'clock to-morrow

Shall I send to thee?

ROMEO

180 At the hour of nine.

JULIET

I will not fail: 'tis twenty years till then.

I have forgot why I did call thee back.

ROMEO

Let me stand here till thou remember it.

JULIET

I shall forget, to have thee *still* stand there,   = always

185 Remembering how I love thy company.

ROMEO

And I'll still stay, to have thee still forget,

Forgetting any other home but this.

JULIET

'Tis almost morning; I would have thee gone:

And yet no further than a *wanton's* bird;   = sportive girl

190   Who lets it hop a little from her hand,

Like a poor prisoner in his twisted *gyves*,   = fetters

And with a silk thread plucks it back again,

So loving-jealous of his liberty.

ROMEO

I would I were thy bird.

JULIET

195   Sweet, so would I:

Yet I should kill thee with *much cherishing*.   = too much caressing

Good night, good night! parting is such sweet sorrow,

That I shall say good night till it be *morrow*.   = morning

[Exit above]

ROMEO

Sleep dwell upon thine eyes, peace in thy breast!   =may sleep dwell upon thine eyes

200   *Would I were* sleep and peace, so sweet to rest!   = I wish I were

Hence will I to my *ghostly father*'s cell,   = go from this place // = spiritual father, Friar Laurence

His help to crave, and *my dear hap to tell*.   = to tell him my good luck

[Exit]

▶▶ STUDY QUESTIONS

Recalling

1. What images does Shakespeare use to describe Juliet's beauty? How does Shakespeare use the traditional images in a fresh way? Please use lines 15-25 as an example to illustrate this point.
2. Shakespeare is said to be the master of word-play. Please explain the word-play in lines 163–166.

B Interpreting

3. Please read lines 89–110 carefully, what do these lines reveal about Juliet?
4. Please read lines 111–130 carefully, what do these lines tell you about both Romeo and Juliet?
5. Why does Juliet propose marriage? Do you think marriage will secure their love?
6. Why do people refer to Romeo and Juliet's love as "young love"?
7. What is attractive about "young love"?

C⟩ *Extending*

8. Romeo and Juliet's love is obviously "love at first sight". Do you believe in "love at first sight"? Why or why not?

9. Shakespeare is often lauded as our contemporary. Please illustrate this point with examples from the play.

10. Please compare the story *Romeo and Juliet* with the Chinese story *Liang Shanbo and Zhu Yingtai*. What is similar? What is different? What difference or similarity strikes you most? What accounts for the similarity and what accounts for the difference?

XI. *The Blue Jar* by Isak Dinesen

▶ ABOUT THE AUTHOR

Isak Dinesen (Karen Blixen)(1885–1962) is the best known, and possibly the greatest, Danish writer of the twentieth century. Her reputation as an author rests on several books written in English under the pseudonym Isak Dinesen, including: *Seven Gothic Tales* (1934), *Winter's Tales* (1942), and *Out of Africa* (1938). The movie *Out of Africa* (1985) celebrates her life as a pioneer coffee farmer in Kenya from 1914 to 1931.

The Blue Jar

1   There once was an immensely rich old Englishman who had been a courier① and a councillor② to the Queen and who now, in his old age, cared for nothing but collecting ancient blue china. To that end he travelled to Persia, Japan and China, and he was everywhere accompanied by his daughter, the Lady Helena. It happened, as they sailed in the China Sea, that the ship caught fire on a still night, and everybody went into the lifeboats and left her. In the dark and confusion the old peer③ was separated from his daughter. Lady Helena got up on deck late, and found the ship quite deserted. In the last moment a young English sailor carried her down into a lifeboat that had been forgotten. To the two fugitives④ it seemed as if fire was following them from all sides, for the phosphorescence⑤ played in the dark sea, and, as they looked up, a falling star ran across the sky, as if it was going to drop into the boat. They sailed for nine days, till they were picked up by a Dutch merchantman, and came home to England.

2   The old lord had believed his daughter to be dead. He now wept with joy, and at once he took her off to a fashionable watering-place so that she might recover from the hardships she had gone through. And as he thought it must be unpleasant to her that a young sailor, who made his bread in the merchant service, should tell the world that he had sailed for nine days alone with a peer's daughter, he paid the boy a fine sum, and made him promise to go shipping in the other hemisphere and never come back. "For what," said the old nobleman, "would be the good of that?"

---

① courier: messenger carrying news or important government papers
② councillor: member of a council
③ peer: member of one of the degrees of nobility, e.g. duke, marquis, earl, viscount, baron
④ fugitive: person running away from justice, degree, etc.
⑤ phosphorescence: luminous radiation

3   When Lady Helena recovered, and they gave her the news of the Court and of her family, and in the end also told her how the young sailor had been sent away never to come back, they found that her mind had suffered from the trials[1], and that she cared for nothing in all the world. She would not go back to her father's castle in its park, nor go to Court, nor travel to any gay town of the continent. The only thing which she now wanted to do was to go, like her father before her, to collect rare blue china. So she began to sail, from one country to the other, and her father went with her.

4   In her search she told people, with whom she dealt, that she was looking for a particular blue color, and would pay any price for it. But although she bought many hundred blue jars and bowls, she would always after a time put them aside and say: "Alas, alas, it is not the right blue." Her father, when they had sailed for many years, suggested to her that perhaps the color which she sought did not exist. "O God, Papa," said she, "how can you speak so wickedly? Surely there must be some of it left from the time when all the world was blue."

5   Her two old aunts in England implored her to come back, still to make a great match. But she answered them: "Nay, I have got to sail. For you must know, dear aunts, that it is all nonsense when learned people tell you that the seas have got a bottom to them. On the contrary, the water, which is the noblest of elements, does, of course, go all through the earth, so that our planet really floats in the ether, like a soap bubble. And there, on the other hemisphere, a ship sails, with which I have got to keep pace. We two are like the reflection of one another, in the deep sea, and the ship of which I speak is always exactly beneath my own ship, upon the opposite side of the globe. You have never seen a big fish swimming underneath a boat, following it like a dark-blue shade in the water. But in that way this ship goes, like the shadow of my ship, and I draw it to and fro wherever I go, as the moon draws the tides, all through the bulk of the earth. If I stopped sailing, what would those poor sailors who made their bread in the merchant service do? But I shall tell you a secret," she said. "In the end my ship will go down, to the centre of the globe, and at the very same hour the other ship will sink as well—for people call it sinking, although I can assure you that there is no up and down in the sea—and there, in the midst of the world, we two shall meet."

6   Many years passed, the old lord died and Lady Helena became old and deaf, but she still sailed. Then it happened, after the plunder of the Summer Palace of the Emperor of China, that a merchant brought her a very old blue jar. The moment she set eyes on it she gave a terrible shriek. "There it is!" she cried. "I have found it at last. This is the true blue. Oh, how light it makes one. Oh, it is as fresh as a breeze, as deep as a deep secret, as full as I say not what." With trembling hands she held the jar to her bosom, and sat for six hours sunk in contemplation of it. Then she said to her doctor and her lady-companion: "Now I can die. And when I am dead you will cut out my heart and lay it in the blue jar. For then everything will be as it was then. All shall be blue around me, and in the midst of the blue world my heart will be innocent and free, and will beat gently, like a wake[2] that sings, like the drops that fall from an oar blade[3]." "Is it not a sweet thing to think that, if only you have patience, all that has ever been, will come back to you?" Shortly afterwards the old lady died.

---

[1] trials: pains
[2] wake: track left by a ship on smooth water
[3] oar blade: flat, wide part of an oar

▶ STUDY QUESTIONS

A ▷ *Recalling*

1. What happened to Lady Helena on the day when she sailed in the China Sea?
2. How did the old Lord "reward" the young sailor for saving his daughter?
3. What changes had taken place to Lady Helena after the incident?

B ▷ *Interpreting*

4. What does Lady Helena's life-long search for the blue jar symbolize?
5. What is the significance of the blue jar to Lady Helena ?
6. How do you interpret Lady Helena's interpretation of two ships sailing on the opposite side of the globe?

C ▷ *Extending*

7. Do you agree that love is most beautiful when it is not fulfilled?
8. How do you like the story?

XII. *The Beggar* by Anton Chekhov

▶ ABOUT THE AUTHOR

Anton Chekhov (1860–1904), Russian, is considered one of the grand masters of the short story. Born into a poor family in the seaport city of Taganrog, Chekhov was the son of a grocer who eventually went bankrupt. "There was no childhood in my childhood," Chekhov once said; his own financial struggles gave him a lifelong sympathy for the poor.

Chekhov began writing to support himself while attending medical school. Once he became a doctor, he chose to practice among the lower classes, even though that meant he could earn little himself. He continued to supplement his income by writing plays and stories, winning acclaim both at home and abroad.

Chekhov's work is known for its realistic blend of comedy and tragedy and for its strong moral tone. Many of his plays—including *Uncle Vanya*, *The Cherry Orchard*, and *The Three Sisters*—are considered classics. His stories are short and simple yet powerful, illustrating his belief that "conciseness is the sister of talent."

The Beggar
Translated from Russian by Marian Tell

1   "Kind sir, have pity; turn your attention to a poor, hungry man! For three days I have had nothing to eat; I haven't five kopecks① for a lodging, I swear it before God. For eight years

―――――――――

① kopecks: Russian coins of small value

I was a village school-teacher and then I lost my place through intrigues①. I fell a victim to calumny②. It is a year now since I have had anything to do—"

2　　　The advocate③ Skvortsoff looked at the ragged, fawn-colored④ overcoat of the suppliant⑤, at his dull, drunken eyes, at the red spot on either cheek, and it seemed to him as if he had seen this man somewhere before.

3　　　"I have now had an offer of a position in the province of Kaluga⑥," the mendicant⑦ went on, "but I haven't the money to get there. Help me kindly; I am ashamed to ask, but—I am obliged to by circumstances."

4　　　Skvortsoff's eyes fell on the man's overshoes, one of which was high and the other low, and he suddenly remembered something.

5　　　"Look here, it seems to me I met you day before yesterday in Sadovaya Street," he said, "but you told me then that you were a student who had been expelled, and not a village school-teacher. Do you remember?"

6　　　"N-no, that can't be so," mumbled the beggar, taken aback. "I am a village school-teacher, and if you like I can show you my papers."

7　　　"Have done with lying! You called yourself a student and even told me what you had been expelled for. Don't you remember?"

8　　　Skvortsoff flushed and turned from the ragged creature with an expression of disgust.

9　　　"This is dishonesty, my dear sir!" he cried angrily. "This is swindling! I shall send the police for you! Even if you are poor and hungry, that does not give you any right to lie brazenly⑧ and shamelessly!"

10　　　The waif⑨ caught hold of the door-handle and looked furtively⑩ round the antechamber, like a detected thief.

11　　　"I'm not lying —" he muttered. "I can show you my papers."

12　　　"Who would believe you?" Skvortsoff continued indignantly. "Don't you know that it's a low, dirty trick to exploit the sympathy which society feels for village school-teachers and students? It's revolting⑪!"

13　　　Skvortsoff lost his temper and began to berate⑫ the mendicant unmercifully. The impudent⑬ lying of the ragamuffin⑭ offended what he, Skvortsoff, most prized in himself: his kindness, his tender heart, his compassion for all unhappy beings. That lie, an attempt to take advantage of the pity of its "subject," seemed to him to profane⑮ the charity which he liked to

---

① intrigues: plots
② calumny: false or malicious statement designed to injure the reputation of sb.
③ advocate: lawyer who argues cases in court
④ fawn-colored: light yellowish brown
⑤ suppliant: the person who begs
⑥ Kaluga: area in west-central Russia
⑦ mendicant: beggar
⑧ brazenly: shamelessly
⑨ waif: a homeless person
⑩ furtively: secretly
⑪ revolting: disgusting
⑫ berate: to blame, to scold
⑬ impudent: shameless
⑭ ragamuffin: a ragged, disreputable person
⑮ profane: to misuse

extend to the poor out of the purity of his heart. At first the waif continued to protest innocence, but soon he grew silent and hung his head in confusion.

14   "Sir!" he said, laying his hand on his heart, "the fact is I—was lying! I am neither a student nor a school-teacher. All that was a fiction. Formerly I sang in a Russian choir and was sent away for drunkenness. But what else can I do? I can't get along without lying. No one will give me anything when I tell the truth. With truth a man would starve to death or die of cold for lack of a lodging. You reason justly, I understand you, but—what can I do?"

15   "What can you do? You ask what you can do?" cried Skvortsoff, coming close to him. "Work! That's what you can do! You must work!"

16   "Work—yes, I know that myself; but where can I find work?"

17   "Rot! You're young and healthy and strong; you could always find work if you only wanted to, but you're lazy and spoiled and drunken! There's a smell about you like a tap-room[1]. You're rotten and false to the core, and all you can do is to lie. When you consent to lower yourself to work, you want a job in an office or in a choir or as a marker at billiards—any employment for which you can get money without doing anything! How would you like to try your hand at manual labor? No, you'll never be a porter or a factory hand; you're a man of pretensions, you are!"

18   "By God, you judge harshly!" cried the beggar with a bitter laugh. "Where can I find manual labor? It's too late for me to be a clerk because in trade one has to begin as a boy; no one would ever take me for a porter because they couldn't order me about; no factory would have me because for that one has to know a trade, and I know none."

19   "Nonsense! You always find some excuse! How would you like to chop wood for me?"

20   "I wouldn't refuse to do that, but in these days even skilled wood-cutters find themselves sitting without bread."

21   "Huh! You loafers[2] all talk that way. As soon as an offer is made you, you refuse it. Will you come and chop wood for me?"

22   "Yes, sir; I will."

23   "Very well; we'll soon find out. Splendid—we'll see—"

24   Skvortsoff hastened along, rubbing his hands, not without a feeling of malice, and called his cook out of the kitchen.

25   "Here, Olga," he said, "take this gentleman into the wood-shed and let him chop wood."

26   The tatterdemalion[3] scarecrow shrugged his shoulders, as if in perplexity, and went irresolutely after the cook. It was obvious from his gait[4] that he had not consented to go and chop wood because he was hungry and wanted work, but simply from pride and shame, because he had been trapped by his own words. It was obvious, too, that his strength had been undermined by vodka and that he was unhealthy and did not feel the slightest inclination for toil.

27   Skvortsoff hurried into the dining room. From its windows one could see the wood-shed and everything that went on in the yard. Standing at the window, Skvortsoff saw the cook and the beggar come out into the yard by the back door and make their way across the dirty snow to

---

① tap-room: a bar room

② loafer: a laze person, an idler

③ tatterdemalion: dressed in rags, tattered in appearance

④ gait: walking manner

the shed. Olga glared wrathfully at her companion, shoved him aside with her elbow, unlocked the shed, and angrily banged the door.

28   "We probably interrupted the woman over her coffee," thought Skvortsoff. "What an ill-tempered creature!"

29   Next he saw the pseudo-teacher[1], pseudo-student seat himself on a log and become lost in thought with his red cheeks resting on his fists. The woman flung down an ax at his feet, spat angrily, and, judging from the expression of her lips, began to scold him. The beggar irresolutely pulled a billet of wood toward him, set it up between his feet, and tapped it feebly with the ax. The billet[2] wavered and fell down. The beggar again pulled it to him, blew on his freezing hands, and tapped it with his ax cautiously, as if afraid of hitting his overshoe or of cutting off his finger. The stick of wood again fell to the ground.

30   Skvortsoff's anger had vanished and he now began to feel a little sorry and ashamed of himself for having set a spoiled, drunken, perchance[3] sick man to work at menial[4] labor in the cold.

31   "Well, never mind," he thought, going into his study from the dining room. "I did it for his own good."

32   An hour later Olga came in and announced that the wood had all been chopped.

33   "Good! Give him half a ruble (chief unit of currency in Russia. One hundred kopecks equal one ruble.)," said Skvortsoff. "If he wants to he can come back and cut wood on the first day of each month. We can always find work for him."

34   On the first of the month the waif made his appearance and again earned half a ruble, although he could barely stand on his legs. From that day on he often appeared in the yard and every time work was found for him. Now he would shovel snow, now put the wood-shed in order, now beat the dust out of rugs and mattresses. Every time he received from twenty to forty kopecks, and once, even a pair of old trousers were sent out to him.

35   When Skvortsoff moved into another house he hired him to help in the packing and hauling of the furniture. This time the waif was sober, gloomy, and silent. He hardly touched the furniture, and walked behind the wagons hanging his head, not even making a pretense of appearing busy. He only shivered in the cold and became embarrassed when the carters jeered at him for his idleness, his feebleness, and his tattered, fancy overcoat. After the moving was over Skvortsoff sent for him.

36   "Well, I see that my words have taken effect," he said, handing him a ruble. "Here's for your pains. I see you are sober and have no objection to work. What is your name?"

37   "Lushkoff."

38   "Well, Lushkoff, I can now offer you some other, cleaner employment. Can you write?"

39   "I can."

40   "Then take this letter to a friend of mine tomorrow and you will be given some copying to do. Work hard, don't drink, and remember what I have said to you. Good-bye!"

41   Pleased at having put a man on the right path, Skvortsoff tapped Lushkoff kindly on the

---

[1] pseudo-teacher: false teacher
[2] billet: a small chunk of wood
[3] perchance: perhaps
[4] menial: lowly and sometimes degrading

shoulder and even gave him his hand at parting. Lushkoff took the letter, and from that day forth came no more to the yard for work.

42   Two years went by. Then one evening, as Skvortsoff was standing at the ticket window of a theater paying for his seat, he noticed a little man beside him with a coat collar of curly fur and a worn sealskin cap. This little individual timidly asked the ticket seller for a seat in the gallery and paid for it in copper coins.

43   "Lushkoff, is that you?" cried Skvortsoff, recognizing in the little man his former wood-chopper. "How are you? What are you doing? How is everything with you?"

44   "All right. I am a notary[1] now and get thirty-five rubles a month."

45   "Thank Heaven! That's fine! I am delighted for your sake. I am very, very glad, Lushkoff. You see, you are my godson, in a sense. I gave you a push along the right path, you know. Do you remember what a roasting I gave you, eh? I nearly had you sinking into the ground at my feet that day. Thank you, old man, for not forgetting my words."

46   "Thank you, too," said Lushkoff. "If I hadn't come to you then I might still have been calling myself a teacher or a student to this day. Yes, by flying to your protection I dragged myself out of a pit."

47   "I am very glad, indeed."

48   "Thank you for your kind words and deeds. You talked splendidly to me then. I am very grateful to you and to your cook. God bless that good and noble woman! You spoke finely then, and I shall be indebted to you to my dying day; but, strictly speaking, it was your cook, Olga, who saved me."

49   "How is that?"

50   "Like this. When I used to come to your house to chop wood she used to begin: 'Oh, you sot[2], you! Oh, you miserable creature! There's nothing for you but ruin.' And then she would sit down opposite me and grow sad, look into my face and weep. 'Oh, you unlucky man! There is no pleasure for you in this world and there will be none in the world to come. You drunkard! You will burn in hell. Oh, you unhappy one!' And so she would carry on, you know, in that strain. I can't tell you how much misery she suffered, how many tears she shed for my sake. But the chief thing was—she used to chop the wood for me. Do you know, sir, that I did not chop one single stick of wood for you? She did it all. Why this saved me, why I changed, why I stopped drinking at the sight of her I cannot explain. I only know that, owing to her words and noble deeds a change took place in my heart; she set me right and I shall never forget it. However, it is time to go now; there goes the hell."

51   Lushkoff bowed and departed to the gallery.

 STUDY QUESTIONS

A▷ *Recalling*

1. What is Skvortsoff's first impression of Lushkoff (the beggar)? What does Lushkoff say to win sympathy? What makes Skvortsoff outrageous?

---

① notary: public clerk responsible for authenticating and certifying legal documents
② sot: a drunkard

2. What is the true cause of Lushkoff's miserable situation? How did he account for his lying?

3. What does Skvortsoff say about job in an office or in a choir or as a marker at billiards and manual labor? What does Lushkoff say about manual work?

4. How does Lushkoff accept his job of cutting wood?

5. How does Olga accept the beggar according to Skvortsoff's observation from the window?

6. How does Skvortsoff feel when he saw the beggar's clumsiness at cutting wood?

7. Please describe the gradual change of Lushkoff in the eyes of Skvortsoff and the changed attitude of Skvortsoff toward Lushkoff.

8. Who has actually changed Lushkoff?

B⟩ *Interpreting*

9. How does Skvortsoff values himself at first? And how will he judge himself after he knows who has really changed Lushkoff?

10. How does Skvortsoff treat Lushkoff? And what is the belief behind? How does Olga treat Lushkoff? What is the belief behind?

11. What is Lushkoff's self image of himself in front of Skvortsoff? And in front of Olga?

12. What power has changed Lushkoff?

C⟩ *Extending*

13. Discuss the best ways to help people in difficulties, such as in poverty, in psychological predicament.

▶▶ LITERARY FOCUS

⟩ *Irony and Surprise Endings*

Irony exists when there is a contrast between the way things seem and the way they really are. When a story has a surprise ending, the ending is ironic because what seems likely to happen is not what actually occurs. Surprise endings are popular in fiction, in part because readers find them entertaining and memorable but also because most fiction attempts to reflect life, and life is often full of surprises. In order to create a surprise ending, authors must carefully manipulate the information they reveal earlier in the story, withholding information that could give away the ending but still providing enough information so that the surprise, when it comes, seems plausible.

▶▶ THINKING ABOUT IRONY AND SURPRISE ENDINGS

Explain the irony behind Chekhov's surprise ending by contrasting what we think has happened with what has actually happened to Lushkoff. How does Chekhov manipulate details of the story to create the surprise ending?

▶▶ APPENDIX 2

The Father

By Björnstjerne Björnson

Translated from Norwegian by James McFarlane and Janet Garton

1   The most powerful man in the parish, of whom this story tells, was called Thord Overaas, One day he stood in the priest's study, tall and serious.

2   "I have got a son," he said. "And I want him baptized."

3   "What is he to be called?"

4   "Finn, after my father."

5   "And the godparents?"

6   Their names were named; they were the best men and women of the village belonging to the man's family.

7   "Is there anything else?" asked the priest. He looked up.

8   The peasant stood for a while. "I would like to have him baptized on his own," he said.

9   "That means on a weekday?"

10   "On Saturday next, 12 noon."

11   "Is there anything else?" asked the priest.

12   "There is nothing else." The peasant twisted his cap as though about to go.

13   Then the priest rose. "Just this," he said and went over to Thord, took his hand and looked him straight in the eyes. "May God grant that the child will be a blessing to you!"

14   Sixteen years after that day Thord stood in the room of the priest.

15   "You are looking well, Thord," said the priest. He saw no change in him.

16   "I have no worries," answered Thord.

17   To this the priest was silent; but a moment later he asked: "What is your errand this evening?"

18   "I come this evening about my son who is to be confirmed tomorrow."

19   "He is a clever lad."

20   "I did not want to pay the priest until I'd heard what place he had been given in the ceremony."

21   "He is in first place."

22   "I am glad to hear it—and here is ten daler[①] for the priest."

23   "Is there anything else?" asked the priest. He looked at Thord.

24   "There is nothing else." Thord left.

25   A further eight years passed, and then a commotion was heard outside the priest's study. For many men had come, with Thord at the head. The priest looked up and recognized him.

26   "You come with many men this evening."

27   "I want to ask for the banns to be called[②] for my son. He is to marry Karen Storliden, daughter of Gudmund, who is standing here."

28   "She is the richest girl in the parish."

---

① daler: dollar

② The banns to be called: marriage proclamations to be made. Announcements were traditionally made in the church for three successive Sundays before the wedding.

29   "What you say is right," answered the peasant. He brushed his hair back with one hand. The priest sat a while as though in thought. He said nothing, but entered the names in his books, and the men signed. Thord placed three daler on the table.

30   "I only want one," said the priest.

31   "I know. But he is my only child. I wanted to do well by him."

32   The priest accepted the money. "This is the third time you stand here on your son's behalf, Thord."

33   "But this marks the finish," said Thord. He folded his pocketbook, said farewell and left. The men followed slowly.

34   Fourteen days after that day, father and son were rowing across the water in calm weather to Storliden to discuss the wedding.

35   This boat seat is not very secure under me," the son said, and he stood up to put it right. That same moment the floorboard he was standing on gave way; he threw up his arms, uttered a cry and fell into the water.

36   "Catch hold of the oar!" shouted the father. He stood up and held it out. But after the son had swum a few strokes, he got a cramp.

37   "Wait!" cried the father, and began rowing. But then the son rolled over on his back, looked long at his father, and sank.

38   Thord could not rightly believe it. He held the boat steady and stared at the spot where his son had gone down, as though he might come up again. A few bubbles rose, then more, then one single big one which burst—then the lake lay once again as smooth as a mirror.

39   For three clays and three nights people watched the father row round that spot without food and without sleep. He was dragging for his son[①]. And on the morning of the third day he found him: and he went and carried him up the hill to his homestead.

40   A year or so might have passed following that day. Then late one autumn evening the priest heard a rattling at the door in the entrance, a cautious fumbling at the latch. The priest opened the door and in stepped a tall bent man, lean and white of hair. The priest looked long at him before he recognized him. It was Thord.

41   "You come late," said the priest and stood quietly before him.

42   "Ah, yes! I come late," said Thord. He sat down. The priest also sat down, as though waiting. There was a long silence.

43   Then Thord said, "I have something here I would like to give to the poor." He rose, placed money on the table, and sat down again. The priest counted it.

44   "This is a lot of money," he said.

45   "It is half of my farm. I sold it today."

46   The priest remained sitting a long time in silence. At length he asked gently: "What will you do now?"

47   "Some better thing."

48   They sat there a while, Thord with his eyes on the floor, the priest with his eyes on him. Then the priest said, slowly and quietly: "Now I think your son has finally been a blessing to you."

49   "Yes, now I think so too," said Thord. He looked up, and two tears ran sadly down his face.

---

① dragging for his son: pulling a net or another object across the bottom of the lake in search of his son's body

▶ FURTHER READING

William Shakespeare, *Romeo and Juliet*

Leo Tolstoy, *Anna Karenina*

Nathaniel Hawthorne, *The Scarlet Letter*

Robert James Waller, *The Bridges of Madison County*

汤显祖，《牡丹亭》

曹雪芹，《红楼梦》

张爱玲，《半生缘》

▶ MOVIES RECOMMENDED

Romeo and Juliet (1968), directed by Franco Zeffirelli

Waterloo Bridge (1940), directed by Mervyn Leroy

Beautiful Life (2000), directed by Nobuhiro Doi and Jiro Shono

When Harry Met Sally (1989), directed by Rob Reiner

Before Sunrise (1995), *Before Sunset* (2004), *Before Midnight* (2013), directed by Richard Linklater

《半生缘》（1997），导演许鞍华

Unit Four Family

I. *The Princess* by Alfred Lord Tennyson

▶▶ ABOUT THE POET

Alfred Lord Tennyson (1809–1892), the English poet, is often regarded as the chief representative of the Victorian Age in poetry. Tennyson succeeded Wordsworth as Poet Laureate in 1850; he was appointed by Queen Victoria and served 42 years. Tennyson's works were melancholic, and reflected the moral and intellectual values of his time, which made them especially vulnerable for later critic, who saw him as a representative of narrow patriotism and sentimentality. But later critics have praised again Tennyson. T. S. Eliot has called him "the great master of metric as well as of melancholia" and that he possessed the finest ear of any English poet since Milton. His major works include: *Poems, Chiefly Lyrical, In Memoriam, Idylls of the King,* etc.

The Princess

1   Yet was there one through whom I loved her, one
    Not learned, save in gracious household ways,
    Not perfect, nay①, but full of tender wants,
    No Angel, but a dearer being, all dipt②

5   In Angel instincts, breathing Paradise,
    Interpreter between the Gods and men,
    Who looked all native to her place, and yet
    On tiptoe seemed to touch upon a sphere
    Too gross③ to tread, and all male minds perforce④

10   Swayed to her from their orbits as they moved,
    And girdled⑤ her with music. Happy he
    With such a mother! faith in womankind
    Beats with his blood, and trust in all things high
    Comes easy to him, and though he trip and fall

15   He shall not blind his soul with clay.

---

① nay: (old use) not
② dipt: the past form of "dip". Here means immerged in, be rich in.
③ gross: coarse, vulgar
④ perforce: necessarily
⑤ girdle: encircle

▶ STUDY QUESTIONS

Recalling

1. Has the mother received much education?
2. In what field is she most adept and gracious?
3. How do the men look at her?

Interpreting

4. In what way is the mother like an angel?
5. What does "a sphere" in Line 8 refer to?
6. What makes the men sway to the mother?

Extending

7. What would you compare your mother to?
8. What makes a mother perfect? How would you compare the role of the mother and that of the father in the children's life?

II. From "On Children"of *The Prophet* by Kahlil Gibran

▶ ABOUT THE POET

Kahlil Gibran (1883–1931), a poet, philosopher, artist, prophet and writer. He was born in Bsharri, Lebanon in 1883. He died in 1931 leaving an amazing legacy in the form of his writings and drawings which have soothed and inspired millions. To many he is a genius whose philosophical and prophetic style convey important messages about life and humanity in a simple, yet beautifully eloquent manner. They are as fresh and meaningful in today's world as when they were first written. His best work is *The Prophet*, a book of 26 poetic essays, which has been translated into over 20 languages.

From "On Children" of *The Prophet*
Translated by Juan Mascaro

1   Your children are not your children.
     They are the sons and daughters of Life's longing for itself.
     They come through you but not from you,
     and though they are with you, and yet they belong not to you.
5   You may give them your love, but not your thoughts.
     For they have their own thoughts.
     You may house their bodies but not their souls,
     for their souls dwell in the house of tomorrow, which you cannot visit, not even in your dreams.
     You may strive to be like them, but seek not to make them like you.

10   For life goes not backward, not tarries[1] with yesterday.

▶▶ STUDY QUESTIONS

A▷ Recalling

1. What should parents do and not do to the children according to the poem?
2. What should the parents expect and not expect from the children?

B▷ Interpreting

3. What is the difference between "come through you" and "come from you"?
4. Who are the children in the poem?

C▷ Extending

5. Think about the poem from the point of view of a daughter or a son. Do you agree with what the poem says?
6. In your opinion, are parents often blind to this truth which is revealed by the poem? If they are, why?

III. *My Father's Song* by Simon J. Ortiz

▶▶ ABOUT THE POET

Simon J. Ortiz (1941–   ) is a contemporary Native American writer who continues to be a strong voice in literature today. He is generally recognized by critics and scholars of American Indian Literature as one of the most talented and accomplished writers of the Native American Renaissance of the 1960s and 1970s. While productive as an essayist and short story writer, his reputation is usually associated with his poetry. His books of poetry include: *Telling and Showing Her: The Earth, The Land* (Just Buffalo Literary Center, 1995); *After and Before the Lightning* (1994); *Woven Stone* (1992); *From Sand Creek: Rising in This Heart Which Is Our America* (1981), for which he received a Pushcart Prize; *A Good Journey* (1977); *Going for the Rain* (1976); and *Naked in the Wind* (1971). His poetry explores the significance of individual origins and journeys, which he sees as forming a vital link in the continuity of life.

My Father's Song

1   Wanting to say things,
     I miss my father tonight.
     His voice, the silent catch[2],
     the depth from his thin chest,

---

① tarry: to stay, to remain
② silent catch: pause during speaking, maybe indicating a question

5   the tremble of emotion
     in something he has just said
     to his son, his song:

     We planted corn one Spring at Acu① —
     we planted several times
10   but this one particular time
     I remember the soft damp sand
     in my hand.

     My father had stopped at one point
     to show me an over turned furrow②;
15   the plowshare had unearthed
     the burrow nest of a mouse③
     in the soft moist sand.

     Very gently, he scooped up tiny pink animals
     into the palm of his hand
20   and told me to touch them.
     We took them to the edge
     of the field and put them in the shade
     of a sand moist clod④.
     I remember the very softness
25   of cool and warm sand and tiny alive mice
     and my father saying things.

▶ STUDY QUESTIONS

A〉 *Recalling*

1. What is the incident described in the poem?
2. With what special emotion does the speaker remember the incident?

B〉 *Interpreting*

3. Please pay special attention to the word usage and see how the word-choice contributes to the tone of the poem.
4. What has the child learned from the father in this little incident?
5. How is the title *My Father's Song* related with the theme of the poem?

C〉 *Extending*

6. Please think about some special moments shared between you and your father. What makes these

---

① Acu: probably a place name
② furrow: long cut in the ground made by a plough
③ the burrow nest of a mouse: the nest of a mouse made in the ground
④ moist clod: wet and sticky earth

moments special?

The Bath
Mary Cassatt, 1890–1891.
Chester Dale Collection.

IV. *A Story Wet as Tears* by Marge Piercy

▶▶ ABOUT THE POETESS

Marge Piercy (1936–) is an American novelist, essayist, and poet best known for fictions with a feminist slant. Her writing stems from a political commitment that began in the 1960s in the Vietnam anti-war movement. In the introduction to a volume of selected poems, *Circles on the Water* (1982), Piercy asserted that she wanted her poems to be "useful." "What I mean by useful is simply that readers will find poems that speak to and for them, will take those poems into their lives and say them to each other and put them up on the bathroom wall and remember bits and pieces of them in stressful or quiet moments...To find ourselves spoken for in art gives dignity to our pain, our anger, our lust, our losses."

A Story Wet as Tears

1   Remember the princess who kissed the frog
     so he became a prince? At first they danced

all weekend, toasted each other in the morning
with coffee, with champagne at night

5   and always with kisses. Perhaps it was
in bed after the first year had ground
around she noticed he had become cold
with her. She had to sleep
with heating pad and down comforter.

10   His manner grew increasingly chilly
and damp when she entered a room.
He spent his time in water sports,
Hydroponics① working on his insect
collection.

15   Then in the third year
when she said to him one day, my dearest,
are you taking your vitamins daily,
you look quite green, he leaped
away from her.

20   Finally on their
fifth anniversary she confronted him.
"My precious, don't you love me any
more?" He replied, "Rivet. Rivet."
Though courtship turns frogs into princes,

25   marriage turns them quietly back.

STUDY QUESTIONS

A> *Recalling*

1. Please find out words in the poem that both apply to the description of a frog and a human being.
2. Please replace the character of the frog in the poem with a human being. Does the story have the same effect?

B> *Interpreting*

3. What does "Rivet. Rivet" mean?
4. Do you think the poem will be better without the last two lines?
5. Please explain the title of the poem.
6. The relationship between the couple changes 1 year later, 3 years later and 5 years later respectively. Do you think the poet chose these numbers randomly or purposefully?
7. What does the poem reveal about marriage and the relationship between man and woman in marriage?

---

① hydroponics: art of growing plants without soil in water

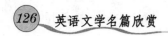
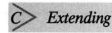

C Extending

8. Please compare the poem with the fairy tale on the appendix page, what makes the fairy tale a fairy tale and the poem "wet as tears"? Do you agree that the reality of marriage is as wet as tears?

▶ APPENDIX 3

The Story of the Frog and the Princess

1   ONCE upon a time there was a king who had a beautiful daughter. She was so wonderful that the sun almost stood still to look at her as it passed over the royal palace.

2   Near the palace was an old forest and in the forest was a deep, dark well. When the day was hot, the little princess would run into the woods, sit beside the cool well, and play for hours with her golden ball. One day as she played, the ball rolled down, down, into the deep well.

3   "Oh, oh, my beautiful ball! My beautiful ball!" cried the princess.

4   "What is the matter, dear princess?" said a voice from the well.

5   The girl looked into the water, but she could see no one. Then the voice called again, "Tell me, princess, I will help you." This time she saw an ugly frog stretch its head above the water.

6   "Why should I tell you, old frog?" asked the princess.

7   "Because I can help the king's daughter," answered the frog.

8   Again the princess burst into tears.

9   "My beautiful ball has fallen into the well," she cried.

10   "Do not weep, beautiful one," said the frog. "I can get your ball, but what will you give me if I bring your toy back to you?"

11   "What do you want," said the princess, "my dresses, my jewels, or my golden crown?"

12   "Dresses, jewels, and golden crowns I do not need," said the frog. "Let me be your playmate, sit at your table, eat from your golden plate, and drink from your golden cup, and I will find your beautiful ball."

13   "I will do all that," she cried, "If you will only get my ball."

14   In a flash the frog dived under the water and brought up the lost toy.

15   "Oh, my beautiful ball! My beautiful ball!" cried the princess. "I will hold you fast this time." And off she ran without a word of thanks.

16   "Stop, stop!" shouted the frog. "Take me with you. I cannot hop as fast as you can run." But on ran the princess and the poor frog had to leap back into the well.

17   The next day the king's daughter was sitting at the table with her father. Suddenly they heard sounds as if something were coming up the marble steps.

18   "Open the door, daughter of the king!" shouted a voice outside.

19   The princess ran to the door. There stood the ugly frog. When she saw it she shut the door quickly and ran to her father.

20   "What is the matter, my child?" asked the king. "Did you see a giant?"

21   "Oh, no!" she answered. "It is an ugly frog. Yesterday my golden ball fell into the well. The frog brought it back to me. But first I promised that he should be my playmate, sit at my table, eat from my golden plate, and drink from my golden cup."

22   "A king's daughter never tells a lie," said her father.

23	Just then they heard the deep, hoarse voice again. It said,

23   Just then they heard the deep, hoarse voice again. It said,

24   "King's daughter

25   King's daughter,

26   Do not forget

27   The promise made

28   In the forest shade."

29   Then the king said, "Let the frog in, daughter. Your promise must be kept."

30   The princess opened the door and the frog hopped right up to her chair.

31   "Take me up, take me up!" cried the frog. "I must eat from our golden plate."

32   The princess did not like to touch it, so she lifted the frog with her napkin and placed it near her plate.

33   The frog seemed to enjoy the dinner but the poor princess could not eat.

34   "I must drink from your cup, I must drink from your cup," cried the hoarse voice again.

35   As the princess lifted her golden cup, her hand touched the frog and it was changed instantly to a handsome boy.

36   "It was an enchanted frog," they all cried in wonder.

37   "You speak truly," said the boy, "I was an enchanted frog. Nine years ago an evil witch changed me into a frog. She said that nothing but the touch of a king's daughter could make me myself again. I am a prince and I wish to be your daughter's playmate."

38   The king was pleased to hear this, and the prince became the playmate and friend of the princess. When they were older the king allowed his daughter to marry the prince.

39   Then the princess took his bride to his father's kingdom. Their golden chariot was drawn by ten white horses, with golden harness and silver plumes.

40   The prince helped his old father rule the kingdom wisely and the people loved the prince dearly. But best of all they loved the beautiful princess who had learned to be kind and gentle to all living things.

V. *The Victims* by Sharon Olds

▶ ABOUT THE POETESS

Sharon Olds (1942–   ) is the author of seven volumes of poetry. Sharon Olds has been much praised for the courage, emotional power, and extraordinary physicality of her work. One reviewer described the appeal of her poems: "What makes these poems gripping is not only their humanity, the recognizable and plausibly complex rendering of character and representative episode, but their language—direct, down to earth, immersed in the essential implements and processes of daily living."

The Victims

1   When Mother divorced you, we were glad. She took it and
took it, in silence, all those years and then
kicked you out, suddenly, and her

kids loved it. Then you were fired, and we
5   grinned inside, the way people grinned when
Nixon's helicopter lifted off the South
Lawn for the last time①. We were tickled②
to think of your office taken away,
your secretaries taken away,
10   your lunches with three double bourbons③,
your pencils, your reams of paper. Would they take your
suits back, too, those dark
carcasses④ hung in your closet, and the black
noses of your shoes with their large pores?
15   She had taught us to take it, to hate you and take it
until we pricked with⑤ her for your
annihilation⑥, Father. Now I
pass the bums⑦ in doorways, the white
slugs⑧ of their bodies gleaming through slits⑨ in their
20   suits of compressed silt⑩, the stained
flippers⑪ of their hands, the underwater
fire of their eyes, ships gone down with the
lanterns lit, and I wonder who took it and
took it from them in silence until they had
25   given it all away and had nothing
left but this.

▶▶ STUDY QUESTIONS

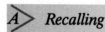 Recalling

1. What has happened between the father and the mother?
2. What is the children's reaction toward it?
3. What has become of the father?

B▷ Interpreting

4. Please explain the meaning of "take" in different lines.

---

① When Richard Nixon resigned the US presidency on August 8, 1974, his exit from the White House (by helicopter from the lawn) was televised live.
② be tickled: be pleased
③ bourbon: a strong kind of alcohol
④ carcass: dead body of an animal; here refers to the suits of the father.
⑤ prick with: to urge, to hope for eagerly
⑥ annihilation: complete destruction, total defeat
⑦ bum: habituated beggar or loafer
⑧ slug: slow-moving creature like a snail but without a shell, here refers to the bodies of the beggars.
⑨ slit: a long, narrow cut
⑩ silt: mud, dirt
⑪ flippers: referring to hands

Line1–2 "she took it and/took it"

Line 8–9 "your office taken away" " your secretaries taken away"

Line 11 "Would they take your/suits back"

Line 15 "She had taught us to take it"

Line 23–24 "I wonder who took it and/took it from them in silence"

5. What is the relationship between lines "the underwater/fire of their eyes" and "ships gone down with the/lanterns lit" (Line 21–23)?

6. Please pick out the images in the poem. What kind of emotion do they convey?

7. Who should be responsible for the father's annihilation?

8. Who are the victims? The victims of what?

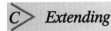

> *Extending*

9. Which character(s) in the poem do you sympathize with? Why?

VI. *The Photos* by Diane Wakoske

▶▶ ABOUT THE POETESS

Diane Wakoske (1932–   ): "One of the two or three most important poets of her generation in America," wrote Hayden Carruth about the extremely prolific and talented Diane Wakoske. Author of more than a dozen full-length collections and many chapbooks, Wakoske is considered one of the most poetically daring writers on the American scene. While she frequently writes about the difficulty of being a woman in an age of changing values, her range encompasses an array of contemporary subject matters and themes. Since 1962, when her first book of poetry appeared, Wakoske has continued to draw her ever-growing readership into the complex world created by her vision.

The Photos

1   My sister in her well-tailored silk blouse hands me
     the photo of my father
     in naval uniform and white hat.
     I say, "Oh, this is the one which Mama used to have on her dresser."

5   My sister controls her face and furtively[1] looks at my mother
     A sad rag of a woman, lumpy and sagging[2] everywhere,
     Like a mattress at the Salvation Army[3], though with no holes or tears
     and says, "No."

     I look again,

---

① furtively: secretly

② sagging: hanging down loosely

③ Salvation Army: a worldwide Christian evangelical organization on quasi-military lines. It is noted for its work with the poor and for its brass bands.

10　And sees that my father is wearing a wedding ring,
　　　Which he never did
　　　When he lived with my mother. And that there is a legend① on it,
　　　"To my dearest wife,
　　　　　Love
15　　　Chief"
　　　And I realize the photo must have belonged to his second wife,
　　　whom he left our mother to marry.

　　　My mother says, with her face as still as the whole unpopulated
　　　part of the
20　　state of North Dakota②,
　　　"May I see it too?" She looks at it.

　　　I look at my tailored③ sister
　　　and my own blue-jeaned self. Have we wanted to hurt our mother,
　　　sharing these pictures on this, one of the few days I ever visit or
25　　spend with family? For her face is curiously haunted,
　　　not now with her usual viperish④ bitterness,
　　　but with something so deep it could not be spoken.

　　　I turn away and say I must go on, as I have a dinner
　　　engagement with friends.
30　　But I drive all the way to Pasadena from Whittier,
　　　thinking of my mother's face; how I could never love her;
　　　how my father
　　　could not love her either. Yet knowing I have inherited
　　　the rag-bag body, stony face with bulldog⑤ jaws.

35　　I drive, thinking of that face.
　　　Jeffers'⑥　California Medea⑦ who inspired me to poetry.
　　　I killed my children,
　　　but there as I am changing lanes on the freeway, necessarily
　　　glancing in the
40　　rearview mirror, I see the face,
　　　not even a ghost, but always with me, like a photo in a
　　　beloved's wallet.

　　　How I hate my destiny.

---

① legend: inscription on a coin or medal
② North Dakota: a former territory of the US
③ tailored: (of a woman's garment) in a simple or plain style with fitted lines
④ viperish: poisonous like a viper (snake)
⑤ bulldog: one of the British breed of dogs, with prominent, undershot jaw; "bulldog" also refers to stubbornly persistent person.
⑥ Robinson Jeffers (1887-1962): American poet who migrated to California from the east retold the Medea story in Solstice, 1935.
⑦ Medea: a sorceress, daughter of Aeëtes and wife of Jason, whom she assisted in obtaining the Golden Fleece. When Jason deserted her, she killed their children.

STUDY QUESTIONS

 Recalling

1. What does the mother look like? What kind of person is she?
2. What does the speaker look like? What kind of person is she?

 Interpreting

3. What myth figure does the speaker compare her mother to? What does that suggest?
4. What is the speaker's feeling towards the mother? Why does she have such feeling?
5. What about the sister? Does she share the motion of the speaker?
6. What does the last line mean?

> Extending

7. Think about the title of the poem. Why does photo come in plural while only one photo is mentioned in the poem?
8. What's your feeling towards your mother?

LITERARY FOCUS

> Tone

Tone is the writer's attitude toward the subject and/or readers or toward him/herself. Tone may be playful, formal, intimate, angry, serious, ironic, outraged, baffled, tender, serene, depressed, etc. Almost all the elements of poetry go into indicating its tone: connotation, imagery, and metaphor; irony and understatement; rhythm, sentence construction, and formal pattern, etc.

THINKING ABOUT TONE

What is the tone in *The Princess, A Story Wet as Tears* and *The Photos* respectively? How is the tone achieved? Please consider elements like word choice, connotation, imagery, rhythm and rhyming, sentence construction, etc.

VII. *My Oedipus Complex* by Frank O'Connor

ABOUT THE AUTHOR

Frank O'Connor (Michael O'Conovan) (1903–1966) was born Michael O'Conovan in Cork, Ireland. He later took the name Frank O'Connor as a pen name. His family's poverty forced him to leave school at age fourteen. O'Connor served in the Irish Republican Army (IRA) during the civil war in Ireland that erupted after the 1922 treaty with Great Britain that resulted in the partitioning of Ireland into two states. The defeat of the IRA and the division of Ireland greatly disappointed O'Connor, feelings which are reflected in his first collection of stories *Guests of the Nation* (1931).

In the 1930s, O'Connor became director of the Abbey Theatre in Dublin, during which time he also wrote several plays and a biography of Michael Collins, the leader of the Irish rebellion against the British. O'Connor published several collections of short stories during his lifetime and several others have been published posthumously, including *Collected Stories* (1981), *The Collar: Stories of Irish Priests* (1993), and *A Frank O'Connor Reader* (1994). His work is marked by its literary realism and its depiction of Irish life. O'Connor was also a noted literary critic and translator of Gaelic poetry into English.

Irish writer Frank O'Connor explains,
far better than Freud might have done…

My Oedipus Complex

1   Father was in the army all through the war—the first war, I mean—so, up to the age of five, I never saw much of him, and what I saw did not worry me. Sometimes I woke and there was a big figure in khaki peering down at me in the candlelight. Sometimes in the early morning I heard the slamming of the front door and the clatter of nailed boots down the cobbles of the lane. These were Father's entrances and exits. Like Santa Claus he came and went mysteriously.

2   In fact, I rather liked his visits, though it was an uncomfortable squeeze between Mother and him when I got into the big bed in the early morning. He smoked, which gave him a pleasant musty smell, and shaved, an operation of astounding interest. Each time he left a trail of souvenirs—model tanks and Gurkha knives with handles made of bullet cases, and German helmets and cap badges and button sticks, and all sorts of military equipment—carefully stowed away in a long box on top of the wardrobe, in case they ever came in handy. There was a bit of the magpie① about Father; he expected everything to come in handy. When his back was turned, Mother let me get a chair and rummage through② his treasures. She didn't seem to think so highly of them as he did.

3   The war was the most peaceful period of my life. The window of my attic faced southeast. My mother had curtained it, but that had small effect. I always woke with the first light and, with all the responsibilities of the previous day melted, feeling myself rather like the sun, ready to illumine and rejoice. Life never seemed so simple and clear and full of possibilities as then. I put my feet out from under the clothes—I called them Mrs. Left and Mrs. Right—and invented dramatic situations for them in which they discussed the problems of the day. At least Mrs. Right did; she was very demonstrative, but I hadn't the same control of Mrs. Left, so she mostly contented herself with nodding agreement③.

4   They discussed what Mother and I should do during the day, what Santa Claus should give a fellow for Christmas, and what steps should be taken to brighten the home. There was

---

① magpie: Here refers to a person collecting things, esp. indiscriminately.
② rummage through: turn things over, move things about, while looking for something
③ The two feet play the parts of two persons arguing. As the body can't control his left foot well, thought it disagrees, it nods rather than shakes its toes.

that little matter of the baby, for instance. Mother and I could never agree about that. Ours was the only house in the terrace without a new baby, and Mother said we couldn't afford one till Father came back from the war because they cost seventeen and six①.

5   That showed how simple she was. The Geneys up the road had a baby, and everyone knew they couldn't afford seventeen and six. It was probably a cheap baby, and Mother wanted something really good, but I felt she was too exclusive. The Geneys' baby would have done us fine.

6   Having settled my plans for the day, I got up, put a chair under the attic window, and lifted the frame high enough to stick out my head. The window overlooked the front gardens of the terrace behind ours, and beyond these it looked over a deep valley to the tall, red brick houses terraced up the opposite hillside, which were all still in shadow, while those at our side of the valley were all lit up, though with long strange shadows that made them seem unfamiliar; rigid and painted.

7   After that I went into Mother's room and climbed into the big bed. She woke and I began to tell her of my schemes. By this time, though I never seemed to have noticed it, I was petrified② in my nightshirt, and I thawed③ as I talked until, the last frost melted, I fell asleep beside her and woke again only when I heard her below in the kitchen, making the breakfast.

8   After breakfast we went into town; heard Mass④ at St. Augustine's and said a prayer for Father, and did the shopping. If the afternoon was fine we either went for a walk in the country or a visit to Mother's great friend in the convent⑤, Mother Saint Dominic. Mother had them all praying for Father, and every night, going to bed, I asked God to send him back safe from the war to us. Little, indeed, did I know what I was praying for!

9   One morning, I got into the big bed, and there, sure enough, was Father in his usual Santa Claus manner, but later, instead of uniform, he put on his best blue suit, and Mother was as pleased as anything. I saw nothing to be pleased about, because, out of uniform, Father was altogether less interesting, but she only beamed, and explained that our prayers had been answered, and off we went to Mass to thank God for having brought Father safely home.

10   The irony of it! That very day when he came in to dinner he took off his boots and put on his slippers, donned the dirty old cap he wore about the house to save him from colds, crossed his legs, and began to talk gravely to Mother, who looked anxious. Naturally, I disliked her looking anxious, because it destroyed her good looks, so I interrupted him.

11   "Just a moment, Larry!" she said gently. This was only what she said when we had boring visitors, so I attached no importance to it and went on talking.

12   "Do be quiet, Larry!" she said impatiently. "Don't you hear me talking to Daddy?" This was the first time I had heard those ominous⑥ words, "talking to Daddy," and I couldn't help feeling that if this was how God answered prayers, he couldn't listen to them very

---

① seventeen and six: the amount of money
② petrify: to become rigid because of coldness
③ thaw: to become warm and soft
④ Mass: 基督教中的圣餐仪式
⑤ convent: a religious community
⑥ ominous: of bad omen, treatening

attentively.

13   "Why are you talking to Daddy?" I asked with as great a show of indifference as I could muster.

14   "Because Daddy and I have business to discuss. Now, don't interrupt again!"

15   In the afternoon, at Mother's request, Father took me for a walk. This time we went into town instead of out in the country, and I thought at first, in my usual optimistic way, that it might be an improvement. It was nothing of the sort. Father and I had quite different notions of a walk in town. He had no proper interest in trams, ships, and horses, and the only thing that seemed to divert him was talking to fellows as old as himself. When I wanted to stop he simply went on, dragging me behind him by the hand; when he wanted to stop I had no alternative but to do the same. I noticed that it seemed to be a sign that he wanted to stop for a long time whenever he leaned against a wall. The second time I saw him do it I got wild. He seemed to be settling himself forever. I pulled him by the coat and trousers, but, unlike Mother who, if you were too persistent, got into a wax and said: "Larry, if you don't behave yourself, I'll give you a good slap," Father had an extraordinary capacity for amiable inattention. I sized him up and wondered would I cry, but he seemed to be too remote to be annoyed even by that. Really, it was like going for a walk with a mountain! He either ignored the wrenching[1] and pummeling[2] entirely, or else glanced down with a grin of amusement from his peak. I had never met anyone so absorbed in himself as he seemed.

16   At teatime, "talking to Daddy" began again, complicated this time by the fact that he had an evening paper, and every few minutes he put it down and told Mother something new out of it. I felt this was foul play. Man for man, I was prepared to compete with him any time for Mother's attention, but when he had it all made up for him by other people it left me no chance. Several times I tried to change the subject without success.

17   "You must be quiet while Daddy is reading, Larry," Mother said impatiently. It was clear that she either genuinely liked talking to Father better than talking to me, or else that he had some terrible hold on her which made her afraid to admit the truth. "Mummy," I said that night when she was tucking me up[3], "do you think if I prayed hard God would send Daddy back to the war?"

18   She seemed to think about that for a moment.

19   "No, dear," she said with a smile. "I don't think He would."

20   "Why wouldn't He, Mummy?"

21   "Because there isn't a war any longer, dear."

22   "But, Mummy, couldn't God make another war, if He liked?"

23   "He wouldn't like to, dear. It's not God who makes wars, but bad people."

24   "Oh!" I said. I was disappointed about that. I began to think that God wasn't quite what He was cracked up[4] to be.

25   Next morning I woke at my usual hour, feeling like a bottle of champagne. I put out my feet and invented a long conversation in which Mrs. Right talked of the trouble she had with

---

① wrench: to pull to a violent twist
② pummel: to beat with fists
③ tuck up: here means to put to bed.
④ crack up: to praise highly, or in an exaggerated way

her own father till she put him in the Home. I didn't quite know what the Home was but it sounded the right place for Father. Then I got my chair and stuck my head out of the attic window. Dawn was just breaking, with a guilty air that made me feel I had caught it in the act. My head bursting with stories and schemes, I stumbled in next door, and in the half-darkness scrambled into the big bed. There was no room at Mother's side so I had to get between her and Father. For the time being I had forgotten about him, and for several minutes I sat bolt upright, racking my brains to know what I could do with him. He was taking up more than his fair share of the bed, and I couldn't get comfortable, so I gave him several kicks that made him grunt and stretch. He made room all right, though. Mother waked and felt for me. I settled back comfortably in the warmth of the bed with my thumb in my mouth.

26   "Mummy!" I hummed, loudly and contentedly.

27   "Sssh! dear," she whispered. "Don't wake Daddy!"

28   This was a new development, which threatened to be even more serious than "talking to Daddy." Life without my early-morning conferences was unthinkable.

29   "Why?" I asked severely.

30   "Because poor Daddy is tired." This seemed to me a quite inadequate reason, and I was sickened by the sentimentality of her "poor Daddy." I never liked that sort of gush; it always struck me as insincere.

31   "Oh!" I said lightly. Then in my most winning tone: "Do you know where I want to go with you today, Mummy?"

32   "No, dear," she sighed.

33   "I want to go down the Glen and fish for thorny-backs with my new net, and then I want to go out to the Fox and Hounds, and —"

34   "Don't-wake-Daddy!" she hissed angrily, clapping her hand across my mouth. But it was too late. He was awake, or nearly so. He grunted and reached for the matches. Then he stared incredulously at his watch.

35   "Like a cup of tea, dear?" asked Mother in a meek, hushed voice I had never heard her use before. It sounded almost as though she were afraid.

36   "Tea?" he exclaimed indignantly. "Do you know what the time is?"

37   "And after that I want to go up the Rathcooney Road," I said loudly, afraid I'd forget something in all those interruptions.

38   "Go to sleep at once, Larry!" she said sharply.

39   I began to snivel①. I couldn't concentrate, the way that pair went on, and smothering my early-morning schemes was like burying a family from the cradle. Father said nothing, but lit his pipe and sucked it, looking out into the shadows without minding Mother or me. I knew he was mad. Every time I made a remark Mother hushed me irritably. I was mortified②. I felt it wasn't fair; there was even something sinister③ in it. Every time I had pointed out to her the waste of making two beds when we could both sleep in one, she had told me it was healthier like that, and now here was this man, this stranger, sleeping with her without the least regard

---

① snivel: to cry from pretended grief, sorrow or fear
② to mortify: to shame, to humiliate
③ sinister: suggesting evil or the likelihood of coming misfortune

for her health! He got up early and made tea, but though he brought Mother a cup he brought none for me.

40   "Mummy," I shouted, "I want a cup of tea, too."

41   "Yes, dear," she said patiently. "You can drink from Mummy's saucer."

42   That settled it. Either Father or I would have to leave the house. I didn't want to drink from Mother's saucer; I wanted to be treated as an equal in my own home, so, just to spite her, I drank it all and left none for her. She took that quietly, too. But that night when she was putting me to bed she said gently:

43   "Larry, I want you to promise me something."

44   "What is it?" I asked.

45   "Not to come in and disturb poor Daddy in the morning. Promise?"

46   "Poor Daddy" again! I was becoming suspicious of everything involving that quite impossible man.

47   "Why?" I asked.

48   "Because poor Daddy is worried and tired and he doesn't sleep well."

49   "Why doesn't he, Mummy?"

50   "Well, you know, don't you, that while he was at the war Mummy got the pennies from the post office?

51   "From Miss MacCarthy?"

52   "That's right. But now, you see, Miss MacCarthy hasn't any more pennies, so Daddy must go out and find us some. You know what would happen if he couldn't?"

53   "No," I said, "tell us."

54   "Well, I think we might have to go out and beg for them like the poor old woman on Fridays. We wouldn't like that, would we?"

55   "No," I agreed. "We wouldn't."

56   "So you'll promise not to come in and wake him?"

57   "Promise."

58   Mind you, I meant that. I knew pennies were a serious matter, and I was all against having to go out and beg like the old woman on Fridays. Mother laid out all my toys in a complete ring round the bed so that, whatever way I got out, I was bound to fall over one of them. When I woke I remembered my promise all right. I got up and sat on the floor and played—for hours, it seemed to me. Then I got my chair and looked out the attic window for more hours. I wished it was time for Father to wake; I wished someone would make me a cup of tea. I didn't feel in the least like the sun; instead, I was bored and so very, very cold! I simply longed for the warmth and depth of the big feather bed. At last I could stand it no longer. I went into the next room. As there was still no room at Mother's side I climbed over her and she woke with a start. "Larry," she whispered, gripping my arm very tightly, "what did you promise?"

59   "But I did, Mummy," I wailed, caught in the very act. "I was quiet for ever so long."

60   "Oh, dear, and you're perished!" she said sadly, feeling me all over. "Now, if I let you stay will you promise not to talk?"

61   "But I want to talk, Mummy," I wailed.

62   "That has nothing to do with it," she said with a firmness that was new to me. "Daddy

wants to sleep. Now, do you understand that?"

63   I understood it only too well. I wanted to talk, he wanted to sleep—whose house was it, anyway?

64   "Mummy," I said with equal firmness, "I think it would be healthier for Daddy to sleep in his own bed."

65   That seemed to stagger her, because she said nothing for a while.

66   "Now, once for all," she went on, "you're to be perfectly quiet or go back to your own bed. Which is it to be?"

67   The injustice of it got me down. I had convicted her out of her own mouth of inconsistency and unreasonableness, and she hadn't even attempted to reply. Full of spite, I gave Father a kick, which she didn't notice but which made him grunt and open his eyes in alarm.

68   "What time is it?" he asked in a panic-stricken voice, not looking at Mother but at the door, as if he saw someone there.

69   "It's early yet," she replied soothingly. "It's only the child. Go to sleep again...Now, Larry," she added, getting out of bed, "you've wakened Daddy and you must go back."

70   This time, for all her quiet air, I knew she meant it, and knew that my principal rights and privileges were as good as lost unless I asserted them at once. As she lifted me, I gave a screech[1], enough to wake the dead, not to mind Father.

71   He groaned. "That damn child! Doesn't he ever sleep?"

72   "It's only a habit, dear," she said quietly, though I could see she was vexed.

73   "Well, it's time he got out of it," shouted Father, beginning to heave in the bed. He suddenly gathered all the bedclothes about him, turned to the wall, and then looked back over his shoulder with nothing showing only two small, spiteful, dark eyes. The man looked very wicked. To open the bedroom door, Mother had to let me down, and I broke free and dashed for the farthest corner, screeching.

74   Father sat bolt upright in bed. "Shut up, you little puppy," he said in a choking voice.

75   I was so astonished that I stopped screeching. Never, never had anyone spoken to me in that tone before. I looked at him incredulously[2] and saw his face convulsed[3] with rage. It was only then that I fully realized how God had codded[4] me, listening to my prayers for the safe return of this monster.

76   "Shut up, you!" I bawled[5], beside myself.

77   "What's that you said?" shouted Father, making a wild leap out of the bed.

78   "Mick, Mick!" cried Mother. "Don't you see the child isn't used to you?"

79   "I see he's better fed than taught," snarled Father, waving his arms wildly. "He wants his bottom smacked."

80   All his previous shouting was as nothing to these obscene[6] words referring to my person. They really made my blood boil.

81   "Smack your own!" I screamed hysterically. "Smack your own! Shut up! Shut up!"

---

① screech: to make a harsh, piercing sound
② incredulously: unbelievingly
③ convulse: to twist
④ cod: to fool, to tease
⑤ bawl: to cry or wail lustily
⑥ obscene: offensive, indecent

82   At this he lost his patience and let fly at[1] me. He did it with the lack of conviction you'd expect of a man under Mother's horrified eyes, and it ended up as a mere tap, but the sheer indignity of being struck at all by a stranger, a total stranger who had cajoled[2] his way back from the war into our big bed as a result of my innocent intercession[3], made me completely dotty[4]. I shrieked and shrieked, and danced in my bare feet, and Father, looking awkward and hairy in nothing but a short gray army shirt, glared down at me like a mountain out for murder. I think it must have been then that I realized he was jealous too. And there stood Mother in her nightdress, looking as if her heart was broken between us. I hoped she felt as she looked. It seemed to me that she deserved it all.

83   From that morning out my life was a hell. Father and I were enemies, open and avowed[5]. We conducted a series of skirmishes[6] against one another, he trying to steal my time with Mother and I his. When she was sitting on my bed, telling me a story, he took to looking for some pair of old boots which he alleged[7] he had left behind him at the beginning of the war. While he talked to Mother I played loudly with my toys to show my total lack of concern.

84   He created a terrible scene one evening when he came in from work and found me at his box, playing with his regimental[8] badges, Gurkha knives and button sticks. Mother got up and took the box from me.

85   "You mustn't play with Daddy's toys unless he lets you, Larry," she said severely. "Daddy doesn't play with yours."

86   For some reason Father looked at her as if she had struck him and then turned away with a scowl[9]. "Those are not toys," he growled, taking down the box again to see had I lifted anything. "Some of those curios are very rare and valuable."

87   But as time went on I saw more and more how he managed to alienate Mother and me. What made it worse was that I couldn't grasp his method or see what attraction he had for Mother. In every possible way he was less winning than I. He had a common accent and made noises at his tea. I thought for a while that it might be the newspapers she was interested in, so I made up bits of news of my own to read to her. Then I thought it might be the smoking, which I personally thought attractive, and took his pipes and went round the house dribbling[10] into them till he caught me. I even made noises at my tea, but Mother only told me I was disgusting. It all seemed to hinge round[11] that unhealthy habit of sleeping together, so I made a point of dropping into their bedroom and nosing round, talking to myself, so that they wouldn't know I was watching them, but they were never up to anything that I could see. In the end it beat me. It seemed to depend on being grown-up and giving people rings, and I realized I'd have to wait. But at the same time I wanted him to see that I was only waiting, not giving up

---

① let fly at: to rush angrily at
② cajole: to persuade with flattery or promises
③ intercession: a prayer to God on behalf of another person
④ dotty: crazy
⑤ avowed: declared, announced
⑥ skirmish: brisk conflict
⑦ allege: to declare with positiveness
⑧ regimental: here means military.
⑨ scowl: gloomy or angry look
⑩ dribble: to smoke
⑪ hinge around: to linger around

the fight.

88 One evening when he was being particularly obnoxious①, chattering away well above my head, I let him have it.

89 "Mummy," I said, "do you know what I'm going to do when I grow up?"

90 "No, dear," she replied. "What?"

91 "I'm going to marry you," I said quietly.

92 Father gave a great guffaw② out of him, but he didn't take me in. I knew it must only be pretence.

93 And Mother, in spite of everything, was pleased. I felt she was probably relieved to know that one day Father's hold on her would be broken.

94 "Won't that be nice?" she said with a smile.

95 "It'll be very nice," I said confidently. "Because we're going to have lots and lots of babies."

96 "That's right, dear," she said placidly③. "I think we'll have one soon, and then you'll have plenty of company."

97 I was no end pleased about that because it showed that in spite of the way she gave in to Father she still considered my wishes. Besides, it would put the Geneys in their place. It didn't turn out like that, though. To begin with, she was very preoccupied—I supposed about where she would get the seventeen and six—and though Father took to staying out late in the evenings it did me no particular good. She stopped taking me for walks, became as touchy as blazes, and smacked me for nothing at all. Sometimes I wished I'd never mentioned the confounded④ baby—I seemed to have a genius for bringing calamity on myself.

98 And calamity⑤ it was! Sonny arrived in the most appalling hulla-baloo⑥ —even that much he couldn't do without a fuss—and from the first moment I disliked him. He was a difficult child— so far as I was concerned he was always difficult—and demanded far too much attention. Mother was simply silly about him, and couldn't see when he was only showing off. As company he was worse than useless. He slept all day, and I had to go round the house on tiptoe to avoid waking him. It wasn't any longer a question of not waking Father. The slogan now was "Don't-wake-Sonny!" I couldn't understand why the child wouldn't sleep at the proper time, so whenever Mother's back was turned I woke him. Sometimes to keep him awake I pinched him as well. Mother caught me at it one day and gave me a most unmerciful flaking⑦.

99 One evening, when Father was coming in from work, I was playing trains in the front garden. I let on⑧ not to notice him; instead, I pretended to be talking to myself, and said in a loud voice: "If another bloody baby comes into this house, I'm going out."

100 Father stopped dead and looked at me over his shoulder. "What's that you said?" he asked sternly.

101 "I was only talking to myself," I replied, trying to conceal my panic. "It's private." He

① obnoxious: highly offensive
② guffaw: noisy laugh
③ placid: pleasantly calm or peaceful
④ confounded: damned
⑤ calamity: great and serious misfortune or disaster
⑥ hulla-baloo: loud, confused noise, commotion
⑦ flaking: criticism
⑧ let on: to pretend

turned and went in without a word.

102   Mind you, I intended it as a solemn warning, but its effect was quite different. Father started being quite nice to me. I could understand that, of course. Mother was quite sickening about Sonny. Even at mealtimes she's get up and gawk[①] at him in the cradle with an idiotic smile, and tell Father to do the same. He was always polite about it, but he looked so puzzled you could see he didn't know what she was talking about. He complained of the way Sonny cried at night, but she only got cross and said that Sonny never cried except when there was something up with him —which was a flaming lie, because Sonny never had anything up with him, and only cried for attention. It was really painful to see how simpleminded she was.

103   Father wasn't attractive, but he had a fine intelligence. He saw through Sonny, and now he knew that I saw through him as well. One night I woke with a start. There was someone beside me in the bed. For one wild moment I felt sure it must be Mother, having come to her senses and left Father for good, but then I heard Sonny in convulsions in the next room, and Mother saying: "There! There! There!" and I knew it wasn't she. It was Father. He was lying beside me, wide-awake, breathing hard and apparently as mad as hell. After a while it came to me what he was mad about. It was his turn now. After turning me out of the big bed, he had been turned out himself. Mother had no consideration now for anyone but that poisonous pup, Sonny.

104   I couldn't help feeling sorry for Father. I had been through it all myself, and even at that age I was magnanimous[②]. I began to stroke him down and say: "There! There!"

105   He wasn't exactly responsive. "Aren't you asleep either?" he snarled.

106   "Ah, come on and put your arm around us, can't you?" I said, and he did, in a sort of way. Gingerly[③], I suppose, is how you'd describe it. He was very bony but better than nothing. Christmas he went out of his way to buy me a really nice model railway.

▶▶ APPENDIX 4

A⟩ *What is OEDIPUS COMPLEX?*

For **Sigmund Freud** (1856–1939), the childhood desire is to sleep with the mother and to kill the father. Freud describes the source of this complex in his *Introductory Lectures* (*Twenty-First Lecture*): "You all know the Greek legend of King Oedipus, who was destined by fate to kill his father and take his mother to wife, who did everything possible to escape the oracle's decree and punished himself by blinding when he learned that he had none the less unwittingly committed both these crimes."According to Freud, Sophocles' play, *Oedipus Rex*, illustrates a formative stage in each individual's psychosexual development, when the young child transfers his love object from the breast (the oral phase) to the mother. At this time, the child desires the mother and resents (even secretly desires the murder) of the father. (The Oedipus complex is closely connected to the castration complex.) Such primal desires are, of course, quickly repressed but, even among the mentally sane, they will arise again in dreams or in literature. Among those individuals who do not progress properly into the genital phase, the Oedipus complex, according to Freud, can still be playing out its psychdrama in various displaced, abnormal, and/or exaggerated ways.

---

① gawk: to stare stupidly
② magnanimous: generous in forgiving insult or injury
③ gingerly: with great care or caution

B▷ Who is Oedipus?

Oedipus is known in Greek mythology for being declared a Greek hero. In the myth of Oedipus, he lived up to the requests of what was called the Delphic oracle and murdered his father, King Laertes out of pure rage and jealousy. As the story evolves, Oedipus unknowingly marries his own mother, Queen Jocasta and creates a family with her.

Resulting from his marriage, Oedipus created three intersecting crossroads. In stating this, it is meant that he engaged in sexual activity with Jocasta and had children as an outcome of their copulation. Therefore, Oedipus helped to create three generations (or crossroads) in which he was a part of all of them.

The Greek meaning of Oedipus' name is "swollen foot". Oidus means swollen and pous means foot. The first syllable of Oedipus' name, "oido", means "I know." Thus his full name could be depicted as know-foot. The meaning of his name reverts to his feet so much particularly because of a special marking he received when he was an infant. When he was young, he had his ankles pierced, therefore, he lives up to his name of "swollen foot" and he even had difficulties in walking.

Ironically enough the term "swollen foot" is meant to be an allusion of an erect penis. Because of this association, it would be simpler to decipher the true meaning of the Oedipus myth. Overall, it has evolved into an entire story about how a boy feels towards his father in a jealous way and how a boy feels towards his mother in a sexual way.

▶▌ STUDY QUESTIONS

A▷ Recalling

1. How do "I" feel about father when he came and went mysteriously like Santa Claus?
2. When do "I" begin to dislike father?
3. Why is the walk between the father and son unsuccessful? What annoyed "I" most? What does the father think of his son?
4. What are some of the best moments the boy shared with his mother?
5. How does the boy compete with his father for the mother's attention?
6. The writer has used a lot of different words to describe mood and emotion. Please make a list of those words and explain what kind of mood or emotion is expressed by each word.

B▷ Interpreting

7. Please show how the boy's attitude towards his father changes.
8. Please show how the boy's attitude towards his mother changes.
9. Does the boy dislike the new-born baby for the same reason he dislikes his father?
10. Please point out some of the "baby-talk" in the story.
11. If the story is told from an adult's point of view, what different effect will it achieve?

C▷ Extending

12. What do you think about the boy's story? Do you think it is only "baby-talk"? What do you think of Freud's explanation? Do you agree with him?

▶▶ LITERARY FOCUS

▷ *Character and Characterization*

A character is a person presented in a dramatic or narrative work and characterization is the process by which a writer makes that character seem real to the reader. There are **Flat character** who is known by one or two traits, **Round character** who is complex and many-sided, **Stock character** who is a stereotyped character (a mad scientist, the absent-minded professor, the cruel mother-in-law), **Static character** who remains the same from the beginning of the plot to the end and **Dynamic (Developing) character** who undergoes permanent change. A hero or heroine, often called the **Protagonist**, is the central character who engages the reader's interest and empathy. The **Antagonist** is the character, force, or collection of forces that stands directly opposed to the protagonist and gives rise to the conflict of the story. A character is presented either through **Direct Presentation** or **Indirect Presentation**. In Direct Presentation the author tells us straight out, by exposition or analysis, or through another character. In Indirect Presentation the author shows us the character in action; the reader infers what a character is like from what she/he thinks, or says, or does. These are also called dramatized characters and they are generally consistent (in behavior), motivated (convincing), and plausible (lifelike).

▶▶ THINKING ABOUT CHARACTER AND CHARACTERIZATION

Think about characters in *A Clean, Well-lighted Place, Rice* and *My Oedipus Complex*. Who is the protagonist? What types of characters are they? Are they flat or round characters? Do they develop? How are the characters presented, through direct or indirect presentation? Are they convincing? Why or why not?

Family of Saltimbanques
Pablo Picasso, 1905.
Chester Dale Collection.

VIII. "Chapter 1" from *Pride and Prejudice* by Jane Austen

▶ ABOUT THE AUTHOR

Jane Austen (1775–1817), English writer, who first gave the novel its modern character through the treatment of everyday life. Although Austen was widely read in her lifetime, she published her works anonymously. The most urgent preoccupation of her young, well-bred heroines is courtship, and finally marriage. Austen's best-known books include *Pride and Prejudice* (1813) and *Emma* (1816). Virginia Woolf called her "the most perfect artist among women."

▶ INTRODUCTION TO *PRIDE AND PREJUDICE*

Pride and Prejudice is the story of Mr. and Mrs. Bennet (minor gentry), their five daughters, and the various romantic adventures at their Hertfordshire residence of Longbourn. The parents' characters are greatly contrasted: Mr. Bennet being a wise and witty gentleman; while Mrs. Bennet is permanently distracted by the issue of marrying off her daughters at any cost. The reason for Mrs. Bennet's obsession is that their estate will pass by law after Mr. Bennet's death to his closest blood relative: his cousin, the Reverend William Collins (a fatuous, tactless and pompous man). Austen's tale is spurred on by the arrival of the young and wealthy bachelor Charles Bingley and his friend Fitzwilliam Darcy. It is the story of the various affections, affectations and engagement shenanigans that develop due to Mrs. Bennet's relentless matchmaking and the dashing Darcy's tempestuous relationship with Elizabeth Bennet who Jane Austen claimed was favourite amongst her literary offspring. Its 1797 earlier version was turned down for publication and it appeared in this form in 1813.

Pride and Prejudice
Chapter 1

1   IT is a truth universally acknowledged, that a single man in possession of a good fortune must be in want of a wife.

2   However little known the feelings or views of such a man may be on his first entering a neighbourhood, this truth is so well fixed in the minds of the surrounding families, that he is considered as the rightful property of some one or other of their daughters.

3   "My dear Mr. Bennet," said his lady to him one day, "have you heard that Netherfield Park is let at last?"

4   Mr. Bennet replied that he had not.

5   "But it is," returned she; "for Mrs. Long has just been here, and she told me all about it."

6   Mr. Bennet made no answer.

7   "Do not you want to know who has taken it?" cried his wife impatiently.

8   "You want to tell me, and I have no objection to hearing it."

9   This was invitation enough.

10   "Why, my dear, you must know, Mrs. Long says that Netherfield is taken by a young man

of large fortune from the north of England; that he came down on Monday in a chaise[①] and four to see the place, and was so much delighted with it that he agreed with Mr. Morris immediately; that he is to take possession before Michaelmas[②], and some of his servants are to be in the house by the end of next week."

11　　"What is his name?"

12　　"Bingley."

13　　"Is he married or single?"

14　　"Oh! single, my dear, to be sure! A single man of large fortune; four or five thousand a year. What a fine thing for our girls!"

15　　"How so? How can it affect them?"

16　　"My dear Mr. Bennet," replied his wife, "how can you be so tiresome! You must know that I am thinking of his marrying one of them."

17　　"Is that his design in settling here?"

18　　"Design! nonsense, how can you talk so! But it is very likely that he may fall in love with one of them, and therefore you must visit him as soon as he comes."

19　　"I see no occasion for that. You and the girls may go, or you may send them by themselves, which perhaps will be still better; for, as you are as handsome as any of them, Mr. Bingley might like you the best of the party."

20　　"My dear, you flatter me. I certainly have had my share of beauty, but I do not pretend to be any thing extraordinary now. When a woman has five grown up daughters, she ought to give over thinking of her own beauty."

21　　"In such cases, a woman has not often much beauty to think of."

22　　"But, my dear, you must indeed go and see Mr. Bingley when he comes into the neighbourhood."

23　　"It is more than I engage for, I assure you."

24　　"But consider your daughters. Only think what an establishment it would be for one of them. Sir William and Lady Lucas are determined to go, merely on that account, for in general, you know they visit no new comers. Indeed you must go, for it will be impossible for us to visit him, if you do not."

25　　"You are over-scrupulous[③], surely. I dare say Mr. Bingley will be very glad to see you; and I will send a few lines by you to assure him of my hearty consent to his marrying which ever he chuses of the girls; though I must throw in a good word for my little Lizzy."

26　　"I desire you will do no such thing. Lizzy is not a bit better than the others; and I am sure she is not half so handsome as Jane, nor half so good humoured as Lydia. But you are always giving her the preference."

27　　"They have none of them much to recommend them," replied he; "They are all silly and ignorant like other girls; but Lizzy has something more of quickness than her sisters."

28　　"Mr. Bennet, how can you abuse your own children in such way? You take delight in vexing[④] me. You have no compassion on my poor nerves."

---

① chaise: a light, open, one horse carriage
② Michaelmas: 29th of September, a Christian holy day in honor of Saint Michael
③ over-scrupulous: too careful, too prudent
④ vex: annoy

29   "You mistake me, my dear. I have a high respect for your nerves. They are my old friends. I have heard you mention them with consideration these twenty years at least."

30   "Ah! You do not know what I suffer."

31   "But I hope you will get over it, and live to see many young men of four thousand a year come into the neighbourhood."

32   "It will be no use to us if twenty such should come, since you will not visit them."

33   "Depend upon it, my dear, that when there are twenty I will visit them all."

34   Mr. Bennet was so odd a mixture of quick parts, sarcastic humour, reserve, and caprice[1], that the experience of three and twenty years had been insufficient to make his wife understand his character. Her mind was less difficult to develop. She was a woman of mean understanding, little information, and uncertain temper. When she was discontented, she fancied herself nervous. The business of her life was to get her daughters married; its solace[2] was visiting and news.

▶ STUDY QUESTIONS

A Recalling

1. How does Mrs. Bennet react towards the arrival of Mr. Bingley?
2. How does Mr. Bennet react towards it?
3. What is Mr. Bennet's response towards his wife's enthusiasm in the event?
4. Which daughter is Mr. Bennet's favorite?

B Interpreting

5. What is Mr. Bennet's character?
6. What is Mrs. Bennet's character?
7. What does this passage say about the relationship between Mr. and Mrs. Bennet?

C Extending

8. What does this passage say about the relationship and position of man and wife in a family? Is that relationship and position between man and wife still true today?

IX. A Selection from *A Doll's House* (Act III) by Henrik Ibsen

▶ ABOUT THE PLAYWRIGHT

Henrik Ibsen (1828–1906), Norwegian playwright and poet who created twenty-six plays and a volume of poetry. He is noted for his nationalistic spirit and for exploring Europe's social problems during the 1800s. Critics both past and present have praised his realistic approach to drama and his well-developed characters. He is best known for creating strong female characters in dramas such as *A Doll's House* and *Hedda Gabler*.

① caprice: a sudden, unpredictable change of one's mind
② solace: comfort

▶ THE SUMMARY OF *A DOLL'S HOUSE*

A▷ *Act I*

A Doll's House opens as Nora Helmer returns from Christmas shopping. Her husband Torvald comes out of his study to banter[①] with her. They discuss how their finances will improve now that Torvald has a new job as a bank manager. Torvald expresses his horror of debt. Nora behaves childishly and he enjoys treating her like a child to be instructed and indulged.

Soon an old friend of Nora's, Kristine Linde, arrives. She is a childless widow who is moving back to the city. Her husband left her no money, so she has tried different kinds of work, and now hopes to find some work that is not too strenuous[②]. Nora confides to Kristine that she once secretly borrowed money from a disgraced lawyer, Nils Krogstad, to save Torvald's life when he was very ill, but she has not told him in order to protect his pride. She told everyone that the money came from her father, who died at about the same time. She has been repaying the debt from her housekeeping budget, and also from some work she got copying papers by hand, which she did secretly in her room, and took pride in her ability to earn money "as if she were a man." Torvald's new job promises to finally liberate her from this debt.

Nora asks Torvald to give Kristine a position as a secretary in the bank, and he agrees, as she has experience in bookkeeping. They leave the house together.

Krogstad arrives and tells Nora that he is worried he will be fired. He asks her to help him keep his job and says that he will fight desperately to keep it. Nora is reluctant to commit to helping him, so Krogstad reveals that he knows she committed forgery[③] on the bond she signed for her loan from him. As a woman, she needed an adult male co-signer, so she said she would have her father do so. However the signature is dated three days after his death, which suggests that it is a forgery. Nora admits that she did forge the signature, so as to spare her dying father further worry about her (she was pregnant, poor, and had a seriously ill husband). Krogstad explains that the forgery betrayed his trust and is also a serious crime. If he told others about it, her reputation would be ruined, as was his after a similar "indiscretion," even though he was never prosecuted. He implies that what he did was in order to provide for his sick wife, who later died.

B▷ *Act II*

Kristine arrives to help Nora repair a dress for a costume party she and Torvald are going to tomorrow. Then Torvald comes home from the bank and Nora pleads with him to reinstate[④] Krogstad at the bank. She claims she is worried that Krogstad will publish libelous[⑤] articles about Torvald and ruin his career. Torvald dismisses her fears and explains that although Krogstad is a good worker and seems to have turned his life around, he insists on firing him because Krogstad is not deferential enough to him in front of other bank personnel. Torvald goes into his study to do some work.

---

① banter: an exchange of light, playful, teasing remarks
② strenuous: demanding great effort, hard work
③ forgery: the crime of falsely making or altering a writing by which the legal rights of another will be affected
④ reinstate: to put back in the former position
⑤ libelous: ill, wicked

Next Dr. Rank, a family friend, arrives. Nora talks about asking him for a favor. Then he reveals that he has entered the terminal stage of tuberculosis of the spine (a contemporary euphemism for congenital syphilis), and that he has always been secretly in love with her. Nora tries to deny the first revelation and make light of it, but she is more disturbed by the second. She tries clumsily to tell him that she is not in love with him, but loves him dearly as a friend.

Desperate after being fired by Torvald, Krogstad arrives at the house. Nora gets Dr. Rank to go in to Torvald's study, so he does not see Krogstad. When Krogstad comes in he declares he no longer cares about the remaining balance of Nora's loan, but that he will preserve the associated bond in order to blackmail Torvald into not only keeping him employed, but giving him a promotion. Nora explains that she has done her best to persuade her husband, but he refuses to change his mind. Krogstad informs Nora that he has written a letter detailing her crime (forging her father's signature of surety on the bond) and puts it in Torvald's mailbox, which is locked.

Nora tells Kristine of her predicament. Kristine says that she and Krogstad were in love before she married, and promises that she will try to convince him to relent.

Torvald comes in and tries to check his mail, but Nora distracts him by begging him to help her with the dance she has been rehearsing for the costume party, as she is so anxious about performing. She dances so badly and acts so worried that Torvald agrees to spend the whole evening coaching her. When the others go in to dinner, Nora stays behind for a few minutes and contemplates suicide to save her husband from the shame of the revelation of her crime, and more importantly to pre-empt any gallant gesture on his part to save her reputation.

C⟩ Act III

Kristine tells Krogstad that she only married her husband because she had no other means to support her sick mother and young siblings, and that she has returned to offer him her love again. She believes that he would not have stooped to unethical behavior if he had not been devastated by her abandonment and in dire financial straits. Krogstad is moved and offers to take back his letter to Torvald. However, Kristine decides that Torvald should know the truth for the sake of his and Nora's marriage.

After literally dragging Nora home from the party, Torvald goes to check his mail, but is interrupted by Dr. Rank, who has followed them. Dr. Rank chats for a while so as to convey obliquely to Nora that this is a final goodbye, as he has determined that his death is near, but in general terms so that Torvald does not suspect what he is referring to. Dr. Rank leaves, and Torvald retrieves his letters. As he reads them Nora steels herself to take her life. Torvald confronts her with Krogstad's letter. Enraged, he declares that he is now completely in Krogstad's power—he must yield to Krogstad's demands and keep quiet about the whole affair. He berates Nora, calling her a dishonest and immoral woman and telling her she is unfit to raise their children. He says that from now on their marriage will be only a matter of appearances.

A maid enters, delivering a letter to Nora. Krogstad has returned the incriminating papers, saying that he regrets his actions. Torvald exults that he is saved as he burns the papers. He takes back his harsh words to his wife and tells her that he forgives her. Nora realizes that her husband is not the strong and gallant man she thought he was, and that he truly loves himself more than he does her.

Torvald explains that when a man has forgiven his wife it makes him love her all the more since it reminds him that she is totally dependent on him, like a child. He dismisses Nora's agonized choice made against her conscience for the sake of his health and her years of secret efforts to free them from the ensuing obligations and danger of loss of reputation, while preserving his peace of mind, as a mere mistake that she made owing to her foolishness, one of her most endearing feminine traits.

Nora tells Torvald that she is leaving him to live alone so she can find out who she is and what she believes and decide what to do with her life. She says she has been treated like a doll to play with, first by her father and then by him. Concerned for the family reputation, Torvald insists that she fulfill her duty as a wife and mother, but Nora says that her first duties are to herself, and she cannot be a good mother or wife without learning to be more than a plaything. She reveals that she had expected that he would want to sacrifice his reputation for hers, and that she had planned to kill herself to prevent him from doing so. She now realizes that Torvald is not at all the kind of person she had believed him to be, and that their marriage has been based on mutual fantasies and misunderstanding.

Torvald is unable to comprehend Nora's point of view, since it contradicts all that he had been taught about the female mind throughout his life. Furthermore, he is so narcissistic that it would be impossible for him to bear to understand how he appears to her, as selfish, hypocritical and more concerned with public reputation than with actual morality. Nora leaves her keys and wedding ring and as Torvald breaks down and begins to cry, baffled by what has happened, Nora leaves the house, slamming the door behind herself.

A Selection from *A Doll's House*

Translated by Nicholas Rudall

ACT III

… …

Helmer

No, don't go—. [*looks in*] What are you doing in there?

Nora

[*from within*] Taking off my fancy dress①.

Helmer

[*standing at the open door*] Yes, do. Try and calm yourself, and make your mind easy again, my frightened little singing-bird. Be at rest, and feel secure; I have broad wings to shelter you under. [*walks up and down by the door.*] How warm and cosy our home is, Nora. Here is shelter for you; here I will protect you like a hunted dove that I have saved from a hawk's claws; I will bring peace to your poor beating heart. It will come, little by little, Nora, believe me. Tomorrow morning you will look upon it all quite differently; soon everything will be just as it was before. Very soon you won't need me to assure you that I have forgiven you; you will yourself feel the certainty that I have done so. Can you suppose I should ever think of such a thing as repudiating② you, or even reproaching you? You have no idea what a true man's heart is like, Nora. There is something so indescribably sweet and satisfying,

---

① fancy dress: the tarantella dress worn by Nora on the dancing ball
② repudiate: to disown, to cast off

to a man, in the knowledge that he has forgiven his wife—forgiven her freely, and with all his heart. It seems as if that had made her, as it were, doubly his own; he has given her a new life, so to speak; and she has in a way become both wife and child to him. So you shall be for me after this, my little scared, helpless darling. Have no anxiety about anything, Nora; only be frank and open with me, and I will serve as will and conscience both to you—. What is this? Not gone to bed? Have you changed your things?

Nora

[*in everyday dress*] Yes, Torvald, I have changed my things now.

Helmer

But what for?—so late as this.

Nora

I shall not sleep tonight.

Helmer

But, my dear Nora—

Nora

[*looking at her watch*] It is not so very late. Sit down here, Torvald. You and I have much to say to one another [*She sits down at one side of the table.*]

Helmer

Nora—what is this?—this cold, set face?

Nora

Sit down. It will take some time; I have a lot to talk over with you.

Helmer

[*sits down at the opposite side of the table*] You alarm me, Nora!—and I don't understand you.

Nora

No, that is just it. You don't understand me, and I have never understood you either—before tonight. No, you mustn't interrupt me. You must simply listen to what I say. Torvald, this is a settling of accounts.

Helmer

What do you mean by that?

Nora

[*after a short silence*] Isn't there one thing that strikes you as strange in our sitting here like this?

Helmer

What is that?

Nora

We have been married now eight years. Does it not occur to you that this is the first time we two, you and I, husband and wife, have had a serious conversation?

Helmer

What do you mean by serious?

Nora

In all these eight years—longer than that—from the very beginning of our acquaintance, we have never exchanged a word on any serious subject.

Helmer

Was it likely that I would be continually and forever telling you about worries that you could not help me to bear?

Nora

I am not speaking about business matters. I say that we have never sat down in earnest together to try and get at the bottom of anything.

Helmer

But, dearest Nora, would it have been any good to you?

Nora

That is just it; you have never understood me. I have been greatly wronged, Torvald—first by papa and then by you.

Helmer

What! By us two—by us two, who have loved you better than anyone else in the world?

Nora

[*shaking her head*] You have never loved me. You have only thought it pleasant to be in love with me.

Helmer

Nora, what do I hear you saying?

Nora

It is perfectly true, Torvald. When I was at home with papa, he told me his opinion about everything, and so I had the same opinions; and if I differed from him I concealed the fact, because he would not have liked it. He called me his doll-child, and he played with me just as I used to play with my dolls. And when I came to live with you—

Helmer

What sort of an expression is that to use about our marriage?

Nora

[*undisturbed*] I mean that I was simply transferred from papa's hands into yours; You arranged everything according to your own taste, and so I got the same tastes as your else I pretended to, I am really not quite sure which—I think sometimes the one and sometimes the other; When I look back on it, it seems to me as if I had been living here like a poor woman—just from hand to mouth; I have existed merely to perform tricks for you, Torvald; But you would have it so; You and papa have committed a great sin against me. It is your fault that I have made nothing of my life.

Helmer

How unreasonable and how ungrateful you are, Nora! Have you not been happy here?

Nora

No, I have never been happy. I thought I was, but it has never really been so.

Helmer

Not—not happy!

Nora

No, only merry. And you have always been so kind to me. But our home has been nothing but a playroom. I have been your doll-wife, just as at home I was papa's doll-child; and here the children have been my dolls. I thought it great fun when you played with me, just as they thought it great fun when I played with them. That is what our marriage has been, Torvald.

Helmer

There is some truth in what you say—exaggerated and strained as your view of it is. But for the future it shall be different. Playtime shall be over, and lesson-time shall begin.

Nora

Whose lessons? Mine, or the children's?

Helmer

Both yours and the children's, my darling Nora.

Nora

Alas, Torvald, you are not the man to educate me into being a proper wife for you.

Helmer

And you can say that!

Nora

And I—how am I fitted to bring up the children?

Helmer

Nora!

Nora

Didn't you say so yourself a little while ago—that you dare not trust me to bring them up?

Helmer

In a moment of anger! Why do you pay any heed to that?

Nora

Indeed, you were perfectly right. I am not fit for the task. There is another task I must undertake first. I must try and educate myself—you are not the man to help me in that. I must do that for myself. And that is why I am going to leave you now.

Helmer

[*springing up*] What do you say?

Nora

I must stand quite alone, if I am to understand myself and everything about me. It is for that reason that I cannot remain with you any longer.

Helmer

Nora, Nora!

Nora

I am going away from here now, at once. I am sure Christine will take me in for the night—

Helmer

You are out of your mind! I won't allow it! I forbid you!

Nora

It is no use forbidding me anything any longer. I will take with me what belongs to myself. I will take nothing from you, either now or later.

Helmer

What sort of madness is this!

Nora

Tomorrow I shall go home—I mean, to my old home. It will be easiest for me to find something to do there.

Helmer

You blind, foolish woman!

Nora

I must try and get some sense, Torvald.

Helmer

To desert your home, your husband and your children! And you don't consider what people will say!

Nora

I cannot consider that at all. I only know that it is necessary for me.

Helmer

It's shocking. This is how you would neglect your most sacred duties.

Nora

What do you consider my most sacred duties?

Helmer

Do I need to tell you that? Are they not your duties to your husband and your children?

Nora

I have other duties just as sacred.

Helmer

That you have not. What duties could those be?

Nora

Duties to myself.

Helmer

Before all else, you are a wife and a mother.

Nora

I don't believe that any longer. I believe that before all else I am a reasonable human being, just as you are—or, at all events, that I must try and become one. I know quite well, Torvald, that most people would think you right, and that views of that kind are to be found in books; but I can no longer content myself with what most people say, or with what is found in books. I must think over things for myself and get to understand them.

Helmer

Can you not understand your place in your own home? Have you not a reliable guide in such matters as that?—Have you no religion?

Nora

I am afraid, Torvald, I do not exactly know what religion is.

Helmer

What are you saying?

Nora

I know nothing but what the clergyman said, when I went to be confirmed. He told us that religion was this, and that, and the other. When I am away from all this, and am alone, I will look into that matter too. I will see if what the clergyman said is true, or at all events if it is true for me.

Helmer

This is unheard of in a girl of your age! But if religion cannot lead you aright, let me try and awaken your conscience. I suppose you have some moral sense? Or—answer me—am I to think you have none?

Nora

I assure you, Torvald, that is not an easy question to answer. I really don't know. The thing perplexes me altogether. I only know that you and I look at it in quite a different light. I am learning, too, that the law is quite another thing from what I supposed; but I find it impossible to convince myself that the law is right. According to it a woman has no right to spare her old dying father, or to save her husband's life. I can't believe that.

Helmer

You talk like a child. You don't understand the conditions of the world in which you live.

Nora

No, I don't. But now I am going to try. I am going to see if I can make out who is right, the world or I.

Helmer

You are ill, Nora; you are delirious[1]; I almost think you are out of your mind.

Nora

I have never felt my mind so clear and certain as tonight.

Helmer

And is it with a clear and certain mind that you forsake your husband and your children?

Nora

Yes, it is.

Helmer

Then there is only one possible explanation.

Nora

What is that?

Helmer

You do not love me anymore.

Nora

No, that is just it.

Helmer

Nora!—and you can say that?

Nora

It gives me great pain, Torvald, for you have always been so kind to me, but I cannot help it. I do not love you any more.

Helmer

[*regaining his composure*] Is that a clear and certain conviction too?

Nora

Yes, absolutely clear and certain. That is the reason why I will not stay here any longer.

Helmer

And can you tell me what I have done to forfeit[2] your love?

Nora

Yes, indeed I can. It was tonight, when the wonderful thing did not happen; then I saw you were not the man I had thought you were.

Helmer

Explain yourself better. I don't understand you.

---

① delirious: mad
② forfeit: to be taken away as a punishment

Nora

I have waited so patiently for eight years; for, goodness knows, I knew very well that wonderful things don't happen every day. Then this horrible misfortune came upon me; and then I felt quite certain that the wonderful thing was going to happen at last. When Krogstad's letter was lying out there, never for a moment did I imagine that you would consent to accept this man's conditions. I was so absolutely certain that you would say to him: Publish the thing to the whole world. And when that was done—

Helmer

Yes, what then?—When I had exposed my wife to shame and disgrace?

Nora

When that was done, I was so absolutely certain, you would come forward and take everything upon yourself, and say: I am the guilty one.

Helmer

Nora—!

Nora

You mean that I would never have accepted such a sacrifice on your part? No, of course not. But what would my assurances have been worth against yours? That was the wonderful thing which I hoped for and feared; and it was to prevent that, that I wanted to kill myself.

Helmer

I would gladly work night and day for you, Nora—bear sorrow and want for your sake. But no man would sacrifice his honour for the one he loves.

Nora

It is a thing hundreds of thousands of women have done.

Helmer

Oh, you think and talk like a heedless child.

Nora

Maybe. But you neither think nor talk like the man I could bind myself to. As soon as your fear was over—and it was not fear for what threatened me, but for what might happen to you—when the whole thing was past, as far as you were concerned it was exactly as if nothing at all had happened. Exactly as before, I was your little skylark, your doll, which you would in future treat with doubly gentle care, because it was so brittle and fragile. [*getting up*] Torvald—it was then it dawned upon me that for eight years I had been living here with a strange man, and had borne him three children—. Oh, I can't bear to think of it! I could tear myself into little bits!

Helmer

[*sadly*] I see, I see; An abyss[①] has opened between us—there is no denying it. But, Nora, would it not be possible to fill it up?

Nora

As I am now, I am no wife for you.

Helmer

I have it in me to become a different man.

Nora

Perhaps—if your doll is taken away from you.

---

① abyss: a deep, immeasurable space, gulf

Helmer

But to part!—to part from you! No, no, Nora, I can't understand that idea.

Nora

[*going out to the right*] That makes it all the more certain that it must be done. [*She comes back with her cloak and hat and a small bag which she puts on a chair by the table.*]

Helmer

Nora, Nora, not now! Wait until tomorrow.

Nora

[*putting on her cloak*] I cannot spend the night in a strange man's room.

Helmer

But can't we live here like brother and sister—?

Nora

[*putting on her hat*] You know very well that would not last long [*puts the shawl round her*] Goodbye, Torvald. I won't see the little ones. I know they are in better hands than mine. As I am now, I can be of no use to them.

Helmer

But some day, Nora—some day?

Nora

How can I tell? I have no idea what is going to become of me.

Helmer

But you are my wife, whatever becomes of you.

Nora

Listen, Torvald. I have heard that when a wife deserts her husband's house, as I am doing now, he is legally freed from all obligations towards her. In any case, I set you free from all your obligations. You are not to feel yourself bound in the slightest way, any more than I shall. There must be perfect freedom on both sides. See, here is your ring back. Give me mine.

Helmer

That too?

Nora

That too.

Helmer

Here it is.

Nora

That's right. Now it is all over. I have put the keys here. The maids know all about everything in the house—better than I do. Tomorrow, after I have left her, Christine will come here and pack up my own things that I brought with me from home. I will have them sent after me.

Helmer

All over! All over!—Nora, shall you never think of me again?

Nora

I know I shall often think of you, the children, and this house.

Helmer

May I write to you, Nora?

Nora

No—never. You must not do that.

Helmer

But at least let me send you—

Nora

Nothing—nothing—

Helmer

Let me help you if you are in want.

Nora

No, I can receive nothing from a stranger.

Helmer

Nora—can I never be anything more than a stranger to you?

Nora

[*taking her bag*] Ah, Torvald, the most wonderful thing of all would have to happen.

Helmer

Tell me what that would be!

Nora

Both you and I would have to be so changed that—. Oh, Torvald, I don't believe any longer in wonderful things happening.

Helmer

But I will believe in it. Tell me! So changed that—?

Nora

That our life together would be a real wedlock. Goodbye. [*She goes out through the hall.*]

Helmer

[*sinks down on a chair at the door and buries his face in his hands*] Nora! Nora! [*looks round, and rises*] Empty. She is gone. [*A hope flashes across his mind.*] The most wonderful thing of all—? [*The sound of a door shutting is heard from below.*]

▶ STUDY QUESTIONS

A *Recalling*

1. How does the husband treat the wife before the blackmail event?
2. What is the reaction of the husband when the wife's "dishonesty" is released? What does the wife expect the husband to do?
3. How does the husband tread the wife when the blackmail is taken back? What is the wife's response?
4. How does the husband respond to the wife's declaration of independence?

B *Interpreting*

5. What makes both the husband and the father treat Nora in a doll-like way?
6. What does Nora want from her husband?

7. What is a "real wedlock" as mentioned by Nora?

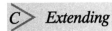 Extending

8. What is the position of woman in the family today?
9. What do you think a woman's position should be?

LITERARY FOCUS

A brief introduction to the essential elements in modern theater:

Plot: This is what happens in the play. Plot refers to the action; the basic storyline of the play. Like the plot of a story, the plot of a play involves characters who face a problem or **conflict**.

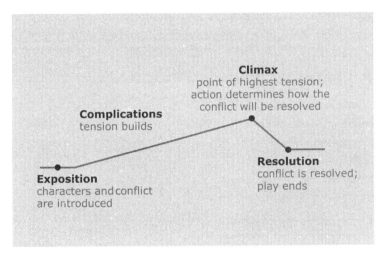

Theme: While plot refers to the action of the play, theme refers to the meaning of the play. Theme is the main idea or lesson to be learned from the play. In some cases, the theme of a play is obvious; other times it is quite subtle.

Characters: Characters are the people (sometimes animals or ideas) portrayed by the actors in the play. It is the characters who move the action, or plot, of the play forward.

Dialogue: This refers to the words written by the playwright and spoken by the characters in the play. The dialogue helps move the action of the play along.

Convention: These are the techniques and methods used by the playwright and director to create the desired stylistic effect.

Genre: Genre refers to the type of play. Some examples of different genres include comedy, tragedy, mystery and historical play.

Audience: This is the group of people who watch the play. Many playwrights and actors consider the audience to be the most important element of drama, as all of the effort put in to writing and producing a play is for the enjoyment of the audience.

▶▶ THINKING ABOUT NORA

A Doll's House made Ibsen many enemies in his time, mostly because of the "strong" female—Nora and the untraditional resolution in the play. Back to Ibsen's time, why did the play arouse great disputes?

▶▶ APPENDIX 5

The alternative ending of *A Doll's House:*

In this ending, Nora is led to her children after having argued with Torvald. Seeing them, she collapses, and the curtain is brought down.

(It was felt by Ibsen's German agent that the original ending would not play well in German theatres; therefore, for the play's German debut, Ibsen was forced to write an alternative ending for it to be considered acceptable. Ibsen later called the ending a disgrace to the original play and referred to it as a "barbaric outrage".)

▶▶ FURTHER READING

Jane Austen, *Pride and Prejudice*
Eugene O'Neill, *Long Day's Journey into Night*
John Updike, *Separating*
Joy Williams, *Taking Care*
Tobias Wolff, *Say Yes*
曹雪芹，《红楼梦》

▶▶ ROCOMMENDED MOVIES

Little Women (1994), directed by Gillian Armstrong
Kramer vs. Kramer (1979), directed by Robert Benton
The Lion King (1994), produced by Walt Disney Feature Animation
Mr. Popper's Penguins (2011), directed by Mark Waters
《千里走单骑》（2004），导演张艺谋

Unit Five   Man and Society

I. Two Poems by W. H. Auden

▶️ ABOUT THE POET

Wystan Hugh Auden (1907–1973), who published as W. H. Auden, was an Anglo-American poet, born in England, later an American citizen, regarded by many critics as one of the greatest writers of the 20th century. His work is noted for its stylistic and technical achievements, its engagement with moral and political issues, and its variety of tone, form and content. The central themes of his poetry are love, politics and citizenship, religion and morals, and the relationship between unique human beings and the anonymous, impersonal world of nature.

The Unknown Citizen
(To JS/07 M 378
This Marble Monument
Is Erected by the State)

1   He was found by the Bureau of Statistics to be
　　 One against whom there was no official complaint,
　　 And all the reports on his conduct agree
　　 That, in the modern sense of an old-fashioned word, he was a saint,
5   For in everything he did he served the Greater Community.
　　 Except for the War till the day he retired
　　 He worked in a factory and never got fired,
　　 But satisfied his employers, Fudge Motors Inc.
　　 Yet he wasn't a scab[①] or odd in his views,
10   For his Union reports that he paid his dues,
　　 (Our report on his Union shows it was sound)
　　 And our Social Psychology workers found
　　 That he was popular with his mates and liked a drink.
　　 The Press are convinced that he bought a paper every day
15   And that his reactions to advertisements were normal in every way.
　　 Policies taken out in his name prove that he was fully insured,
　　 And his Health-card shows he was once in a hospital but left it cured.
　　 Both Producers Research and High-Grade Living declare
　　 He was fully sensible to the advantages of the Installment Plan[②]
20   And had everything necessary to the Modern Man,

---

① scab: a rascal, person who is a nuisance or threat other people and society
② Installment Plan: the plan in which a debt or other sum payable is divided for payment at successive fixed times

A phonograph[1], a radio, a car and a frigidaire.
Our researchers into Public Opinion are content
That he held the proper opinions for the time of year;
When there was peace, he was for peace: when there was war, he went.

25   He was married and added five children to the population,
Which our Eugenicist[2] says was the right number for a parent of his generation.
And our teachers report that he never interfered with their education.
Was he free? Was he happy? The question is absurd:
Had anything been wrong, we should certainly have heard.

STUDY QUESTIONS

Recalling

1. What has the Bureau of Statistics found about this man?
2. Please explain "in the modern sense of an old-fashioned word, he was a saint".

B Interpreting

3. According to what is suggested by the poem, is it easy to be a good citizen? Why or why not?
4. Is it necessary to be a so-called "good citizen"?
5. The poem presents many facts about this "good citizen". In spite of all these facts, the man still remains "unknown". Why?
6. What does the last line mean?
7. What, in your opinion, is the overall tone of this poem? Explain why you come to this conclusion.
8. Please pay attention to the rhyming of the poem. What special effect does it produce?

Extending

9. How do you judge yourself? Do you use the same standard? If not, what is your standard?

Musee des Beaux Arts[3]

1   About suffering they were never wrong,
The Old Masters: how well they understood
Its human position; how it takes place
While someone else is eating or opening a window or just walking dully along;
5   How, when the aged are reverently, passionately waiting
For the miraculous birth, there always must be
Children who did not specially want it to happen, skating
On a pond at the edge of the wood:
They never forgot
10   That even the dreadful martyrdom must run its course
Anyhow in a corner, some untidy spot

---

① phonograph: sound producing machine
② eugenicist: a specialist in the study of methods in improving the quality of human race, esp. by selective breeding
③ Musee des Beaux Arts: Museum of Fine Arts (in Brussels) where Brueghel's *The Fall of Icarus* hangs

Where the dogs go on with their doggy life and the torturer's horse
Scratches its innocent behind on a tree.
In Breughel's Icarus, for instance: how everything turns away

15 Quite leisurely from the disaster; the plowman may
Have heard the splash, the forsaken cry,
But for him it was not an important failure; the sun shone
As it had to on the white legs disappearing into the green
Water; and the expensive delicate ship that must have seen

20 Something amazing, a boy falling out of the sky,
Had somewhere to get to and sailed calmly on.

STUDY QUESTIONS

A Recalling

1. Whom do "The Old Masters" refer to?
2. How many examples are given to show how suffering takes place?
3. Please find out the contrasts in the poem.

B Interpreting

4. What do the contrasts suggest?
5. Do you agree that about suffering the old masters are never wrong?
6. What is the tone of the poem?
7. Auden is describing his feeling when looking at Breughel's picture about the moment Icarus falling into the sea. Can we look at the picture in a different way?

C Extending

8. *Musee des Beaux Arts* is written in free verse, meaning that the poem is essentially "free" of meter, regular rhythm, or a rhyme scheme. How do the irregular rhyme scheme and length of lines help to add expression to the meaning?
9. Please compare this poem with *The Unknown Citizen*. What kind of relationship between man and society is revealed in each poem? Judging from these two poems, do you have some idea of the poet's attitude toward society?

LITERARY FOCUS

Free Verse

Free verse is just what it says it is—poetry that is written without proper rules about form, rhyme, rhythm, meter, etc. The greatest American writer of free verse is probably Walt Whitman. His great collection of free verse was titled *Leaves of Grass* and it was published in 1855.

In free verse the writer makes his/her own rules. The writer decides how the poem should look, feel, and sound. Henry David Thoreau, a great philosopher, explained it this way, "...perhaps it is because he hears a different drummer. Let him step to the music which he hears, however measured or far away." It may take you a while to "hear your own drummer," but free verse can be a great way to "get things off your chest" and express what you really feel.

▶ THINKING ABOUT FREE VERSE

1. Please read *Song of Myself, Variations on the Word Love* and *The Victims* and discuss whether "free verse" is really free.
2. Do you prefer free verse or verse with strict rhyme and rhythm? Why?

▶ APPENDIX 6

The Flight of Icarus

1 A long time ago in ancient Greece there lived a famous mechanic by the name of Deadalus. On a visit to the island of Crete the king of the island King Minos became very upset with him and ordered him locked up in a tower that faced the sea. Daedalus managed to escape from this tower with the help of his son Icarus only to be caught and imprisoned once again! Several times he tried to bribe himself onto a vessel and escape but every time he failed, as King Minos had a strict edict for all ships to be carefully searched upon departing from the island of Crete.

2 Deadalus' spirit however could not be subdued and the genius artist said to his son, "The King may control the land and the sea yet he does not control the sky, we must escape from the sky!" Deadalus told his son to collect all the gulls feathers he could find from the beaches around Crete and bring them to him. Deadalus then melted wax forming the skeleton of a bird's wings to which he would attach the feathers. He then took all the feathers tying the large one's to the skeletal structure, and pressing the small one's into the wings.

3 When Deadalus had completed the wings he placed them on his back and oh to his surprise! Deadalus rose high above the ground and as he flapped his wings he soared through the heavens. Deadalus then quickly made another set of wings, smaller then his own for his son. His son's wings though smaller were constructed far better and appeared more elegant, they were fitting for the son that he so dearly loved.

4 On a clear day Deadalus decided it was time to teach is son how to fly. He told the boy to mimic the birds in their actions, to be graceful and to not beat the wings too heavily. As Icarus put on the wings he sailed far out above the sea flying up high and then diving low above the sea like a child with a new toy.

5 Deadalus watched his son with concern as he knew that the wings were far from a toy. He called on his son and as his son returned he told him, "Son, it is time for us to attempt our escape, you must stay by side, never venturing far away, as if you fly too low your wings will become damp from the fog, if you fly too high the wax on the wings will melt from the sun." Icarus smiled at his father and told him that there was no reason for him to worry.

6 Soon Deadalus and Icarus flew high above the land and the people of Crete watched in amazement as they thought they were witnessing the flight of Gods. On occasion Deadalus would look back towards his son making sure that all was fine with his son. As they flew above the sea they came upon Samos and Delos to their left.

7   Icarus became excited feeling the wind run through his hair and he began to beat his wings wildly which made him go higher and higher. Deadalus yelled at his son, "Stop, you are going too high your wings will melt!" Icarus was too far from his father and could hear nothing his father said, instead he beat his wings faster and faster going ever higher into the sky. Deadalus tried to follow his son but alas his wings were far heavier and would not allow him to soar as high as his son.

8   The sun began to beat down on the wings of Icarus, and slowly they began to melt. Icarus noticed the wings coming apart, but in his joy kept on beating the wings faster and faster bringing him ever further towards the sun. Soon all the feathers had fallen from the wings of Icarus and the boy plunged down into the Aegean Sea.

9   Deadalus looked for his son but could see him nowhere. He then looked down at the sea and his heart broke as he saw the feathers of his son's wings floating on the sea. Deadalus dove towards the sea snatching his son's body out of the water but alas it was too late. Deadalus carried the body of his son as both their feet dragged on the sea below, as a result of the great weight now placed on his wings by the two bodies they now supported. Deadalus took the body of his son and buried it on an island called Icaria in his son's memory.

10   Deadalus then flew for one last time to the island of Sicily. In Sicily he made a temple to the God Apollo, and in the temple he hung the wings as an offering to the god never to fly again.

Landscape with the Fall of Icarus
Pieter Brueghel, 1558.
Musees Royaux des Beaux-Arts de Belgique, Brussels.

II. *Mending Wall* by Robert Frost

▶▶ ABOUT THE POET

Robert Frost (1874–1963), American poet. He drew his images from the New England countryside and his language from New England speech. Although Frost's images and voice often seem familiar and old, his observations have an edge of skepticism and irony that make his work, upon rereading, never as old-fashioned, easy, or carefree as it first appears. In being both traditional and skeptical, Frost's poetry helped provide a link between the American poetry of the 19th century and that of the 20th century.

Frost was one of the most popular poets in America during his lifetime and was frequently called the country's unofficial poet laureate. He read his poem *The Gift Outright* at the 1961 inauguration of John F. Kennedy. Frost preferred traditional rhyme and meter in poetry; his famous dismissal of free verse was, "I'd just as soon play tennis with the net down."

Mending Wall

1   Something there is that doesn't love a wall,
　　That sends the frozen-ground-swell under it,
　　And spills the upper boulders① in the sun,
　　And makes gaps even two can pass abreast②.
5   The work of hunters is another thing:
　　I have come after them and made repair
　　Where they have left not one stone on a stone,
　　But they would have the rabbit out of hiding,
　　To please the yelping dogs. The gaps I mean,
10 No one has seen them made or heard them made,
　　But at spring mending-time we find them there.
　　I let my neighbor know beyond the hill;
　　And on a day we meet to walk the line
　　And set the wall between us once again.
15 We keep the wall between us as we go.
　　To each the boulders that have fallen to each.
　　And some are loaves and some so nearly balls
　　We have to use a spell to make them balance:
　　"Stay where you are until our backs are turned!"
20 We wear our fingers rough with handling them.
　　Oh, just another kind of out-door game,

① boulders: large piece of rock, large stone
② abreast: side by side

One on a side. It comes to little more:
There where it is we do not need the wall:
He is all pine and I am apple orchard.

25   My apple trees will never get across
And eat the cones under his pines, I tell him.
He only says, "Good fences make good neighbors" .
Spring is the mischief in me, and I wonder
If I could put a notion in his head:

30   "Why do they make good neighbors? Isn't it
Where there are cows?
But here there are no cows.
Before I built a wall I'd ask to know
What I was walling in or walling out,

35   And to whom I was like to give offence.
Something there is that doesn't love a wall,
That wants it down." I could say "Elves" ① to him,
But it's not elves exactly, and I'd rather
He said it for himself. I see him there

40   Bringing a stone grasped firmly by the top
In each hand, like an old-stone savage armed.
He moves in darkness as it seems to me,
Not of woods only and the shade of trees.
He will not go behind his father's saying,

45   And he likes having thought of it so well
He says again, "Good fences make good neighbors."

STUDY QUESTIONS

 Recalling

1. What happened to the wall?
2. Who may have suggested mending the wall?
3. Who may have started building the wall in the first place?
4. Do the two neighbours actually need a wall?

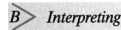 *Interpreting*

5. What does the speaker mean when he says "Stay where you are until our backs are turned!"?
6. What does line "I see him there/Bringing a stone grasped firmly by the top/In each hand, like an old-stone savage armed." suggest?
7. What does "He moves in darkness as it seems to me" indicate?
8. What was walled in and what was walled out?
9. The poem says "Something there is that doesn't love a wall". What is it?

① elves: spirits, fairies

10. What is the speaker's attitude towards the "wall"? What is the neighbour's attitude?

11. What is the symbolic meaning of "wall"?

12. What is the tone of the poem?

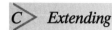 Extending

13. Do you need a wall when dealing with people?

III. *Trust* by Andy Rooney

▶ ABOUT THE AUTHOR

Andy Rooney (1919–2011) was an American radio and television writer. He is known to millions for his wry, humorous and sometimes controversial essays that have been the signature end piece of *60 Minutes* for decades.

In addition to his *60 Minutes* essays, he has written a national newspaper column for Tribune Media Services since 1979, published articles in major magazines, and is the author of 13 books, the most recent, *Years of Minutes*.

"The most felicitous nonfiction writer in television" is how *Time* magazine once described Rooney, who has won the Writers Guild Award for Best Script of the Year six times—more than any other writer in the history of the medium.

Trust

1　　　Last night I was driving from Harrisburg① to Lewisburg, Pa②, a distance of about eighty miles. It was late, I was late and if anyone asked me how fast I was driving, I'd have to plead the Fifth Amendment to avoid self-incrimination③. Several times I got stuck behind a slow-moving truck on a narrow road with a solid white line on my left, and I was clinching my fists with impatience.

2　　　At one point along an open highway, I came to a crossroads with a traffic light. I was alone on the road by now, but as I approached the light, it turned red and I braked to a halt. I looked left, right and behind me. Nothing. Not a car, no suggestion of headlights, but there I sat, waiting for the light to change, the only human being for at least a mile in any direction.

3　　　I started wondering why I refused to run the light.④ I was not afraid of being arrested, because there was obviously no cop around, and there certainly would have been no danger in going through it.

---

① Harrisburg: capital of Pennsylvania, a state in the eastern US
② Lewisburg, Pa: a borough in central Pennsylvania, 85km north of Harrisburg
③ I'd have to plead the Fifth Amendment to avoid self-incrimination: the Fifth Amendment is an amendment to the US Constitution providing chiefly that no person be required to testify against himself or herself in a criminal case. "plead" means "to cite in legal defense". "self-incrimination" is the act of accusing oneself of a crime. What the author implies here is that he was driving very fast, so fast that he actually exceeded the speed limit and thus violated the traffic regulations.
④ to run the light: to drive on in spite of the red traffic light

4   Much later that night, after I'd met with a group in Lewisburg and had climbed into bed near midnight, the question of why I'd stopped for that light came back to me. I think I stopped because it's part of a contract we all have with each other. It's not only the law, but it's an agreement we have, and we trust each other to honor it: we don't go through red lights. Like most of us, I'm more apt to be restrained from doing something bad by the social convention that disapproves of it than by any law against it.

5   It's amazing that we ever trust each other to do the right thing, isn't it? And we do, too. Trust is our first inclination. We have to make a deliberate decision to mistrust someone or to be suspicious or skeptical. Those attitudes don't come naturally to us.

6   It's a damn good thing too, because the whole structure of our society depends on mutual trust, not distrust. This whole thing we have going for us would fall apart if we didn't trust each other most of the time. In Italy, they have an awful time getting any money for the government, because many people just plain^{①} don't pay their income tax. Here the Internal Revenue Service^{②} makes some gestures^{③} toward enforcing the law, but mostly they just have to trust that we'll pay what we owe. There has often been talk of a tax revolt in this country, most recently among unemployed auto workers in Michigan, and our government pretty much admits if there was a widespread tax revolt here, they wouldn't be able to do anything about it.

7   We do what we say we'll do; we show up when we say we'll show up; we deliver when we say we'll deliver; and we pay when we say we'll pay. We trust each other in these matters, and when we don't do what we've promised, it's a deviation from the normal. It happens often that we don't act in good faith^{④} and in a trustworthy manner, but we still consider it unusual, and we're angry or disappointed with the person or organization that violates the trust we have in them. (I'm looking for something good to say about mankind today.)

8   I hate to see a story about a bank swindler who has jiggered the books^{⑤} to his own advantage, because I trust banks. I don't like them, but I trust them. I don't go in and demand that they show me my money all the time just to make sure they still have it.

9   It's the same buying a can of coffee or a quart of milk. You don't take the coffee home and weigh it to make sure it's a pound. There isn't time in life to distrust every person you meet or every company you do business with. I hated the company that started selling beer in eleven-ounce bottles years ago. One of the million things we take on trust is that a beer bottle contains twelve ounces.

10   It's interesting to look around and at people and compare their faith or lack of faith in other people with their success or lack of success in life. The patsies^{⑥}, the suckers^{⑦}, the people who always assume everyone else is as honest as they are, make out better^{⑧} in the long run than the people who distrust everyone—and they're a lot happier even if they get taken once in a while^{⑨}.

---

① plain: here means clearly and simply.
② the Internal Revenue Service: the division of the US Department of the Treasury that collects internal revenues
③ make some gestures: to performs an action for show, knowing that it will have no effect
④ in good faith: honestly and sincerely
⑤ jigger the books: to alter the written records of business accounts in order to get something done illegally or unethically
⑥ the patsies: (informal, chiefly American English) people who are easily taken advantage of, especially by being cheated or blamed for something
⑦ suckers: (informal) easily deceived people
⑧ make out better: to get along better
⑨ even if they get taken once in a while: even if they are cheated once in a while

11   I was so proud of myself for stopping for that red light, and inasmuch as no one would ever have known what a good person I was on the road from Harrisburg to Lewisburg, I had to tell someone.

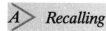

STUDY QUESTIONS

A) *Recalling*

1. Was the speaker in a hurry during his driving to Harrisburg?
2. Why did the speaker stop the car?

B) *Interpreting*

3. How do you understand the distinction between law and the agreement people of a society trust each other to honour, as discussed in Paragraph 4? How much does such an agreement mean to a society?
4. How do you explain the trust people have for each other? Do you agree with the speaker when he says in Paragraph 5 that attitudes of mistrust do not come naturally to us?
5. Think of instances in our own social life of mutual trust and also of mistrust.
6. What do you think of the speaker's life philosophy that it always pays to be more trusting than mistrusting?
7. In the ending of the story, the speaker says "I was so proud of myself for stopping for that red light". How do you explain that?

C) *Extending*

8. Think about the current situation in Chinese society. Are people more trusting or mistrusting? Why do you think so?

LITERARY FOCUS

Nonfiction

Writing about real people, events, and ideas—is the broadest category of literature. Under this huge umbrella come autobiographies, biographies, memoirs, diaries, letters, essays, speeches, travelogues, news articles, and many more types of writing. Like works of fiction, all these types of writing can be inventive and creative, even though they deal with real, rather than imaginary, subjects.

Because they tell stories, autobiographies, memoirs, biographies, and narrative essays share many characteristics of fiction. Like fictional stories, they may include such elements as setting, characters, theme, plot, and conflict. They also are organized like fictional stories. A writer might choose to present events in **chronological order,** or the order in which they occurred. Or the writer might use a **flashback**, going back in time to present incidents that happened before the beginning of the story.

THINKING ABOUT NONFICTION

Under which category of nonfiction will you put *Trust*? What is the purpose of the article?

IV. *The Man Who Married Himself* by Charlie Fish

▶❙ **ABOUT THE AUTHOR**

Charlie Fish (1980–   ) was born in Mount Kisco, New York, and has moved between New England and old England several times (he now lives in London). Since completing a law degree in 2002 he has done a variety of jobs. Now he is the editor of FICTION on the WEB, and he can be contacted at charlie@fictionontheweb.co.uk.

The Man Who Married Himself

1   "Why not?"

2   With those two words, my good friend Reverend[1] Zatarga changed the course of my life. When he said them to me, he had just spent two hours on the telephone with Bishop Fleming discussing various sections of the Bible in excruciatingly[2] fine detail. He pointed out that Leviticus[3] warns Christians not to marry their sister, aunt, mother, mother-in-law, daughter or even their granddaughter (should they be tempted). But nowhere in the good book is there a rule against marrying oneself. So when I told Reverend Zatarga that was exactly what I wanted to do, he eventually conceded those two fateful words:

3   "Why not?"

4   Of course, the Bible also neglects to forbid anyone from marrying great-grandmothers, tables or pet fish. I wouldn't be surprised to learn that Bishop Fleming ended up marrying his beloved French poodle as a result of all this. Or his blanket—after all he's been sleeping with it for years. Anyway, once I convinced the good Reverend to let me marry the man of my dreams, I had to convince my mother and father. I'd have to say that between an international religion, firmly established for two millennia, and my own humble parents, my parents were far more difficult to persuade.

5   My mother just wouldn't take it seriously at first. OK, very few people took it seriously, but I needed her to know I meant it. She kept asking me silly things like "Why marry—you can just live with yourself?" or "What will you wear for the wedding?"

6   And sadly, it drove my father quite mad. Literally. For years after the wedding he spent days typing up articles for a wide variety of news journals, record books and space administration newsletters claiming that he was the first person to have had sex in space. He seemed quite convinced, despite the fact that the closest he had come to space was the big button on his computer keyboard. When asked who he had allegedly[4] had sex with, he would usually pause briefly for dramatic effect, turn his wild eyes towards you and yell shrilly: "Myself!"

7   I would have hoped that I could trust my best friends to be sympathetic towards my cause, but I think it was all a bit of a joke for them. They were often supportive, but after the wedding they just spent a lot of time making fun of me. Some of the wedding presents I received from them were quite demeaning: pornographic magazines, silk gloves, even a ceiling mirror. And I'm

---

① Reverend: used as a title of a clergyman
② excruciatingly: acutely
③ Leviticus: one book of the Bible
④ allegedly: according to what he said

disappointed in them for not stifling their mirth^① when Reverend Zatarga recited the marriage vows: "Will you keep yourself as a husband, to live as one in marriage? Will you love and comfort yourself, obey and honour yourself in sickness and in health, and be faithful to yourself as long as you shall live?" I swear one of my friends wet himself laughing.

8 I had a great honeymoon in Las Vegas^②, gambling away^③ all my savings with nobody to nag me about how much money I was spending. I had a penthouse^④ suite in the Luxor hotel for the night of consummation^⑤...

9 I had many reasons for getting married when I did, apart from the tax benefits of course (trying to make the tax inspector understand that I was my own spouse was hell, though). Ever since I understood the concept of wedlock, I longed for a partner that I could trust. I wanted to have someone with me always, to whom I could tell all my deepest, darkest secrets without having them laugh at me. Unfortunately, although getting girlfriends was usually not too big a problem for me, I tended to have excruciatingly^⑥ bad taste. Then I realised that my perfect partner was closer to home than anyone could have realised.

10 Altogether, I think the marriage was a great success for the most part. I rarely argued with my spouse; in fact I found myself to be the best conversation holder around. The few times that I did argue, I always won. And the sex was, well—it was whatever I made of it. There was some media intrusion of course, lots of cheap journalists trying to cash in^⑦ on this unusual union. I found some of their articles amusing, and others quite offensive, especially the ones dubbing me the most conceited and/or narcissistic^⑧ man in the world. I don't think I'm such an egotist, I just happen to enjoy my company.

11 I suppose it was a hormonal^⑨ thing, a stage of life or something, that made me suddenly crave a child. The cliche is that I realised I was mortal, and I therefore wanted to pass on my genes. So after many days weighing up the pros and cons^⑩ I decided to split up from my husband in order to find a wife. I had a chat with Reverend Zatarga, and he informed me that I couldn't just file for a divorce on a moment's notice^⑪. I had to have legitimate justification. Curiously, wanting a baby wasn't on the list of good reasons to divorce.

12 As the good Reverend explained, I could only divorce if I had been living apart from my spouse for at least a year which would be difficult without major surgery or if my spouse had treated me cruelly or been imprisoned for at least a year. I wasn't particularly willing to beat myself up a bit or lounge^⑫ around in prison just so I could divorce myself. That left one option: Adultery. I just had to have sex with someone other than myself; normal, straight, human sex, and I could be free from the bonds of marriage.

---

① stifling their mirth: keeping back or suppressing their laughter
② Las Vegas: a city of southeast Nevada near the California and Arizona borders. It is a manor tourist center known for its casinos.
③ gambling away: to lose by gambling
④ penthouse: an apartment or building on the roof of a building
⑤ consummation: fulfilling. Here the fulfilling of marriage.
⑥ excruciatingly: extremely painful
⑦ cash in: to take advantage of
⑧ narcissistic: loving oneself
⑨ hormonal: have something to do with hormone.
⑩ the pros and cons: the arguments for and against (sth.)
⑪ on a moment's notice: within a short time
⑫ lounge around: to pass time idly or indolently

13   And so it was that I reluctantly removed my wedding ring and started searching for a mate. My friends were cruel about it, saying that I was separating to stop myself from going blind. I think my mother was relieved when I told her that my relationship with myself was coming to an end. My father just paused for dramatic effect, turned his wild eyes towards me and yelled shrilly: "Myself!" Maybe he really is on another world.

14   I expected it to take me quite a while to find someone who was both willing to sleep with me and who hadn't read the newspapers enough to know that I was already married, but I soon found a plain-faced Malaysian girl who was relatively easy to seduce. The sex was, to be honest, rather disappointing. It seemed that she knew almost nothing of what turns a man on①, whereas by that point I myself had become quite an expert. I suppose it wasn't great for her either — I wasn't practised in pleasuring members of the fairer sex②.

15   The divorce was easy after that. It seemed that the church was keen to split me apart, as if my marriage had been a big mistake. I felt quite lonely for several months after the break-up. At least the local psychiatrist (specialising in multiple personality disorders) stopped sending me his damned business cards every week.

16   It took me nearly a decade to find a good wife who didn't think she'd be marrying into a threesome. Most of that time was just waiting for the media to forget about "The Man Who Married Himself". Meanwhile, I wrote an autobiography with that very title. Included in the book was a detailed account of my marriage to myself, including the ups and downs of living with myself, how I dealt with everyone's criticism of me and my husband, and some intimate details of my relationship. I think it was these sections that made the book a real success when it was published some years later. People were just curious to read about the implications of such an unusual marriage. I suppose it made people think. They would read my book and ask themselves: "Am I easy to live with? If I had to live with me, could I do it?" They all stopped searching for their Mister or Little Miss Right for just a moment to ask themselves if they would ever make a good spouse for anyone.

17   I didn't hear of any copycat③ self-marriages, which probably either means the media lost interest or the church is determined not to let it happen again. Anyway, that's all behind me now. My wife and I have just moved into a new home, big enough to accommodate our new child when he is born. I am happy now. In fact, right now I can't wipe the smile off my face. You see, our next door neighbours are Bishop Fleming and his lovely wife, the French poodle.

▶▶ STUDY QUESTIONS

  Recalling

1. Who is the narrator of the story?
2. What is the narrator's role in the marriage with himself (wife or husband)?
3. On what basis does Bishop Fleming accept this unusual marriage?
4. What is the mother's reaction towards this marriage?
5. What is the father's reaction?

---

① turn sb. on: (cause sb. to) to have a great pleasure or excitement
② the fairer sex: the female
③ copycat: a person who copies, imitates

6. What are the friends' reactions?

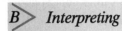 **Interpreting**

7. Why is it far more difficult to persuade the parents to accept the marriage?

8. Why do you think "I" come up with this idea of "marrying myself" rather than just remain single? What is the difference between "marrying oneself" and "remain single"?

9. Why do "I" feel lonely after "I" have divorced "myself"?

10. What is the tone of the story?

 Extending

11. What are the implications of the story?

12. Do you believe that it is easier to live with oneself than living with another person? Why or why not?

V. *Dead Men's Path* by Chinua Achebe

▶▶ ABOUT THE AUTHOR

Chinua Achebe [che noo's a cha'ba] (born in 1930), a Nigerian, Chinua Achebe is one of Africa's most influential and widely published writers. He has written twenty-one novels, short-stories and collections of poetry. His first and best-known post-colonial landmark novel, *Things Fall Apart* (1958) was published at the age of 28, and has proved popular not just in Nigeria, but throughout Africa and the rest of the world. Achebe has also won acclaim for *Arrow of God*, which is winner of the New Statesman-Jock Campbell Award, *Christmas in Biafra*, joint winner of the first Commonwealth Prize, and *Anthills of the Savannah* (1987), a finalist for the prestigious Booker Prize in England.

▶▶ NIGERIA AND THE IBO

The West African nation of Nigeria is the homeland of more than two hundred different native tribes. The largest of these are the Hausa and Fulani, who live mainly in the north; the Yoruba, in the southwest; and the Ibo, in the southeast. Each group has its own language, but their common language is English, reflecting close to a century of British rule that ended in 1960. Chinua Achebe, though fluent in the Ibo language, usually writes in English.

Most Nigerians are Moslems or Christians, although ancient tribal beliefs still persist. The Ibos, for example, traditionally believed in a god so powerful that he had to be approached through lesser deities, each affiliated with a different Ibo village. Today most Ibos are Christians; however, especially when Achebe was growing up, many Ibo villagers still showed respect for their local deity. Sometimes, as in the upcoming story, the old ways came into conflict with new Western ideas.

Dead Men's Path

1   Michael Obi's hopes were fulfilled much earlier than he had expected. He was appointed headmaster of Ndume Central School in January 1949. It had always been an unprogressive school, so the Mission authorities decided to send a young and energetic man to run it. Obi accepted this responsibility with enthusiasm. He had many wonderful ideas and this was an opportunity to put them into practice. He had had sound secondary school education which designated[①] him a "pivotal[②] teacher" in the official records and set him apart from the other headmasters in the mission field. He was outspoken in his condemnation of the narrow views of these older and often less-educated ones.

2   "We shall make a good job of it, shan't we?" he asked his young wife when they first heard the joyful news of his promotion.

3   "We shall do our best," she replied. "We shall have such beautiful gardens and everything will be just modern and delightful..." In their two years of married life she had become completely infected by his passion for "modern methods" and his denigration[③] of "these old and superannuated[④] people in the teaching field who would be better employed as traders in the Onitsha market." She began to see herself already as the admired wife of the young headmaster, the queen of the school.

4   The wives of the other teachers would envy her position. She would set the fashion in everything...Then, suddenly, it occurred to her that there might not be other wives. Wavering between hope and fear, she asked her husband, looking anxiously at him.

5   "All our colleagues are young and unmarried," he said with enthusiasm, which for once she did not share. "Which is a good thing," he continued.

6   "Why?"

7   "Why? They will give all their time and energy to the school."

8   Nancy was downcast. For a few minutes she became skeptical about the new school; but it was only for a few minutes. Her little personal misfortune could not blind her to her husband's happy prospects. She looked at him as he sat folded up in a chair. He was stoop-shouldered and looked frail. But he sometimes surprised people with sudden bursts of physical energy. In his present posture, however, all his bodily strength seemed to have retired behind his deep-set eyes, giving them an extraordinary power of penetration. He was only twenty-six, but looked thirty or more. On the whole, he was not unhandsome.

9   "A penny for your thoughts, Mike," said Nancy after a while, imitating the woman's magazine she read.

10   "I was thinking what a grand opportunity we've got at last to show these people how a school should be run."

11   Ndume School was backward in every sense of the word. Mr. Obi put his whole life into the work, and his wife hers too. He had two aims. A high standard of teaching was insisted upon, and the school compound was to be turned into a place of beauty. Nancy's dream-gardens came

---

① designate: here to signify, to mark
② pivotal: of vital or critical importance
③ denigration: criticism
④ superannuated: out of date, obsolete

to life with the coming of the rains, and blossomed. Beautiful hibiscus[①] and allamanda hedges in brilliant red and yellow marked out the carefully tended school compound from the rank neighborhood bushes.

12   One evening as Obi was admiring his work he was scandalized to see an old woman from the village hobble[②] right across the compound, through a marigold flower-bed and the hedges. On going up there he found faint signs of an almost disused path from the village across the school compound to the bush on the other side.

13   "It amazes me," said Obi to one of his teachers who had been three years in the school, "that you people allowed the villagers to make use of this footpath. It is simply incredible." He shook his head.

14   "The path," said the teacher apologetically, "appears to be very important to them. Although it is hardly used, it connects the village shrine[③] with their place of burial."

15   "And what has that got to do with the school?" asked the headmaster.

16   "Well, I don't know," replied the other with a shrug of the shoulders. "But I remember there was a big row[④] some time ago when we attempted to close it."

17   "That was some time ago. But it will not be used now," said Obi as he walked away. "What will the Government Education Officer think of this when he comes to inspect the school next week? The villagers might, for all I know, decide to use the schoolroom for a pagan ritual during the inspection."

18   Heavy sticks were planted closely across the path at the two places where it entered and left the school premises[⑤]. These were further strengthened with barbed wire[⑥].

19   Three days later the village priest of Ani[⑦] called on the headmaster. He was an old man and walked with a slight stoop. He carried a stout[⑧] walking-stick which he usually tapped on the floor, by way of emphasis, each time he made a new point in his argument.

20   "I have heard," he said after the usual exchange of cordialities[⑨], "that our ancestral footpath has recently been closed..."

21   "Yes, replied Mr. Obi. "We cannot allow people to make a highway of our school compound."

22   "Look here, my son," said the priest bringing down his walking-stick, "this path was here before you were born and before your father was born. The whole life of this village depends on it. Our dead relatives depart by it and our ancestors visit us by it. But most important, it is the path of children coming in to be born..."

23   Mr. Obi listened with a satisfied smile on his face.

24   "The whole purpose of our school," he said finally, "is to eradicate[⑩] just such beliefs as that. Dead men do not require footpaths. The whole idea is just fantastic. Our duty is to teach

---

① hibiscus: 木槿树
② hobble: to walk lamely
③ shrine: any place or building devoted to some saint, holy person, deity or sacred relics
④ row: a noisy dispute or quarrel
⑤ premises: a building together with its grounds and surrounding areas
⑥ barbed wire: 装有倒钩的
⑦ ani: an Etruscan divinity
⑧ stout: heavily built, thick
⑨ cordialities: greetings
⑩ eradicate: to destroy completely

your children to laugh at such ideas."

25　　　"What you say may be true," replied the priest, "But we follow the practices of our fathers. If you reopen the path we shall have nothing to quarrel about. What I always say is: let the hawk perch and let the eagle perch[①]." He rose to go.

26　　　"I am sorry," said the young headmaster. "But the school compound cannot be a thoroughfare[②]. It is against our regulations. I would suggest your constructing another path, skirting[③] our premises. We can even get our boys to help in building it. I don't suppose the ancestors will find the little detour[④] too burdensome."

27　　　"I have no more words to say," said the old priest, already outside.

28　　　Two days later a young woman in the village died in childbed. A diviner[⑤] was immediately consulted and he prescribed heavy sacrifices to propitiate[⑥] ancestors insulted by the fence.

29　　　Obi woke up next morning among the ruins of his work. The beautiful hedges were torn up not just near the path but right round the school, the flowers trampled to death and one of the school buildings pulled down...That day, the white Supervisor came to inspect the school and wrote a nasty report on the state of the premises but more seriously about the "tribal-war situation developing between the school and the village, arising in part from the misguided zeal of the new headmaster."

STUDY QUESTIONS

 Recalling

1. How did Obi accept his new responsibility as the headmaster of the Ndume Central School? About what is the new headmaster, Michael Obi, "outspoken" ?

2. How did his wife respond to his prospect of being the school headmaster? What is she enthusiastic about?

3. What are the two aims of Obi, the new school headmaster?

4. What did Obi discover one day and what action did he take?

5. What did the village priest say about the path across the school compound? How did Obi reply to the priest's interpretation of the path?

6. What is the solution suggested by the priest? And Obi?

7. What is the result of the disagreement?

B *Interpreting*

8. Why did the supervisor call Obi's zeal "misguided"? Is he somewhat misguided by his wife? Do you agree his zeal is "misguided"? If so, what should be the right direction for his zeal?

9. How does the "dead men's path" affect the school children? How do you look at this influence?

---

① let the hark perch and let the eagle perch: Here means to let the others believe what they want to believe.

② thoroughfare: a passage or way through

③ skirt: to avoid

④ detour: a roundabout or circuitous way

⑤ diviner: a person who divines, prophet

⑥ propitiate: to appease, to make peace with

C▷ *Extending*

10. What would you do if you were the schoolmaster?

VI. *The Bad Zouave* by Alphonse Daudet

▶▶ ABOUT THE AUTHOR

Alphonse Daudet (1840—1897) was a French novelist. He was the father of writers Léon Daudet and Lucien Daudet. Alphonse Daudet was born in Nîmes, France. In 1866, Daudet's *Lettres de mon moulin* (*Letters from My Windmill*), written in Clamart, near Paris, won the attention of many readers. His works struck a note, not new certainly in English literature, but comparatively new in French. His creativeness resulted in characters that were real and also typical. His novels include: *Le Nabab* (1877), *Les Rois en exil* (1879), *Numa Roumestan* (1881), *Sapho* (1884), *L'Immortel* (1888), and many plays. Daudet also wrote for children, including *La Belle Nivernaise*, the story of an old boat and her crew.

The Bad Zouave[①]

Translated by Katharine Prescott Wormeley

1   That evening the big blacksmith, Lory of Sainte-Marie-aux-Mines, was not happy.

2   When the smithy fire had gone down and the sun had set, it was his custom to sit on a bench before his door, tasting that grateful weariness which is the reward of heavy labor and of a hot day's work. Before he sent home his apprentices, he would drink several deep glasses of cool beer with them, while he watched the workers coming out of the factories.

3   But that evening the good blacksmith remained at his forge[②] until it was time for his supper, and even then he went as if he regretted to leave. As his old wife looked at him, she thought.

4   "What can have happened to him? Can he have received bad news from the regiment[③] and be hiding it from me? Perhaps the older of the boys is sick——"

5   But she dared not question him, and busied herself quieting three little tow-headed rascals[④], brown as ears of parched corn, who were laughing around the table as they crunched their good salad of black radishes[⑤] and cream.

6   At last the blacksmith pushed back his plate in a rage and cried,

---

① Zouave: (sometimes lowercase) one of a former body of infantry in the French army, composed originally of Algerians, distinguished for their dash, hardiness, and picturesque Oriental uniform

② forge: the workshop of a blacksmith; smithy

③ regiment: (military) a unit of ground forces, consisting of two or more battalions or battle groups, a headquarters unit, and certain supporting units

④ rascal: a base, dishonest, or unscrupulous person. Here refers to the two little children.

⑤ radish: the crisp, pungent, edible root of the plant, Raphanus sativus, of the mustard family, usually eaten raw

7   "Ah, what brutes[1], what curs[2]!"

8   "Come, Lory, who are you talking about?" said his wife. He shouted,

9   "I am talking of five or six scamps[3] who were seen this morning parading the town in their French uniforms, arm in arm with the Bavarians[4] —more of those fellows who have—how do they say it?—'chosen Prussian citizenship.' And to think that every day we seeing such false Alsatians[5] come back! What can they have given the scoundrels[6] to drink anyway?"

10   The mother tried to defend them.

11   "My poor husband, what do you expect? Those boys are not entirely to blame. They are sent to Algeria, so far away in Africa! They get home-sick out there, and their temptation is very strong to come back and not be soldiers any longer."

12   Lory struck the table a heavy blow with his fist.

13   "Be still, mother! You women-folk understand nothing at all. You live so much with children and so little for anything else that you become exactly the size of your cubs[7]. I tell you, those fellows are ragamuffins[8], renegades[9], the worst sort of scoundrels! If bad luck ever made our own Christian[10] capable of such infamous[11] conduct, as surely as my name is George Lory, seven years chasseur[12] in the army of France, I would run him through the body with my saber[13]!"

14   Terrible to look upon, he half rose from his chair and pointed to his long chasseur's saber, which hung under a picture of his son in the uniform of a zouave, taken out there in Africa.

15   But merely to look at that honest Alsatian face,—burned almost black by the sun, the strong light making the colours stand out vividly against the blank whiteness around—that was enough to quiet him suddenly. He began to laugh.

16   "I am a fine fellow to be losing my head this way! As if our Christian could dream of turning Prussian—Christian, who bowled[14] over such a lot of them in the war!"

17   Brought back to good humour by this idea, the good smith managed to make a cheerful meal, and set out right after it to empty a couple of glasses at the Ville de Strasbourg.

18   The old woman was now left alone. She had put the small blond scamps[15] to bed; they

---

① brute: a nonhuman creature; beast
② cur: a mean, cowardly person
③ scamp: an unscrupulous and often mischievous person; rascal; rogue; scalawag
④ Bavarian: a native or inhabitants in Bavaria
⑤ Alsatian: the inhabitants of Alsace
⑥ scoundrel: an unprincipled, dishonorable person; villain
⑦ cub: the young of certain animals. Here refers to children.
⑧ ragamuffin: a ragged, disreputable person; tatterdemalion
⑨ renegade: a person who deserts a party or cause for another
⑩ Christian: the name of the older son of Lory
⑪ infamous: shameful, deserving bad reputation
⑫ chasseur: member of a unit specially trained and equipped for swift deployment
⑬ saber: a heavy, one-edged sword, usually slightly curved, used especially by cavalry
⑭ bowl: to knock, to strike
⑮ scamp: her little children

could be heard twittering in the next room like a nestful of birds getting ready for sleep. She picked up her work, and set to darning① before the door on the garden side of the house. Once in a while she sighed, and she thought,

19   "Of course—there can be no doubt of it—they are scoundrels and renegades—but, what of it? Their mothers are glad to see them again."

20   And she thought of the time when her own boy had not yet gone to join the army and stood there just at that hour of the day, getting ready to work in the garden. She looked at the well where he refilled his watering cans: her boy, in his blouse, with his long hair, that beautiful hair which had been cut short when he entered the Zouaves.

21   Suddenly she trembled. The little gate at the back—the gate which led to the fields, —had been opened. The dogs had not barked, though the man who had just entered slunk② along the walk like a thief, and slipped in among the beehives③.

22   "Good-day, mother!"

23   His uniform all awry④, there stood before her Christian, her son, anxious, shame-faced, and thick-tongued. The wretched boy had come back with the others and for the last hour had been prowling⑤ about the house, waiting for his father to go out. She wanted to scold him, but she had not the courage. How long it was since she had seen him, had hugged him! And then he went on to give her such good reasons for his return! —how he had grown weary for his native countryside, for the smithy: —weary of living always so far away from them all, and of the discipline—much harsher of late—as well as of his comrades, who called him "Prussian" because of his Alsatian accent. She believed every word he said. She had only to look at him to believe him. Deep in their talk, they went into the lower room. The little ones woke up, and ran in their nightshirts and bare feet to embrace the big brother. He was urged to eat, but he was not hungry. He was only thirsty, always thirsty; and he gulped great draughts of water on top of all the beer and white wine for which he had paid that morning at the inn.

24   But some one was coming into the yard. It was the black-smith returning.

25   "Christian, here comes your father. Quick, hide until I have time to talk with him and explain."

26   She pushed the boy behind the great porcelain stove and again set herself to sewing with trembling hands. But as ill fortune would have it, the Zouave's cap lay upon the table, and it was the first thing Lory noticed as he entered. The mother's pallor⑥, and her agitation⑦ —he understood it all.

27   "Christian is here!" he cried, in a terrible voice. Taking down his saber with a mad gesture, he rushed towards the stove where crouched the Zouave, pale, sobered, and steadying himself

---

① darning: to mend, as torn clothing, with rows of stitches, sometimes by crossing and interweaving rows to span a gap
② slunk: past tense of slink, to move or go in a furtive way, as from fear, cowardice or shame
③ beehive: a habitation or dwelling-place constructed for bees, usually either dome-shaped or box-shaped
④ awry: with a turn or twist to one side
⑤ prowl: to go about stealthily
⑥ pallor: unusual or extreme paleness, as from fear, ill health, or death; wanness
⑦ agitation: a state of excitement, disturbance, or worry

against the wall to keep from falling.

28   The mother threw herself between them.

29   "Lory, Lory! Don't kill him! He came back because I wrote that you needed him at the forge!"

30   She riveted① her hold upon his arm, and dragged him back, sobbing. The children, in the darkness of their room, began to cry when they heard those voices full of anger and tears, and so thick that they did not know them.

31   The smith stood still and looked at his wife.

32   "Oh!" he said. "So it was you who made him come back! Very well. It is time he went to bed. I shall decide to-morrow what I must do."

33   Christian woke next morning from a sleep filled with nightmares and broken by causeless terrors, to find himself in the room he had used as a child. Already warm and well up in the sky, the sun sent its rays across the blossoming hops② and through the small leaded panes③ of the window. Hammers were ringing on the anvil④ below. His mother sat by his pillow: she had been so afraid of her husband's anger that she had not stirred from there all night. Nor had the father gone to bed. Till the first dawn, he had walked through the house weeping, sighing, opening and closing closets. He now entered his son's room. He was very grave and dressed for a journey. He wore his high gaiters⑤ and his big hat, and carried his heavy mountain stick with its iron ferule⑥. He went straight to the bed.

34   "Come, get up!"

35   Dazed⑦, the boy made as if to get his Zouave equipment.

36   "No, not that!" said the father, sternly.

37   The mother, all apprehension⑧, said,

38   "But, my dear, he has no other things."

39   "Give him mine. I shall not need them again."

40   While the boy dressed, Lory carefully packed the uniform, with its little vest and its huge red trousers. As soon as he had made the package, he slung about his neck the tin box which contained the schedule of coaches⑨.

41   "Now let us go down," he said; and all three without a word descended to the smithy.

---

① rivet: to fasten or fix firmly
② hop: a kind of plant
③ pane: one of the divisions of a window or the like, consisting of a single plate of glass in a frame
④ anvil: a heavy iron block with a smooth face, on which metals are hammered into desired shapes
⑤ gaiter: a covering of cloth or leather for the ankle and instep and sometimes the lower leg, worn over the shoe or boot
⑥ ferule: a metal ring, tube, or cap placed over the end of a stick, handle, or post for added strength or stability or to increase wear
⑦ daze: to stun or stupefy with a blow or shock
⑧ apprehension: fear of future trouble or evil
⑨ the schedule of the coaches: here refers to the equipments for travelling.

42　　　The blast roared. Everyone was at work. When Christian saw once more that great open shed① of which he had so often thought off there in Algeria, he recalled his childhood and the long hours he had played out there, between the heat of the road and the sparks from the forge that glittered amid the black dust.

43　　　He felt a sudden flood of tenderness, a great longing to be pardoned by his father; but whenever he raised his eyes, he met an inexorable② look.

44　　　At last the blacksmith made up his mind to speak.

45　　　"Boy," he said, "there stands the anvil with the tools. They are all yours. And so is all this." He indicated the little garden which lay beyond, filled with sunshine and with bees, and framed by the sooty square of the door.

46　　　"The hives, the vine, the house itself,—they are all yours. You sacrificed your honour for these things. The least you can do is to take care of them. Now you are master here. As for myself, I shall go away. You owe five years to France: I am going to pay them for you."

47　　　"Lory, Lory!' cried the poor old wife, "where are you going?"

48　　　"Father!" begged the son.

49　　　But the blacksmith was already on his way. He walked with great strides and did not turn back.

50　　　At Sidi-bel-Abbés, the dépôt of the Third Zouaves, there enlisted some days later a volunteer who gave his age as fifty-five years.

▶ STUDY QUESTIONS

 Recalling

1. What did Lory see that day? How did he react?
2. What is the wife's attitude toward the event?
3. Where is the older son Christian? What is the father's feeling towards him?
4. How did Christian react when he saw his mother? And his father?
5. How did the mother react when she saw her son? And how did the father react?
6. What did the father do in the end?

 Interpreting

7. What is the main character trait of the father? And the mother?
8. How do you look at the son's retreat?
9. How do you look at the father's action in the end?
10. How do you interpret the title *The Bad Zouave*?

C **Extending**

11. What is the major conflict in the story? How is the conflict solved?

---

① shed: a structure built for shelter or storage
② inexorable: unyielding; unalterable

12. How do you look at war? Are you willing to fight in the war? Will you let your children to fight in the war?

▶ LITERARY FOCUS

> *Theme*

The theme in a piece of fiction is its controlling idea or its central insight. It is the author's underlying meaning or main idea that he is trying to convey. The theme may be the author's thoughts about a topic or view of human nature. The title of the short story usually points to what the writer is saying and he may use various figures of speech to emphasize his theme, such as: symbol, allusion, simile, metaphor, hyperbole, or irony. Theme is more specific than topic. For example, under the topic of love themes can be as various as: love is fallacy; love is blind; love conquers everything; love transcends a person; love is all; love is not everything; love is selfish; love is selfless, etc.

▶ THINKING ABOUT THEME

What is the theme of *The Man Who Married Himself, Dead Men's Path,* and *The Bad Zouave* respectively?

VII. *Two Friends* by Guy de Maupassant

▶ ABOUT THE AUTHOR

Henri René Albert Guy de Maupassant (French pronunciation: [gid(ə) mopasɑ̃]; 1850–1893) was a popular French writer, considered one of the fathers of the modern short story and one of the form's finest exponents.

Maupassant was a protégé of Flaubert and his stories are characterized by economy of style and efficient, effortless dénouements. Many are set during the Franco-Prussian War of the 1870s, describing the futility of war and the innocent civilians who, caught up in events beyond their control, are permanently changed by their experiences. He wrote some 300 short stories, six novels, three travel books, and one volume of verse. His first published story, *Boule de Suif* (*Ball of Fat*, 1880), is often considered his masterpiece. Maupassant's clever plotting has greatly influenced Somerset Maugham and O. Henry.

Two Friends

Taken from *The Entire Original Maupassant Short Stories*
Translated by Albert M. C. McMaster, B. A.
A. E. Henderson, B. A
Mme. Quesada and Others

Besieged[①] Paris was in the throes[②] of famine. Even the sparrows on the roofs and the rats in the

---

① besieged: to be surrounded by military force to bring about its surrender
② throe: agony or pain

sewers① were growing scarce. People were eating anything they could get.

As Monsieur Morissot, watchmaker by profession and idler for the nonce②, was strolling along the boulevard③ one bright January morning, his hands in his trousers pockets and stomach empty, he suddenly came face to face with an acquaintance—Monsieur Sauvage, a fishing chum④.

Before the war broke out Morissot had been in the habit, every Sunday morning, of setting forth with a bamboo rod in his hand and a tin box on his back. He took the Argenteuil⑤ train, got out at Colombes⑥, and walked thence to the Ile Marante⑦. The moment he arrived at this place of his dreams he began fishing, and fished till nightfall.

Every Sunday he met in this very spot Monsieur Sauvage, a stout⑧, jolly⑨, little man, a draper⑩ in the Rue Notre Dame de Lorette⑪, and also an ardent⑫ fisherman. They often spent half the day side by side, rod in hand and feet dangling over the water, and a warm friendship had sprung up between the two.

Some days they did not speak; at other times they chatted; but they understood each other perfectly without the aid of words, having similar tastes and feelings.

In the spring, about ten o'clock in the morning, when the early sun caused a light mist to float on the water and gently warmed the backs of the two enthusiastic anglers⑬, Morissot would occasionally remark to his neighbor:

"My, but it's pleasant here."

To which the other would reply:

"I can't imagine anything better!"

And these few words sufficed to make them understand and appreciate each other.

In the autumn, toward the close of day, when the setting sun shed a blood-red glow over the western sky, and the reflection of the crimson clouds tinged the whole river with red, brought a glow to the faces of the two friends, and gilded the trees, whose leaves were already turning at the first chill touch of winter, Monsieur Sauvage would sometimes smile at Morissot, and say:

"What a glorious spectacle!"

And Morissot would answer, without taking his eyes from his float:

"This is much better than the boulevard, isn't it?"

As soon as they recognized each other they shook hands cordially, affected at the thought of meeting under such changed circumstances.

Monsieur Sauvage, with a sigh, murmured:

"These are sad times!"

Morissot shook his head mournfully.

① sewer: the underground pipe to carry off waster water and refuse
② for the nonce: for the present
③ boulevard: a broad avenue in a city
④ chum: a close friend
⑤ Argenteuil: a city in North France, on the Seine near Paris
⑥ Colombes: a city in North France, North West of Paris
⑦ Ili Marante: the name of an island
⑧ stout: heavily built
⑨ jolly: merry, gay
⑩ draper: a dealer in cloth
⑪ Notre Dame de Lorette: a station in Paris
⑫ ardent: devoted, passionate
⑬ angler: a person who fishes with a hook and line

"And such weather! This is the first fine day of the year."

The sky was, in fact, of a bright, cloudless blue.

They walked along, side by side, reflective and sad.

"And to think of the fishing!" said Morissot. "What good times we used to have!"

"When shall we be able to fish again?" asked Monsieur Sauvage.

They entered a small cafe and took an absinthe[1] together, then resumed their walk along the pavement.

Morissot stopped suddenly.

"Shall we have another absinthe?" he said.

"If you like," agreed Monsieur Sauvage.

And they entered another wine shop.

They were quite unsteady when they came out, owing to the effect of the alcohol on their empty stomachs. It was a fine, mild day, and a gentle breeze fanned their faces.

The fresh air completed the effect of the alcohol on Monsieur Sauvage. He stopped suddenly, saying:

"Suppose we go there?"

"Where?"

"Fishing."

"But where?"

"Why, to the old place. The French outposts are close to Colombes. I know Colonel Dumoulin, and we shall easily get leave to pass."

Morissot trembled with desire.

"Very well. I agree."

And they separated, to fetch their rods and lines.

An hour later they were walking side by side on the-highroad. Presently they reached the villa occupied by the colonel. He smiled at their request, and granted it. They resumed their walk, furnished with a password.

Soon they left the outposts behind them, made their way through deserted Colombes, and found themselves on the outskirts of the small vineyards which border the Seine. It was about eleven o'clock.

Before them lay the village of Argenteuil, apparently lifeless. The heights of Orgement and Sannois dominated the landscape. The great plain, extending as far as Nanterre, was empty, quite empty-a waste of dun-colored soil and bare cherry trees.

Monsieur Sauvage, pointing to the heights, murmured:

"The Prussians are up yonder!"

And the sight of the deserted country filled the two friends with vague misgivings[2].

The Prussians! They had never seen them as yet, but they had felt their presence in the neighborhood of Paris for months past—ruining France, pillaging[3], massacring, starving them. And a kind of superstitious terror mingled with the hatred they already felt toward this unknown, victorious nation.

"Suppose we were to meet any of them?" said Morissot.

---

① absinthe: a kind of strong alcohol
② misgiving: suspicion or fear of future trouble
③ pillage: to strip ruthlessly of money or goods by open violence

"We'd offer them some fish," replied Monsieur Sauvage, with that Parisian[①] light-heartedness which nothing can wholly quench[②].

Still, they hesitated to show themselves in the open country, overawed[③] by the utter silence which reigned around them.

At last Monsieur Sauvage said boldly:

"Come, we'll make a start; only let us be careful!"

And they made their way through one of the vineyards, bent double, creeping along beneath the cover afforded by the vines, with eye and ear alert.

A strip of bare ground remained to be crossed before they could gain the river bank. They ran across this, and, as soon as they were at the water's edge, concealed themselves among the dry reeds.

Morissot placed his ear to the ground, to ascertain, if possible, whether footsteps were coming their way. He heard nothing. They seemed to be utterly alone.

Their confidence was restored, and they began to fish.

Before them the deserted Ile Marante hid them from the farther shore. The little restaurant was closed, and looked as if it had been deserted for years.

Monsieur Sauvage caught the first gudgeon[④], Monsieur Morissot the second, and almost every moment one or other raised his line with a little, glittering, silvery fish wriggling[⑤] at the end; they were having excellent sport.

They slipped their catch gently into a close-meshed bag lying at their feet; they were filled with joy—the joy of once more indulging in a pastime of which they had long been deprived.

The sun poured its rays on their backs; they no longer heard anything or thought of anything. They ignored the rest of the world; they were fishing.

But suddenly a rumbling[⑥] sound, which seemed to come from the bowels of the earth, shook the ground beneath them: the cannon were resuming their thunder.

Morissot turned his head and could see toward the left, beyond the banks of the river, the formidable[⑦] outline of Mont-Valerien, from whose summit arose a white puff of smoke.

The next instant a second puff followed the first, and in a few moments a fresh detonation[⑧] made the earth tremble.

Others followed, and minute by minute the mountain gave forth its deadly breath and a white puff of smoke, which rose slowly into the peaceful heaven and floated above the summit of the cliff.

Monsieur Sauvage shrugged his shoulders.

"They are at it again!" he said.

Morissot, who was anxiously watching his float bobbing up and down, was suddenly seized with the angry impatience of a peaceful man toward the madmen who were firing thus, and remarked indignantly:

"What fools they are to kill one another like that!"

---

① Parisian: characteristic of Paris
② quench: destroy
③ overawed: to be overcome, overwhelmed by fear
④ gudgeon: a kind of fish
⑤ wriggle: to twist to and fro
⑥ rumbling: deep, heavy and continuous
⑦ formidable: arousing feeling of awe or admiration because of grandeur, strength, etc
⑧ detonation: an explosion

"They're worse than animals," replied Monsieur Sauvage.

And Morissot, who had just caught a bleak[1], declared:

"And to think that it will be just the same so long as there are governments!"

"The Republic would not have declared war," interposed[2] Monsieur Sauvage.

Morissot interrupted him:

"Under a king we have foreign wars; under a republic we have civil war."

And the two began placidly[3] discussing political problems with the sound common sense of peaceful, matter-of-fact citizens—agreeing on one point: that they would never be free. And Mont-Valerien thundered ceaselessly, demolishing the houses of the French with its cannon balls, grinding lives of men to powder, destroying many a dream, many a cherished hope, many a prospective happiness; ruthlessly causing endless woe and suffering in the hearts of wives, of daughters, of mothers, in other lands.

"Such is life!" declared Monsieur Sauvage.

"Say, rather, such is death!" replied Morissot, laughing.

But they suddenly trembled with alarm at the sound of footsteps behind them, and, turning round, they perceived close at hand four tall, bearded men, dressed after the manner of livery[4] servants and wearing flat caps on their heads. They were covering the two anglers with their rifles.

The rods slipped from their owners' grasp and floated away down the river.

In the space of a few seconds they were seized, bound, thrown into a boat, and taken across to the Ile Marante.

And behind the house they had thought deserted were about a score of German soldiers.

A shaggy-looking[5] giant, who was bestriding[6] a chair and smoking a long clay pipe, addressed them in excellent French with the words:

"Well, gentlemen, have you had good luck with your fishing?"

Then a soldier deposited at the officer's feet the bag full of fish, which he had taken care to bring away. The Prussian smiled.

"Not bad, I see. But we have something else to talk about. Listen to me, and don't be alarmed:

"You must know that, in my eyes, you are two spies sent to reconnoitre[7] me and my movements. Naturally, I capture you and I shoot you. You pretended to be fishing, the better to disguise your real errand. You have fallen into my hands, and must take the consequences. Such is war."

"But as you came here through the outposts you must have a password for your return. Tell me that password and I will let you go."

The two friends, pale as death, stood silently side by side, a slight fluttering of the hands alone betraying their emotion.

"No one will ever know," continued the officer. "You will return peacefully to your homes, and the secret will disappear with you. If you refuse, it means death-instant death. Choose!"

They stood motionless, and did not open their lips.

---

① bleak: here, a kind of fish
② interpose: to put in a remark in the midst of a conversation
③ placidly: pleasantly calm or peaceful
④ livery: a uniform
⑤ shaggy-looking: rough and untidy
⑥ bestride: to place the legs on both sides of sth.
⑦ reconnoirtre: to survey or inspect

The Prussian, perfectly calm, went on, with hand outstretched toward the river:

"Just think that in five minutes you will be at the bottom of that water. In five minutes! You have relations, I presume?"

Mont-Valerien still thundered.

The two fishermen remained silent. The German turned and gave an order in his own language. Then he moved his chair a little way off, that he might not be so near the prisoners, and a dozen men stepped forward, rifle in hand, and took up a position, twenty paces off.

"I give you one minute," said the officer; "not a second longer."

Then he rose quickly, went over to the two Frenchmen, took Morissot by the arm, led him a short distance off, and said in a low voice:

"Quick! the password! Your friend will know nothing. I will pretend to relent①."

Morissot answered not a word.

Then the Prussian took Monsieur Sauvage aside in like manner, and made him the same proposal.

Monsieur Sauvage made no reply.

Again they stood side by side.

The officer issued his orders; the soldiers raised their rifles.

Then by chance Morissot's eyes fell on the bag full of gudgeon lying in the grass a few feet from him.

A ray of sunlight made the still quivering fish glisten like silver. And Morissot's heart sank. Despite his efforts at self-control his eyes filled with tears.

"Good-by, Monsieur Sauvage," he faltered.

"Good-by, Monsieur Morissot," replied Sauvage.

They shook hands, trembling from head to foot with a dread beyond their mastery.

The officer cried:

"Fire!"

The twelve shots were as one.

Monsieur Sauvage fell forward instantaneously. Morissot, being the taller, swayed slightly and fell across his friend with face turned skyward and blood oozing② from a rent③ in the breast of his coat.

The German issued fresh orders.

His men dispersed, and presently returned with ropes and large stones, which they attached to the feet of the two friends; then they carried them to the river bank.

Mont-Valerien, its summit now enshrouded in smoke, still continued to thunder.

Two soldiers took Morissot by the head and the feet; two others did the same with Sauvage. The bodies, swung lustily by strong hands, were cast to a distance, and, describing a curve, fell feet foremost into the stream.

The water splashed high, foamed, eddied, then grew calm; tiny waves lapped the shore.

A few streaks of blood flecked the surface of the river.

The officer, calm throughout, remarked, with grim④ humor:

---

① relent: to become more mild or to change one' s mind
② ooze: to flow slowly
③ rent: opening
④ grim: sinister or ghastly

"It's the fishes' turn now!"

Then he retraced his way to the house.

Suddenly he caught sight of the net full of gudgeons, lying forgotten in the grass. He picked it up, examined it, smiled, and called:

"Wilhelm!"

A white-aproned soldier responded to the summons, and the Prussian, tossing him the catch of the two murdered men, said:

"Have these fish fried for me at once, while they are still alive; they'll make a tasty dish."

Then he resumed his pipe.

▶ STUDY QUESTIONS

A ▷ Recalling

1. What is the social background of the story?
2. What makes Monsieur Sauvage and Monsieur Morissot become good friends?
3. In what situation do the two friends meet again?
4. Please describe the changing feelings of the two friends after they have taken the risk and arrived at their old fishing spot.
5. Please describe their emotions when they know they are to die soon.

B ▷ Interpreting

6. What factors contribute to the two friend's decision of going fishing again?
7. Why are Morissot's eyes full of tears at the sight of the glistening fish?
8. Please discuss the effects of the war on the two friends, Colonel Dumoulin and the Prussian officer.
9. What does the story say about war? About man? About man in war?

C ▷ Extending

10. Does the narrator have a position (taking side) when narrating the story? Why or why not?

VIII. *The Law of Life* by Jack London

▶ ABOUT THE AUTHOR

John Griffith "Jack" London (1876–1916) was an American author, journalist, and social activist. He was a pioneer in the then-burgeoning world of commercial magazine fiction and was one of the first fiction writers to obtain worldwide celebrity and a large fortune from his fiction alone. He is best remembered as the author of *Call of the Wild* and *White Fang*, both set in the Klondike Gold Rush, as well as the short stories *To Build a Fire*, *An Odyssey of the North*, and *Love of Life*. He also wrote of the South Pacific in such stories as *The Pearls of Parlay* and *The Heathen*, and of the San Francisco Bay area in *The Sea Wolf*.

London was a passionate advocate of unionization, socialism, and the rights of workers and wrote several powerful works dealing with these topics such as his dystopian novel, *The Iron Heel* and his non-fiction exposé, *The People of the Abyss*.

The Law of Life

1 Old Koskoosh listened greedily. Though his sight had long since faded, his hearing was still acute, and the slightest sound penetrated to the glimmering intelligence which yet abode behind the withered forehead, but which no longer gazed forth upon the things of the world. Ah! that was Sit-cum-to-ha, shrilly anathematizing① the dogs as she cuffed② and beat them into the harnesses. Sit-cum-to-ha was his daughter's daughter, but she was too busy to waste a thought upon her broken grandfather, sitting alone there in the snow, forlorn and helpless. Camp must be broken. The long trail waited while the short day refused to linger. Life called her, and the duties of life, not death. And he was very close to death now.

2 The thought made the old man panicky for the moment, and he stretched forth a palsied③ hand which wandered tremblingly over the small heap of dry wood beside him. Reassured that it was indeed there, his hand returned to the shelter of his mangy furs, and he again fell to listening. The sulky④ crackling of half-frozen hides⑤ told him that the chief's moose-⑥ skin lodge had been struck, and even then was being rammed and jammed⑦ into portable compass. The chief was his son, stalwart⑧ and strong, head man of the tribesmen, and a mighty hunter. As the women toiled with the camp luggage, his voice rose, chiding⑨ them for their slowness. Old Koskoosh strained his ears. It was the last time he would hear that voice. There went Geehow's lodge! And Tusken's! Seven, eight, nine; only the shaman's could be still standing. There! They were at work upon it now. He could hear the shaman grunt as he piled it on the sled. A child whimpered⑩, and a woman soothed it with soft, crooning⑪ gutturals⑫. Little Koo-tee, the old man thought, a fretful child, and not overstrong. It would die soon, perhaps, and they would burn a hole through the frozen tundra⑬ and pile rocks above to keep the wolverines⑭ away. Well, what did it matter? A few years at best, and as many an empty belly as a full one. And in the end, Death waited, ever-hungry and hungriest of them all.

3 What was that? Oh, the men lashing the sleds and drawing tight the thongs⑮. He listened, who would listen no more. The whip-lashes⑯ snarled and bit among the dogs. Hear them

---

① anathematize: to curse
② cuff: to beat
③ palsied: paralysed and shaky
④ sulky: dull
⑤ hide: the skin of some animal used as covering
⑥ moose: 驼鹿
⑦ be rammed and jammed: to be squeezed
⑧ stalwart: strongly or stoutly built
⑨ chide: to express disapproval of, to scold
⑩ whimper: to cry with low, broken sound
⑪ crooning: to sing or hum in a soft, soothing voice
⑫ guttural: harsh, as pronounced from the throat
⑬ tundra: 冻土
⑭ wolverine: 狗熊
⑮ thong: a strip of leather used to fasten something
⑯ whip-lash: the thing used to beat the dogs

whine[1]! How they hated the work and the trail[2]! They were off! Sled after sled churned[3] slowly away into the silence. They were gone. They had passed out of his life, and he faced the last bitter hour alone. No. The snow crunched beneath a moccasin; a man stood beside him; upon his head a hand rested gently. His son was good to do this thing. He remembered other old men whose sons had not waited after the tribe. But his son had. He wandered away into the past, till the young man's voice brought him back.

4   "Is it well with you?" he asked.

5   And the old man answered, "It is well."

6   "There be wood beside you," the younger man continued, "and the fire burns bright. The morning is gray, and the cold has broken. It will snow presently. Even now is it snowing."

7   "Ay, even now is it snowing."

8   "The tribesmen hurry. Their bales[4] are heavy, and their bellies flat with lack of feasting. The trail is long and they travel fast. go now. It is well?"

9   "It is well. I am as a last year's leaf, clinging lightly to the stem. The first breath that blows, and I fall. My voice is become like an old woman's. My eyes no longer show me the way of my feet, and my feet are heavy, and I am tired. It is well."

10   He bowed his head in content till the last noise of the complaining snow had died away, and he knew his son was beyond recall. Then his hand crept out in haste to the wood. It alone stood between him and the eternity that yawned[5] in upon him. At last the measure of his life was a handful of fagots[6]. One by one they would go to feed the fire, and just so, step by step, death would creep upon him. When the last stick had surrendered up its heat, the frost would begin to gather strength. First his feet would yield, then his hands; and the numbness would travel, slowly, from the extremities to the body. His head would fall forward upon his knees, and he would rest. It was easy. All men must die.

11   He did not complain. It was the way of life, and it was just. He had been born close to the earth, close to the earth had he lived, and the law thereof was not new to him. It was the law of all flesh. Nature was not kindly to the flesh. She had no concern for that concrete thing called the individual. Her interest lay in the species, the race. This was the deepest abstraction old Koskoosh's barbaric mind was capable of, but he grasped it firmly. He saw it exemplified in all life. The rise of the sap, the bursting greenness of the willow bud, the fall of the yellow leaf— in this alone was told the whole history. But one task did Nature set the individual. Did he not perform it, he died. Did he perform it, it was all the same, he died. Nature did not care; there were plenty who were obedient, and it was only the obedience in this matter, not the obedient, which lived and lived always. The tribe of Koskoosh was very old. The old men he had known when a boy, had known old men before them. Therefore it was true that the tribe lived, that

① whine: to utter a low, usually nasal complaining cry or sound
② trail: here refers to the moving.
③ churn: to move in agitation
④ bale: package
⑤ yawn: to open wide
⑥ fagot: 柴把，束薪

it stood for the obedience of all its members, way down into the forgotten past, whose very resting-places were unremembered. They did not count; they were episodes. They had passed away like clouds from a summer sky. He also was an episode, and would pass away. Nature did not care. To life she set one task, gave one law. To perpetuate① was the task of life, its law was death. A maiden was a good creature to look upon, full-breasted and strong, with spring② to her step and light in her eyes. But her task was yet before her. The light in her eyes brightened, her step quickened, she was now bold with the young men, now timid, and she gave them of her own unrest. And ever she grew fairer and yet fairer to look upon, till some hunter, able no longer to withhold himself, took her to his lodge to cook and toil for him and to become the mother of his children. And with the coming of her offspring her looks left her. Her limbs dragged and shuffled③, her eyes dimmed and bleared④, and only the little children found joy against the withered cheek of the old squaw⑤ by the fire. Her task was done. But a little while, on the first pinch⑥ of famine or the first long trail, and she would be left, even as he had been left, in the snow, with a little pile of wood. Such was the law. He placed a stick carefully upon the fire and resumed his meditations. It was the same everywhere, with all things. The mosquitoes vanished with the first frost. The little tree-squirrel crawled away to die. When age settled upon the rabbit it became slow and heavy, and could no longer outfoot its enemies. Even the big bald-face grew clumsy and blind and quarrelsome, in the end to be dragged down by a handful of yelping huskies⑦. He remembered how he had abandoned his own father on an upper reach of the Klondike one winter, the winter before the missionary came with his talk-books and his box of medicines. Many a time had Koskoosh smacked his lips over the recollection of that box, though now his mouth refused to moisten. The "painkiller" had been especially good. But the missionary was a bother after all, for he brought no meat into the camp, and he ate heartily, and the hunters grumbled. But he chilled his lungs on the divide by the Mayo⑧, and the dogs afterwards nosed the stones away and fought over his bones.

12   Koskoosh placed another stick on the fire and harked back⑨ deeper into the past. There was the time of the Great Famine, when the old men crouched empty-bellied to the fire, and let fall from their lips dim traditions of the ancient day when the Yukon⑩ ran wide open for three winters, and then lay frozen for three summers. He had lost his mother in that famine. In the summer the salmon⑪ un had failed, and the tribe looked forward to the winter and the coming of the caribou⑫. Then the winter came, but with it there were no caribou. Never had the like been known, not even in the lives of the old men. But the caribou did not come, and it was the seventh year, and the rabbits had not

---

① perpetuate: to prevent from extinction
② spring: an elastic or bouncing quality that makes walk light
③ shuffle: to walk with clumsy steps
④ blear: to become dim
⑤ squaw: (slang, often offensive) woman
⑥ pinch: sharp, painful stress, as of hunger, need or anything trying circumstances
⑦ husky: Eskimo dog
⑧ Mayo: a county in the northwestern Republic of Ireland
⑨ hark back: to return to some previous subject
⑩ Yukon: a river flowing northwest and then southwest from nortwestern Canada through Alaska to the Bering Sea.
⑪ salmon: 三文鱼
⑫ caribou: 北美驯鹿

replenished[1], and the dogs were naught but bundles of bones. And through the long darkness the children wailed and died, and the women, and the old men; and not one in ten of the tribe lived to meet the sun when it came back in the spring. That was a famine!

13   But he had seen times of plenty, too, when the meat spoiled on their hands, and the dogs were fat and worthless with overeating—times when they let the game go unkilled, and the women were fertile[2] and the lodges were cluttered with sprawling men-children and women-children. Then it was the men became high-stomached, and revived ancient quarrels, and crossed the divides to the south to kill the Pellys[3], and to the west that they might sit by the dead fires of the Tananas[4]. He remembered, when a boy, during a time of plenty, when he saw a moose pulled down by the wolves. Zing-ha lay with him in the snow and watched—Zing-ha, who later became the craftiest of hunters, and who, in the end, fell through an air-hole on the Yukon. They found him, a month afterward, just as he had crawled halfway out and frozen stiff to the ice.

14   But the moose. Zing-ha and he had gone out that day to play at hunting after the manner of their fathers. On the bed of the creek[5] they struck the fresh track of a moose, and with it the tracks of many wolves. "An old one," Zing-ha, who was quicker at reading the sign, said— "an old one who cannot keep up with the herd. The wolves have cut him out from his brothers, and they will never leave him." And it was so. It was their way. By day and by night, never resting, snarling on his heels, snapping at his nose, they would stay by him to the end. How Zing-ha and he felt the blood-lust quicken! The finish would be a sight to see!

15   Eager-footed, they took the trail, and even he, Koskoosh, slow of sight and an unversed[6] tracker, could have followed it blind, it was so wide. Hot were they on the heels of the chase, reading the grim tragedy, fresh-written, at every step. Now they came to where the moose had made a stand. Thrice the length of a grown man's body, in every direction, had the snow been stamped about and uptossed. In the midst were the deep impressions of the splay-hoofed game[7], and all about, everywhere, were the lighter footmarks of the wolves. Some, while their brothers harried[8] the kill, had lain to one side and rested. The full-stretched impress of their bodies in the snow was as perfect as though made the moment before. One wolf had been caught in a wild lunge[9] of the maddened victim and trampled to death. A few bones, well picked, bore witness.

16   Again, they ceased the uplift of their snowshoes at a second stand. Here the great animal had fought desperately. Twice had he been dragged down, as the snow attested[10], and twice had he shaken his assailants[11] clear[12] and gained footing once more. He had done his task long since, but none the less was life dear to him. Zing-ha said it was a strange thing, a moose once down

---

① replenish: to supply what is lacking
② fertile: reproductive
③ Pellys: people living along the Pelly river, flowing northwest to the Yukon River
④ Tananas: people living along the Tanana River which flows northwest from eastern Alaska to the Yukon River
⑤ creek: stream
⑥ unversed: not skillful
⑦ splay-hoofed game: a game that is spreading wide
⑧ harry: to attack repeatedly
⑨ lunge: a sudden forward movement
⑩ attest: to give proof or evidence of
⑪ assailant: wolf that attacks
⑫ shake...clear: to get rid of...

to get free again; but this one certainly had. The shaman① would see signs and wonders in this when they told him.

17 And yet again, they come to where the moose had made to mount the bank and gain the timber. But his foes had laid on from behind, till he reared and fell back upon them, crushing two② deep into the snow. It was plain the kill was at hand, for their brothers had left them untouched. Two more stands were hurried past, brief in time-length and very close together. The trail was red now, and the clean stride of the great beast had grown short and slovenly③. Then they heard the first sounds of the battle—not the full-throated chorus of the chase, but the short, snappy bark which spoke of④ close quarters⑤ and teeth to flesh. Crawling up the wind, Zing-ha bellied it through the snow, and with him crept he, Koskoosh, who was to be chief of the tribesmen in the years to come. Together they shoved aside the under branches of a young spruce and peered forth. It was the end they saw.

18 The picture, like all of youth's impressions, was still strong with him, and his dim eyes watched the end played out as vividly as in that far-off time. Koskoosh marvelled at this, for in the days which followed, when he was a leader of men and a head of councillors, he had done great deeds and made his name a curse in the mouths of the Pellys, to say naught of the strange white man he had killed, knife to knife, in open fight.

19 For long he pondered on the days of his youth, till the fire died down and the frost bit deeper. He replenished it with two sticks this time, and gauged⑥ his grip on life by what remained. If Sit-cum-to-ha had only remembered her grandfather, and gathered a larger armful, his hours would have been longer. It would have been easy. But she was ever a careless child, and honored not her ancestors from the time the Beaver, son of the son of Zing-ha, first cast eyes upon her. Well, what mattered it? Had he not done likewise in his own quick youth? For a while he listened to the silence. Perhaps the heart of his son might soften, and he would come back with the dogs to take his old father on with the tribe to where the caribou ran thick and the fat hung heavy upon them.

20 He strained his ears, his restless brain for the moment stilled. Not a stir, nothing. He alone took breath in the midst of the great silence. It was very lonely. Hark! What was that? A chill passed over his body. The familiar, long-drawn howl⑦ broke the void, and it was close at hand. Then on his darkened eyes was projected the vision of the moose—the old bull moose—the torn flanks⑧ and bloody sides, the riddled⑨ mane⑩, and the great branching horns, down low and tossing to the last. He saw the flashing forms of gray, the gleaming eyes, the lolling⑪ tongues,

---

① shaman: a person who works as intermediary between natural and supernatural worlds, using magic to cure illness, foretell the future, etc.
② two: here refers to two wolves.
③ slovenly: here suggests the moose's steps become unsteady and tired.
④ speak of: to tell, to suggest
⑤ quarter: here refers to the stage of combat.
⑥ gauge: to measure
⑦ howl: the cry of a dog or a wolf
⑧ flank: the side of a person or an animal , between the ribs and the hip
⑨ riddled: here means to be pierced with holes.
⑩ mane: the long hair around the face and neck of a lion, here referring to that of a moose
⑪ loll: to hang loosely

the slavered[1] fangs. And he saw the inexorable[2] circle close in till it became a dark point in the midst of the stamped snow.

21   A cold muzzle[3] thrust against his cheek, and at its touch his soul leaped back to the present. His hand shot into the fire and dragged out a burning faggot. Overcome for the nonce by his hereditary fear of man, the brute retreated, raising a prolonged call to his brothers; and greedily they answered, till a ring of crouching, jaw-slobbered[4] gray was stretched round about. The old man listened to the drawing in[5] of this circle. He waved his brand wildly, and sniffs turned to snarls; but the panting brutes refused to scatter. Now one wormed his chest forward, dragging his haunches[6] after, now a second, now a third; but never a one drew back. Why should he cling to life? He asked, and dropped the blazing stick into the snow. It sizzled[7] and went out. The circle grunted uneasily, but held its own. Again he saw the last stand of the old bull moose, and Koskoosh dropped his head wearily upon his knees. What did it matter after all? Was it not the law of life?

STUDY QUESTIONS

A > *Recalling*

1. Who is Koskoosh? Why is he left behind, alone?
2. How does he take it (his being left behind)?
3. What is the son's attitude toward his father's being left alone?
4. What events has Koskoosh recalled when sitting alone?
5. How is Koskoosh's life ended?

B > *Interpreting*

6. What does each of the recalled events suggest?
7. Although a lot of persons and animals are presented, there are actually only two types of them. What are the two types?
8. At one moment, Koskoosh wished his son would come back and bring him along. What does that suggest?
9. What law of life does the story try to reveal? Do you believe in it? Why or why not?

C > *Extending*

10. What would you do if you were the son of Koskoosh?

FURTHER READING

Miguel de Cervantes, *Don Quixote*

---

① slaver: to water, to let liquid fall without being controlled
② inexorable: ruthless, that can't be persuaded
③ muzzle: the front part of an animal's face
④ slobber: to have mouth liquid run from one's mouth
⑤ draw in: to encircle
⑥ haunch: either of the back legs of a four-legged animal
⑦ sizzle: to make a hissing sound

Leo Tolstoy, *War and Peace*
William Golding, *Lord of the Flies*
Gabriel García Márquez, *A Very Old Man with Enormous Wings*
莫言，《生死疲劳》
贾平凹，《古炉》

▶▶ RECOMMENDED MOVIES

Gone with the Wind (1939), directed by Victor Fleming
Big Fish (2003), directed by Tim Burton
The Pianist (2002), directed by Roman Polanski
The Reader (2008), directed by Stephen Daldry
《霸王别姬》（1993），导演陈凯歌

Unit Six   Contemplations

I. *The Lamb* by William Blake

▶ ABOUT THE POET

William Blake (1757–1827) was an English poet, painter, and printmaker. Largely unrecognised during his lifetime, Blake is now considered a seminal figure in the history of the poetry and visual arts of the Romantic Age. Considered mad by contemporaries for his idiosyncratic views, Blake is held in high regard by later critics for his expressiveness and creativity, and for the philosophical and mystical undercurrents within his work.

The Lamb

1   Little Lamb who made thee
Dost thou know who made thee
Gave thee life & bid thee feed.
By the stream & o'er the mead[①];
5   Gave thee clothing of delight,
Softest clothing wooly bright;
Gave thee such a tender voice,
Making all the vales rejoice!
Little Lamb who made thee
10   Dost thou know who made thee

Little Lamb I'll tell thee,
Little Lamb I'll tell thee!
He is called by thy name,
For he calls himself a Lamb[②]:
15   He is meek[③] & he is mild,
He became a little child:
I a child & thou a lamb,
We are called by his name.
Little Lamb God bless thee.
20   Little Lamb God bless thee.

---

① mead: meadow, grassland
② he calls himself a Lamb: In the Bible, Jesus calls himself the Lamb
③ meek: gentle, kind

▶▶ STUDY QUESTIONS

Recalling

1. Please describe the image of the lamb.
2. What is the image of "He"?

Interpreting

3. Who is the speaker?
4. Please describe the speaker.
5. What is shared by the speaker, the lamb and "He"?
6. What connects the speaker, the lamb and "He"?
7. Who is the "He"?
8. What is the mood of the poem?
9. What does the poet try to say through the poem?

Extending

10. Can you feel the existence of "He"?
11. If there is a "He", who is closer to Him, the adults or the children?

II. *God's Grandeur* by Gerard Manley Hopkins

▶▶ ABOUT THE POET

Gerard Manley Hopkins (1844–1889) was an English poet, Roman Catholic convert, and Jesuit priest, whose posthumous fame established him among the leading Victorian poets. His experimental explorations in prosody (especially sprung rhythm) and his use of imagery established him as a daring innovator in a period of largely traditional verse.

God's Grandeur

1   The world is charged with the grandeur of God.
    It will flame out, like shining from shook foil①;
    It gathers to a greatness, like the ooze of oil②
    Crushed. Why do men then now not reck his rod③?
5   Generations have trod, have trod, have trod④;

---

① like shining from shook foil: like the brightness from shaking gold foil
② ooze of oil: oil coming out from the ground slowly, in great amount
③ reck his rod: literally, to take heed, to mind his rod. Figuratively, to mind God's anger
④ trod: to trample or crush under foot, indicating human being's heartless overuse of the earth

And all is seared with trade①; bleared②, smeared③ with toil;
And wears man's smudge④ and shares man's smell: the soil
Is bare now, nor can foot feel, being shod⑤.

And for all this, nature is never spent;
10   There lives the dearest freshness deep down things;
And though the last lights off the black West went
Oh, morning, at the brown brink eastward, springs—
Because the Holy Ghost⑥ over the bent
World broods⑦ with warm breast and with ah! bright wings.

STUDY QUESTIONS

A Recalling

1. Find out similes and metaphors in the poem. What are being compared?
2. How do human beings regard God's grandeur?
3. How does God tread human beings?

B Interpreting

4. Where does the turn occur in the poem?
5. What does the turn suggest?
6. Where does God's grandeur lie according to the poem?

C Extending

7. Can you feel God's grandeur? To you, where does God's grandeur lie?
8. What is special about the form of the poem? How does the form contribute to what it tries to say?

III. *Design* by Robert Frost

Design

1   I found a dimpled⑧ spider, fat and white,
On a white heal-all⑨, holding up a moth
Like a white piece of rigid satin⑩ cloth—

---

① seared with trade: "sear" literally means to burn injuriously. Here means to destroy the earth with commercialism.
② blear: to blur, to make dim
③ smear: to stain, to make dirty
④ smudge: dirty mark
⑤ nor can foot feel, being shod: It means that the foot cannot feel the soil because of being put shoes on.
⑥ the Holy Ghost: God
⑦ brood: to sit upon eggs to hatch, as a bird. Here God is compared to a big bird who hatches the world patiently with love and hope.
⑧ dimpled: with one part of the surface depressed
⑨ heal-all: a kind of flower
⑩ satin: 缎子

Assorted^① characters of death and blight^②

5 Mixed ready to begin the morning right,
Like the ingredients of a witches' broth^③ —
A snow-drop spider, a flower like a froth,
And dead wings carried like a paper kite.

What had that flower to do with being white,

10 The wayside^④ blue and innocent heal-all?
What brought the kindred^⑤ spider to that height,
Then steered^⑥ the white moth thither in the night?
What but design of darkness to appall? —
If design govern in a thing so small.

▶▶ STUDY QUESTIONS

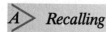

A Recalling

1. Please describe the spider, the heal-all flower and the moth. What is similar about them?
2. What is the incident?
3. What thoughts does the incident arouse in the speaker's mind?

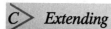

B Interpreting

4. Why is the flower compared to be the froth and the moth's wings are compared to be the paper kite?
5. What is the significance of the color "white"?
6. Please illustrate the significance of the word "appall".
7. How does the "design of darkness" work according to the poem?

C Extending

8. This poem has similar form with *God's Grandeur*. What is unusual about this form? Why both Hopkins and Robert Frost choose this form? By accident? Or for some common purpose?
9. Compare this poem with *The Lamb* and *God's Grandeur*. What is similar and what is different?
10. What are the beliefs behind the above mentioned poems?

IV. *Gimpel the Fool* by Isaac Bashevis Singer

▶▶ ABOUT THE AUTHOR

Isaac Bashevis Singer (1902–1991) was a Polish-born Jewish-American author. He was a leading figure in the Yiddish literary movement and won the Nobel Prize in Literature in 1978.

---

① assorted: here means well-arranged.
② blight: the death of plant tissues
③ broth: soup of meat or fish and vegetables
④ wayside: road-side
⑤ kindred: having similar qualities, related
⑥ steer: to guide the course of

He won two U.S. National Book Awards, one in Children's Literature for his memoir *A Day Of Pleasure: Stories of a Boy Growing Up in Warsaw* and one in Fiction for his collection *A Crown of Feathers and Other Stories*. Isaac Bashevis Singer was one of the great storytellers of the twentieth century. His writing is a unique blend of religious morality and social awareness combined with an investigation of personal desires. Though not primarily nostalgic, Singer's work hearkened back to a former time. The setting for much of the work was his native Poland, and the writing addressed existential and spiritual questions through folk tales and parables.

Gimpel the Fool
Translated by Saul Bellow

I

1   I am Gimpel the fool. I don't think myself a fool. On the contrary. But that's what folks call me. They gave me the name while I was still in school. I had seven names in all: imbecile[1], donkey, flax-head[2], dope[3], glump[4], ninny[5], and fool. The last name stuck. What did my foolishness consist of? I was easy to take in. They said, "Gimpel, you know the rabbi's[6] wife has been brought to childbed?" So I skipped school. Well, it turned out to be a lie. How was I supposed to know? She hadn't had a big belly. But I never looked at her belly. Was that really so foolish? The gang laughed and hee-hawed[7], stomped[8] and danced and chanted a good-night prayer. And instead of the raisins[9] they give when a woman's lying in[10], they stuffed my hand full of goat turds[11]. I was no weakling[12]. If I slapped someone he'd see all the way to Cracow[13]. But I'm really not a slugger[14] by nature. I think to myself: Let it pass. So they take advantage of me.

2   I was coming home from school and heard a dog barking. I'm not afraid of dogs, but of course I never want to start up with them. One of them may be mad, and if he bites there's not a Tartar[15] in the world who can help you. So I made tracks[16]. Then I looked around and saw the whole market place wild with laughter. It was no dog at all but Wolf-Leib the Thief. How was I supposed to know it was he? It sounded like a howling bitch.

---

[1] imbecile: a stupid person
[2] flax-head: indicating the color of the hair which is pale yellow
[3] dope: (informal) a stupid person
[4] glump: a person who is unwilling to talk or sociable, being gloomy and silent
[5] ninny: (informal) a foolish person
[6] rabbi: a Jewish priest
[7] hee-hawed: making sounds like that of a donkey
[8] stomp: to walk or dance with heavy steps
[9] raisin: sweet dried grape
[10] lie in: here means to give birth.
[11] turd: the solid waste material passed from the body
[12] weakling: a weak person
[13] Cracow: a city in South Poland
[14] slugger: a person who strikes hard
[15] Tartar: a member of the Mongolian or Turkish tribes, considered to be savage or strong
[16] make tracks: to go in a hurry

3   When the pranksters[①] and leg-pullers[②] found that I was easy to fool, every one of them tried his luck with me. "Gimpel the Czar is coming to Frampol; Gimpel, the moon fell down in Turbeen; Gimpel, little Hodel Furpiece found a treasure behind the bathhouse." And I like a golem[③] believed everyone. In the first place, everything is possible, as it is written in the Wisdom of the Fathers, I've forgotten just how. Second, I had to believe when the whole town came down on me! If I ever dared to say, "Ah, you're kidding!" there was trouble. People got angry. "What do you mean! You want to call everyone a liar?" What was I to do? I believed them, and I hope at least that did them some good.

4   I was an orphan. My grandfather who brought me up was already bent toward the grave. So they turned me over to a baker, and what a time they gave me there! Every woman or girl who came to bake a batch of noodles had to fool me at least once. "Gimpel, there's a fair in heaven; Gimpel, the rabbi gave birth to a calf in the seventh month; Gimpel, a cow flew over the roof and laid brass eggs." A student from the yeshiva came once to buy a roll, and he said, "You, Gimpel, while you stand here scraping with your baker's shovel the Messiah has come. The dead have arisen." "What do you mean?" I said. "I heard no one blowing the ram's horn[④]!" He said, "Are you deaf?" And all began to cry, "We heard it, we heard!" Then in came Rietze the Candle-dipper and called out in her hoarse voice, "Gimpel, your father and mother have stood up from the grave. They're looking for you."

5   To tell the truth, I knew very well that nothing of the sort had happened, but all the same, as folks were talking, I threw on my wool vest and went out. Maybe something had happened. What did I stand to lose by looking? Well, what a cat music went up! And then I took a vow to believe nothing more. But that was no go either. They confused me so that I didn't know the big end from the small.

6   I went to the rabbi to get some advice. He said, "It is written, better to be a fool all your days than for one hour to be evil. You are not a fool. They are the fools. For he who causes his neighbor to feel shame loses Paradise himself." Nevertheless the rabbi's daughter took me in. As I left the rabbinical court she said, "Have you kissed the wall yet?" I said, "No; what for?" She answered, "It's the law; you've got to do it after every visit." Well, there didn't seem to be any harm in it. And she burst out laughing. It was a fine trick. She put one over on me, all right.

7   I wanted to go off to another town, but then everyone got busy matchmaking, and they were after me so they nearly tore my coat tails off. They talked at me and talked until I got water on the ear. She was no chaste maiden, but they told me she was virgin pure. She had a limp, and they said it was deliberate, from coyness[⑤]. She had a bastard[⑥], and they told me the child was her little brother. I cried, "You're wasting your time. I'll never marry that whore." But they said indignantly, "What a way to talk! Aren't you ashamed of yourself? We can take you to the rabbi and have you fined for giving her a bad name." I saw then that I wouldn't

---

① prankster: a mischievous or malicious person who plays tricks or practical jokes at the expanse of others
② leg-puller: person who loves making fun of other people
③ golem: a stupid or clumsy person
④ blow the ram's horn: according to the *Bible: Revelation*, ram's horn will be blown on the Final Judgment.
⑤ coyness: being shy and modest
⑥ bastard: the illegitimate child

escape them so easily and I thought: They're set on making me their butt[1]. But when you're married the husband's the master, and if that's all right with her it's agreeable to me too. Besides, you can't pass through life unscathed[2], nor expect to.

8   I went to her clay house, which was built on the sand, and the whole gang hollering[3] and chorusing, came after me. They acted like bear-baiters[4]. When we came to the well they stopped all the same. They were afraid to start anything with Elka. Her mouth would open as if it were on a hinge[5], and she had a fierce tongue. I entered the house. Lines were strung from wall to wall and clothes were drying. Barefoot she stood by the tub, doing the wash. She was dressed in a worn hand-me-down gown of plush[6]. She had her hair put up in braids and pinned across her head. It took my breath away, almost, the reek[7] of it all.

9   Evidently she knew who I was. She took a look at me and said, "Look who's here! He's come, the drip[8]. Grab a seat."

10   I told her all; I denied nothing. "Tell me the truth," I said, "are you really a virgin; and is that mischievous Yechiel actually your little brother? Don't be deceitful with me, for I'm an orphan."

11   "I'm an orphan myself," she answered, "and whoever tries to twist you up[9], may the end of his nose take a twist. But don't let them think they can take advantage of me. I want a dowry of fifty guilders[10], and let them take up a collection[11] besides. Otherwise they can kiss my you-know-what." She was very plainspoken. I said, "It's the bride and not the groom who gives a dowry." Then she said, "Don't bargain with me. Either a flat 'yes' or a flat 'no'— Go back where you came from."

12   I thought: No bread will ever be baked from this dough[12]. But ours is not a poor town. They consented to everything and proceeded with the wedding. It so happened that there was a dysentery epidemic at the time. The ceremony was held at the cemetery gates, near the little corpse-washing hut. The fellows got drunk. While the marriage contract was being drawn up I heard the most pious high rabbi ask, "Is the bride a widow or a divorced woman?" And the sexton's[13] wife answered for her, "Both a widow and divorced." It was a black moment for me. But what was I to do, run away from her under the marriage canopy[14]?

13   There was singing and dancing. An old granny danced opposite me, hugging a braided

---

① butt: the target of ridicule
② unscratched: unharmed
③ holler: to shout
④ bear-baiter: person who set dogs to fight with the captive bear
⑤ on a hinge: hinge is what the door is fixed on and what makes the door turn. "her mouth is on a hinge" means she is ready to utter fierce words.
⑥ plush: 长毛绒
⑦ reek: the strong, unpleasant smell
⑧ drip: (slang) an unattractive, boring, colorless person
⑨ twist sb. up: (informal) to cheat, to swindle
⑩ guilder: a silver or nickel coin or monetary unit of Netherlands until the euro was adopted
⑪ let them take up a collection: to let them collect some money
⑫ no break will ever be baked from this dough: I can never make anything out of her.
⑬ sexton: an official of the church
⑭ canopy: here means roof or cover.

white chalah①. The master of revels② made a "God'a mercy" in memory of the bride's parents. The schoolboys threw burrs③, as on Tishe b'Av fast day④. There were a lot of gifts after the sermon: a noodle board, a kneading trough⑤, a bucket, brooms, ladies, household articles galore⑥. Then I took a look and saw two strapping⑦ young men carrying a crib⑧. "What do we need this for?" I asked. So they said, "Don't rack your brains about it. It's all right, it'll come in handy." I realized I was going to be rooked⑨. Take it another way though, what did I stand to lose? I reflected: I'll see what comes of it. A whole town can't go altogether crazy.

II

14   At night I came where my wife lay, but she wouldn't let me in. "Say, look here, is this what they married us for?" I said. And she said, "My monthly has come." "But yesterday they took you to the ritual bath, and that's afterward, isn't it supposed to be?" "Today isn't yesterday," said she, "and yesterday's not today. You can beat it if you don't like it." In short, I waited.

15   Not four months later she was in childbed. The townsfolk hid their laughter with their knuckles. But what could I do? She suffered intolerable pains and clawed at the walls. "Gimpel," she cried, "I'm going. Forgive me!" The house filled with women. They were boiling pans of water. The screams rose to the welkin⑩.

16   The thing to do was to go the House of Prayer to repeat Psalms, and that was what I did.

17   The townsfolk liked that, all right. I stood in a corner saying Psalms and prayers, and they shook their heads at me. "Pray, pray!" they told me. "Prayer never made any woman pregnant." One of the congregation put a straw to my mouth and said, "Hay for the cows." There was something to that too, by God!

18   She gave birth to a boy. Friday at the synagogue⑪ the sexton stood up before the Ark, pounded on the reading table, and announced, "The wealthy Reb Gimpel invites the congregation to a feast in honor of the birth of a son." The whole House of Prayer rang with laughter. My face was flaming. But there was nothing I could do. After all, I was the one responsible for the circumcision⑫ honors and rituals.

19   Half the town came running. You couldn't wedge⑬ another soul in. Women brought

---

① chalah: a loaf of bread eaten on the Sab bath
② revel: an occasion of merrymaking or festivity with dancing, etc.
③ throw burrs: to make whirring sounds
④ Tishe b'Av fast day: a holiday commemorating the Roman destruction of the Second Temple in A.D. 70
⑤ kneading trough: 揉面槽
⑥ galore: in plentiful amounts
⑦ strapping: powerfully-built, robust
⑧ crib: a bed for a baby
⑨ be rooked: be cheated
⑩ welkin: (poetic) the sky
⑪ synagogue: the Jewish house of worship
⑫ circumcision: a religious ritual
⑬ wedge in: to pack in

peppered chickpeas①, and there was a keg② of beer from the tavern③. I ate and drank as much as anyone, and they all congratulated me. Then there was a circumcision, and I named the boy after my father, may he rest in peace. When all were gone and I was left with my wife alone, she thrust her head through the bed-curtain and called me to her.

20   "Gimpel," said she, "why are you silent? Has your ship gone and sunk?"

21   "What shall I say?" I answered. "A fine thing you've done to me! If my mother had known of it she'd have died a second time."

22   She said, "Are you crazy, or what?"

23   "How can you make such a fool," I said, "of one who should be the lord and master?"

24   "What's the matter with you?" she said. "What have you taken it into your head to imagine?"

25   I saw that I must speak bluntly and openly. "Do you think this is the way to use an orphan?" I said. "You have borne a bastard."

26   She answered, "Drive this foolishness out of your head. The child is yours."

27   "How can he be mine?" I argued. "He was born seventeen weeks after the wedding."

28   She told me then that he was premature. I said, "Isn't he a little too prema-ture?" She said she had had a grandmother who carried just as short a time and she resembled this grandmother of hers as one drop of water does another. She swore to it with such oaths that you would have believed a peasant at the fair if he had used them. To tell the plain truth, I didn't believe her; but when I talked it over next day with the schoolmaster he told me that the very same thing had happened to Adam and Eve. Two they went up to bed, and four they descended.

29   "There isn't a woman in the world who is not the granddaughter of Eve," he said.

30   That was how it was; they argued me dumb. But then, who really knows how such things are?

31   I began to forget my sorrow. I loved the child madly, and he loved me too. As soon as he saw me he'd wave his little hands and want me to pick him up, and when he was colicky④ I was the only one who could pacify him. I bought him a little bone teething ring and a little gilded cap. He was forever catching the evil eye from some-one, and then I had to run to get one of those abracadabras⑤ for him that would get him out of it. I worked like an ox. You know how expenses go up when there's an infant in the house. I don't want to lie about it; I didn't dislike Elka either, for that matter. She swore at me and cursed, and I couldn't get enough of her. What strength she had! One of her looks could rob you of the power of speech. And her orations! Pitch and sulphur⑥, that's what they were full of, and yet somehow also full

---

① chickpea: 鹰嘴豆
② keg: a small barrel
③ tavern: pub
④ colicky: 腹绞痛
⑤ abracadabras: magical words of incantation. Here refers to the little toys.
⑥ pitch and sulphur: literally, in Chinese is 沥青和硫磺. Figuratively, her language is full of darkness and anger.

of charm. I adored her every word. She gave me bloody wounds though.

32   In the evening I brought her a white loaf as well as a dark one, and also poppyseed[①] rolls I baked myself. I thieved because of her and swiped everything I could lay hands on: macaroons[②], raisins, almonds, cakes. I hope I may be forgiven for stealing from the Saturday pots the women left to warm in the baker's oven. I would take out scraps of meat, a chunk of pudding, a chicken leg or head, a piece of tripe[③], whatever I could nip[④] quickly. She ate and became fat and handsome.

33   I had to sleep away from home all during the week, at the bakery. On Friday nights when I got home she always made an excuse of some sort. Either she had heartburn, or a stitch[⑤] in the side, or hiccups, or headaches. You know what women's excuses are. I had a bitter time of it. It was rough. To add to it, this little brother of hers, the bastard, was growing bigger. He'd put lumps[⑥] on me, and when I wanted to hit back she'd open her mouth and curse so powerfully I saw a green haze[⑦] floating before my eyes. Ten times a day she threatened to divorce me. Another man in my place would have taken French leave[⑧] and disappeared. But I'm the type that bears it and says nothing. What's one to do? Shoulders are from God, and burdens too.

34   One night there was a calamity in the bakery; the oven burst, and we almost had a fire. There was nothing to do but go home, so I went home. Let me, I thought, also taste the joy of sleeping in bed in midweek. I didn't want to wake the sleeping mite[⑨] and tiptoed into the house. Coming in, it seemed to me that I heard not the snoring of one but, as it were, a double snore, one a thin enough snore and the other like the snoring of a slaughtered ox. Oh, I didn't like that! I didn't like it at all. I went up to the bed, and things suddenly turned black. Next to Elka lay a man's form. Another in my place would have made an uproar, and enough noise to rouse the whole town, but the thought occurred to me that I might wake the child. A little thing like that—why frighten a little swallow, I thought. All right then, I went back to the bakery and stretched out on a sack of flour and till morning I never shut an eye. I shivered as if I had had malaria[⑩]. "Enough of being a donkey," I said to myself. "Gimpel isn't going to be a sucker[⑪] all his life. There's a limit even to the foolishness of a fool like Gimpel."

35   In the morning I went to the rabbi to get advice, and it made a great commotion in the town. They sent the beadle[⑫] for Elka right away. She came, carrying the child. And what do you think she did? She denied it, denied everything, bone and stone! "He's out of his head," she said. "I know nothing of dreams or divinations." They yelled at her, warned her, hammered

---

① poppyseed: 罂粟籽
② macaroon: a small flat cake made mainly of sugar, eggs, and crushed almonds
③ tripe: 牛肚
④ nip: to catch in a tight sharp hold between two points or surfaces
⑤ stitch: a sharp spasmodic pain in the side resulting from running or exercising
⑥ put lumps on me: make me suffer
⑦ haze: a light mist or smoke
⑧ take French leave: a departure without permission or notice
⑨ mite: a small child
⑩ malaria: 疟疾
⑪ sucker: a person who is easily deceived
⑫ beadle: an official who in former times helped a priest in keeping order in church

on the table, but she stuck to her guns[1]: it was a false accusation, she said.

36   The butchers and the horse-traders took her part. One of the lads from the slaughterhouse came by and said to me, "We've got our eye on you, you're a marked man." Meanwhile the child started to bear down[2] and soiled[3] itself. In the rabbinical court there was an Ark of the Covenant, and they couldn't allow that, so they sent Elka away.

37   I said to the rabbi, "What shall I do?" "You must divorce her at once," said he.

38   "And what if she refuses?" I asked.

39   He said, "You must serve the divorce. That's all you'll have to do."

40   I said, "Well, all right, Rabbi. Let me think about it."

41   "There's nothing to think about," said he. "You mustn't remain under the same roof with her."

42   "And if I want to see the child?" I asked. "Let her go, the harlot," said he, "and her brood[4] of bastards with her."

43   The verdict he gave was that I mustn't even cross her threshold—never again, as long as I should live.

44   During the day it didn't bother me so much. I thought: It was bound to happen, the abscess[5] had to burst. But at night when I stretched out upon the sacks I felt it all very bitterly. A longing took me, for her and for the child. I wanted to be angry, but that's my misfortune exactly, I don't have it in me to be really angry. In the first place this was how my thoughts went—there's bound to be a slip sometimes. You can't live without errors. Probably that lad who was with her led her on and gave her presents and what not, and women are often long on hair and short on sense, and so he got around her. And then since she denies it so, maybe I was only seeing things? Hallucinations[6] do happen. You see a figure or a mannikin[7] or something, but when you come up closer it's nothing, there's not a thing there. And if that's so, I'm doing her an injustice. And when I got so far in my thoughts I started to weep. I sobbed so that I wet the flour where I lay. In the morning I went to the rabbi and told him that I had made a mistake. The rabbi wrote on with his quill[8], and he said that if that were so he would have to reconsider the whole case. Until he had finished I wasn't to go near my wife, but I might send her bread and money by messenger.

III

45   Nine months passed before all the rabbis could come to an agreement. Letters went back and forth. I hadn't realized that there could be so much erudition[9] about a matter like this.

---

[1] to stick to one's guns: to insist one's position in the face of opposition
[2] bear down: here to show the intension of excreting
[3] soil: to make dirty
[4] brood: group of. Here it is used in a derogative way.
[5] abscess: 脓疮
[6] hallucination: a false perception, an illusion
[7] manikin: phantom, ghost
[8] quill: pen that is made of bird's feather
[9] erudition: having or showing extensive scholarship

46　　Meanwhile Elka gave birth to still another child, a girl this time. On the Sabbath I went to the synagogue and invoked a blessing on her. They called me up to the *Torah*[①], and I named the child for my mother-in-law—may she rest in peace. The louts[②] and loudmouths of the town who came into the bakery gave me a going over[③]. All Frampol[④] refreshed its spirits because of my trouble and grief. However, I resolved that I would always believe what I was told. What's the good of not believing? Today it's your wife you don't believe; tomorrow it's God Himself you won't take stock in.

47　　By an apprentice who was her neighbor I sent her daily a corn or a wheat loaf, or a piece of pastry, rolls or bagels, or, when I got the chance, a slab of pudding, a slice of honeycake, or wedding strudel[⑤]—whatever came my way. The apprentice was a goodhearted lad, and more than once he added something on his own. He had formerly annoyed me a lot, plucking my nose and digging me in the ribs, but when he started to be a visitor to my house he became kind of friendly. "Hey, you, Gimpel," he said to me, "you have a very decent little wife and two fine kids. You don't deserve them."

48　　"But the things people say about her," I said.

49　　"Well, they have long tongues," he said, "and nothing to do with them but babble. Ignore it as you ignore the cold of last winter."

50　　One day the rabbi sent for me and said, "Are you certain, Gimpel, that you were wrong about your wife?"

51　　I said, "I'm certain."

52　　"Why, but look here! You yourself saw it."

53　　"It must have been a shadow," I said.

54　　"The shadow of what?"

55　　"Just one of the beams, I think."

56　　"You can go home then. You owe thanks to the Yanover rabbi. He found an obscure reference in Maimonides[⑥] that favored you."

57　　I seized the rabbi's hand and kissed it.

58　　I wanted to run home immediately. It's no small thing to be separated for so long a time from wife and child. Then I reflected: I'd better go back to work now, and go home in the evening. I said nothing to anyone, although as far as my heart was concerned it was like one of the Holy Days. The women teased and twitted[⑦] me as they did every day, but my thought was: Go on, with your loose talk. The truth is out, like the oil upon the water. Maimonides says it's

---

① *Torah*: the Jewish holy book
② lout: rough young man
③ give me a going over: to remind me of the shame
④ Frampol: a town in Poland
⑤ strudel: a kind of cake made of light pastry with fruit inside
⑥ Maimonides: Jewish scholastic philosopher and rabbi, one of the manor theologians of Judaism
⑦ twit: to make funny of because of foolish behavior

right, and therefore it is right!

59   At night, when I had covered the dough to let it rise, I took my share of bread and a little sack of flour and started homeward. The moon was full and the stars were glistening, something to terrify the soul. I hurried onward, and before me darted a long shadow. It was winter, and a fresh snow had fallen. I had a mind to sing, but it was growing late and I didn't want to wake the householders. Then I felt like whistling, but I remembered that you don't whistle at night because it brings the demons out. So I was silent and walked as fast as I could.

60   Dogs in the Christian yards barked at me when I passed, but I thought: Bark your teeth out! What are you but mere dogs? Whereas I am a man, the husband of a fine wife, the father of promising children.

61   As I approached the house my heart started to pound as though it were the heart of a criminal. I felt no fear, but my heart went thump! thump! Well, no drawing back. I quietly lifted the latch and went in. Elka was asleep. I looked at the infant's cradle. The shutter was closed, but the moon forced its way through the cracks. I saw the newborn child's face and loved it as soon as I saw it immediately—each tiny bone.

62   Then I came nearer to the bed. And what did I see but the apprentice lying there beside Elka. The moon went out all at once. It was utterly black, and I trembled. My teeth chattered. The bread fell from my hands, and my wife waked and said, "Who is that, ah?"

63   I muttered, "It's me."

64   "Gimpel?" she asked. "How come you're here? I thought it was forbidden."

65   "The rabbi said," I answered and shook as with a fever.

66   "Listen to me, Gimpel," she said, "go out to the shed and see if the goat's all right. It seems she's been sick." I have forgotten to say that we had a goat. When I heard she was unwell I went into the yard. The nanny goat was a good little creature. I had a nearly human feeling for her.

67   With hesitant steps I went up to the shed and opened the door. The goat stood there on her four feet. I felt her everywhere, drew her by the horns, examined her udders[①], and found nothing wrong. She had probably eaten too much bark[②]. "Good night, little goat," I said. "Keep well." And the little beast answered with a "Maa" as though to thank me for the good will.

68   I went back. The apprentice had vanished. "Where," I asked, "is the lad?"

69   "What lad?" my wife answered.

70   "What do you mean?" I said. "The apprentice. You were sleeping with him."

71   "The things I have dreamed this night and the night before," she said, "may they come true and lay you low, body and soul! An evil spirit has taken root in you and dazzles your

---

① udders: baglike organ of a cow, female goat, etc., from which milk is produced
② bark: the strong utter cover of a tree

sight." She screamed out, "You hateful creature! You moon calf[1]! You spook[2]! You uncouth[3] man! Get out, or I'll scream all Frampol out of bed!"

72   Before I could move, her brother sprang out from behind the oven and struck me a blow on the back of the head. I thought he had broken my neck. I felt that something about me was deeply wrong, and I said, "Don't make a scandal. All that's needed now is that people should accuse me of raising spooks and dybbuks[4]." For that was what she had meant. "No one will touch bread of my baking."

73   In short, I somehow calmed her.

74   "Well," she said, "that's enough. Lie down, and be shattered by wheels."

75   Next morning I called the apprentice aside. "Listen here, brother!" I said. And so on and so forth. "What do you say?" He stared at me as though I had dropped from the roof or something.

76   "I swear," he said, "you'd better go to an herb doctor or some healer. I'm afraid you have a screw loose[5], but I'll hush it up[6] for you." And that's how the thing stood.

77   To make a long story short, I lived twenty years with my wife. She bore me six children, four daughters and two sons. All kinds of things happened, but I neither saw nor heard. I believed, and that's all. The rabbi recently said to me, "Belief in itself is beneficial. It is written that a good man lives by his faith."

78   Suddenly my wife took sick. It began with a trifle, a little growth upon the breast. But she evidently was not destined to live long; she had no years. I spent a fortune on her. I have forgotten to say that by this time I had a bakery of my own and in Frampol was considered to be something of a rich man. Daily the healer came, and every witch doctor in the neighborhood was brought. They decided to use leeches[7], and after that to try cupping[8]. They even called a doctor from Lublin, but it was too late. Before she died she called me to her bed and said, "Forgive me, Gimpel."

79   I said, "What is there to forgive? You have been a good and faithful wife."

80   "Woe, Gimpel!" she said. "It was ugly how I deceived you all these years. I want to go clean to my Maker, and so I have to tell you that the children are not yours."

81   If I had been clouted[9] on the head with a piece of wood it couldn' t have bewildered me more.

82   "Whose are they?" I asked. "I don't know," she said. 'There were a lot...but they're not yours." And as she spoke she tossed her head to the side, her eyes turned glassy, and it was all up with Elka. On her whitened lips there remained a smile.

---

① moon calf: a foolish person
② spook: (informal) ghost
③ uncouth: awkward or impolite in speech and behaviour
④ dybbuk: the soul of a sinner that has transmigrated into the body a living person
⑤ have a screw loose: something wrong with the brain
⑥ hush it up: to keep a secret of it
⑦ to use leeches: to use leeches to suck the blood as a method of medial treatment
⑧ cupping: the process of drawing blood from the body by scarification or the application of a cupping glass, as for relieving of internal congestion
⑨ clout: to knock

83　　I imagined that, dead as she was, she was saying, "I deceived Gimpel. That was the meaning of my brief life."

IV

84　　One night, when the period of mourning was done, as I lay dreaming on the flour sacks, there came the Spirit of Evil himself and said to me, "Gimpel, why do you sleep?"

85　　I said, "What should I be doing? Eating kreplach①?"

86　　"The whole world deceives you," he said, "and you ought to deceive the world in your turn."

87　　"How can I deceive the world?" I asked him.

88　　He answered, "You might accumulate a bucket of urine every day and at night pour it into the dough. Let the sages of Frampol eat filth."

89　　"What about the judgment in the world to come?" I said.

90　　"There is no world to come," he said. "They've sold you a bill of goods and talked you into believing you carried a cat in your belly. What nonsense!"

91　　"Well then," I said, "and is there a God?"

92　　He answered, "There is no God either."

93　　"What," I said, "is there, then?"

94　　"A thick mire②."

95　　He stood before my eyes with a goatish beard and horn, long-toothed, and with a tail. Hearing such words, I wanted to snatch him by the tail, but I tumbled for the flour sacks and nearly broke a rib. Then it happened that I had to answer the call of nature, and, passing, I saw the risen dough, which seemed to say to me, "Do it!" In brief, I let myself be persuaded.

96　　At dawn the apprentice came. We kneaded the bread, scattered caraway③ seeds on it, and set it to bake. Then the apprentice went away, and I was left sitting in the little trench by the oven, on a pile of rags. Well, Gimpel, I thought, you've revenged yourself on them for all the shame they've put on you. Outside the frost glittered, but it was warm beside the oven. The flames heated my face. I bent my head and fell into a doze.

97　　I saw in a dream, at once, Elka in her shroud. She called to me, "What have you done, Gimpel?"

98　　I said to her, "It's all your fault," and started to cry.

99　　"You fool!" she said. "You fool! Because I was false is everything false too? I never deceived anyone but myself. I'm paying for it all, Gimpel. They spare you nothing here."

100　　I looked at her face. It was black; I was startled and waked, and remained sitting dumb. I sensed that everything hung in the balance. A false step now and I'd lose Eternal Life. But God

---

① kreplach: small filled dough casings usu. served in soup
② thick mire: deep mud
③ caraway: 香旱芹

gave me His help. I seized the long shovel and took out the loaves, carried them into the yard, and started to dig a hole in the frozen earth.

101   My apprentice came back as I was doing it. "What are you doing, boss?" he said, and grew pale as a corpse.

102   "I know what I'm doing," I said, and I buried it all before his very eyes. Then I went home, took my hoard[①] from its hiding place, and divided it among the children. "I saw your mother tonight," I said. "She's turning black, poor thing."

103   They were so astounded they couldn't speak a word.

104   "Be well," I said, "and forget that such a one as Gimpel ever existed." I put on my short coat, a pair of boots, took the bag that held my prayer shawl in one hand, my stock in the other, and kissed the mezuzah[②]. When people saw me in the street they were greatly surprised.

105   "Where are you going?" they said.

106   I answered, "Into the world." And so I departed from Frampol. I wandered over the land, and good people did not neglect me. After many years I became old and white; I heard a great deal, many lies and falsehoods, but the longer I lived the more I understood that there were really no lies. Whatever doesn't really happen is dreamed at night. It happens to one if it doesn't happen to another, tomorrow if not today, or a century hence if not next year. What difference can it make? Often I heard tales of which I said, "Now this is a thing that cannot happen." But before a year had elapsed I heard that it actually had come to pass somewhere.

107   Going from place to place, eating at strange tables, it often happens that I spin yarns—improbable things that could never have happened—about devils, magicians, windmills, and the like. The children run after me, calling, "Grandfather, tell us a story." Sometimes they ask for particular stories, and I try to please them. A fat young boy once said to me, "Grandfather, it's the same story you told us before." The little rogue, he was right.

108   So it is with dreams too. It is many years since I left Frampol, but as soon as I shut my eyes I am there again. And whom do you think I see? Elka. She is standing by the washtub, as at our first encounter, but her face is shining and her eyes are as radiant as the eyes of a saint, and she speaks outlandish[③] words to me, strange things. When I wake I have forgotten it all. But while the dream lasts I am comforted. She answers all my queries, and what comes out is that all is right. I weep and implore, "Let me be with you." And she consoles me and tells me to be patient. The time is nearer than it is far. Sometimes she strokes and kisses me and weeps upon my face. When I awaken I feel her lips and taste the salt of her tears.

109   No doubt the world is entirely an imaginary world, but it is only once removed from the true world. At the door of the hovel[④] where I lie, there stands the plank on which the dead are taken away. The gravedigger Jew has his spade ready. The grave waits and the worms

---

① hoard: a store (esp.) of something valuable to the owner
② mezuzah: a piece of parchment inscribed on one side with the biblical passages and on the other with name of God, enclosed in a case and attached to a doorpost to ward off evil
③ outlandish: strange
④ hovel: a small dirty place where people live

are hungry; the shrouds are prepared—I carry them in my beggar's sack. Another shnorrer[1] is waiting to inherit my bed of straw. When the time comes I will go joyfully. Whatever may be there, it will be real, without complication[2], without ridicule, without deception. God be praised: there even Gimpel cannot be deceived.

▶ STUDY QUESTIONS

A〉 *Recalling*

1. Please describe the occasions when Gimpel was fooled. Who fooled him on each occasion?
2. How did Gimpel account for his being fooled on each occasion?
3. What idea came to Gimpel's head after he heard the confessions of his wife?
4. What has become of him in the end?

B〉 *Interpreting*

5. What virtues of Gimpel are revealed on each occasion of his being fooled or deceived?
6. What did the fooling stories say about people?
7. What role does religion play in the story?
8. What is the significance of first-person narration in the story?
9. What is your opinion of Gimpel? Have you found people like him around you?

C〉 *Extending*

10. What does the story say about truth? Who is closer to truth?

***The Gleaners* [*Des glaneuses*]**
Jean-François Millet, 1857.
Musée d'Orsay, Paris.

---

① shnorrer: a shameless beggar
② complication: something that complicates

V. *To Hell with Dying* by Alice Walker

▶ ABOUT THE AUTHOR

Alice Malsenior Walker (born on February 9, 1944) is an American author, poet, womanist, and activist. She is best known for the critically acclaimed novel *The Color Purple* (1982) for which she won the National Book Award and the Pulitzer Prize.

To Hell with Dying

1   "To hell with dying," my father would say. "These children want Mr. Sweet!"

2   Mr. Sweet was a diabetic① and an alcoholic and a guitar player and lived down the road from us on a neglected cotton farm. My older brothers and sisters got the most benefit from Mr. Sweet, for when they were growing up he had quite a few years ahead of him and so was capable of being called back from the brink of death any number of times—whenever the voice of my father reached him as he lay expiring. "To hell with dying, man," my father would say, pushing the wife away from the bedside (in tears although she knew the death was not necessarily the last one unless Mr. Sweet really wanted it to be) "These children want Mr. Sweet!" And they did want him, for at a signal from Father they would come crowding around the bed and throw themselves on the covers, and whoever was the smallest at the time would kiss him all over his wrinkled brown face and tickle him so that he would laugh all down in his stomach, and his mustache, which was long and sort of straggly②, would shake like Spanish moss and was also that color.

3   Mr. Sweet had been ambitious as a boy, wanted to be a doctor or lawyer or sailor, only to find that black men fare better if they are not. Since he could become none of these things he turned to fishing as his only earnest career and playing the guitar as his only claim to doing anything extraordinarily well. His son, the only one that he and his wife, Miss Mary, had, was shiftless③ as the day is long and spent money as if he were trying to see the bottom of the mint④, which Mr. Sweet would tell him was the clean brown palm of his hand. Miss Mary loved her "baby," however, and worked hard to get him the "li'l necessaries" of life, which turned out mostly to be women.

4   Mr. Sweet was a tall, thinnish man with thick kinky⑤ hair going dead white. He was dark brown, his eyes were squinty⑥ and sort of bluish, and he chewed Brown Mule tobacco. He was constantly on the verge of being blind drunk, for he brewed his own liquor and was not in the least a stingy⑦ sort of man, and was always very melancholy and sad, though frequently when

---

① diabetic: 糖尿病的
② straggly: messy
③ shiftless: lazy and lacking the desire to succeed
④ mint: a place coins officially made by the government
⑤ kinky: twisting
⑥ squinty: 斜视
⑦ stingy: reluctant to give, not generous

he was "feelin' good" he'd dance around the yard with us, usually keeling over[①] just as my mother came to see what the commotion was.

5   Toward all of us children he was very kind, and had the grace to be shy with us, which is unusual in grown-ups. He had great respect for my mother for she never held his drunkenness against him and would let us play with him even when he was about to fall in the fireplace from drink. Although Mr. Sweet would sometimes lose complete or nearly complete control of his head and neck so that he would loll[②] in his chair, his mind remained strangely acute and his speech not too affected. His ability to be drunk and sober at the same time made him an ideal playmate, for he was as weak as we were and we could usually best him in wrestling, all the while keeping a fairly coherent conversation going.

6   We never felt anything of Mr. Sweet's age when we played with him. We loved his wrinkles and would draw some on our brows to be like him, and his white hair was my special treasure and he knew it and would never come to visit us just after he had had his hair cut off at the barbershop. Once he came to our house for something, probably to see my father about fertilizer for his crops because, although he never paid the slightest attention to his crops, he liked to know what things would be best to use on them if he ever did. Anyhow, he had not come with his hair since he had just had it shaved off at the barbershop. He wore a huge straw hat to keep off the sun and also to keep his head away from me. But as soon as I saw him I ran up and demanded that he take me up and kiss me with his funny beard which smelled so strongly of tobacco. Looking forward to burying my small fingers into woolly hair I threw away his hat only to find he had done something to his hair, that it was no longer there! I let out a squall[③] which made my mother think that Mr. Sweet had finally dropped me in the well or something and from that day I've been wary of men in hats. However, not long after, Mr. Sweet showed up with his hair grown out and just as white and kinky and impenetrable as it ever was.

7   Mr. Sweet used to call me his princess, and I believed it. He made me feel pretty at five and six, and simply outrageously devastating[④] at the blazing age of eight and a half. When he came to our house with his guitar the whole family would stop whatever they were doing to sit around him and listen to him play. He liked to play "Sweet Georgia Brown", and all sorts of sweet, sad, wonderful songs which he sometimes made up. It was from one of these songs that I heard that he had had to marry Miss Mary when he had in fact loved somebody else (now living in Chicago, or De-story, Michigan). He was not sure that Joe Lee, her "baby", was also his baby. Sometimes he would cry and that was an indication that he was about to die again. And so we would all get prepared, for we were sure to be called upon.

8   I was seven the first time I remember actually participating in one of Mr. Sweet's "revivals"—my parents told me I had participated before, I had been the one chosen to kiss him and tickle him long before I knew the rite of Mr. Sweet's rehabilitation[⑤]. He had come to our house, it was a few years after his wife's death and he was very sad, and also, typically, very

---

① keel over: to fall over sideways
② loll: to be in a lazy loose position
③ squall: screaming
④ devastating: destroying
⑤ rehabilitation: here means revival.

drunk. He sat on the floor next to me and my older brother, the rest of the children were grown up and lived elsewhere, and he began to play his guitar and cry. I held his woolly head in my arms and wished I could have been old enough to have been the woman he loved so much and that I had not been lost years and years ago.

9   When he was leaving, my mother said to us that we'd better sleep light that night for we'd probably have to go over to Mr. Sweet's before daylight. And we did. For soon after we had gone to bed one of the neighbors knocked on our door and called my father and said that Mr. Sweet was sinking fast and if he wanted to get in a word before the crossover he'd better shake a leg and get over to Mr. Sweet's house. All the neighbors knew to come to our house if something was wrong with Mr. Sweet, but they did not know how we always managed to make him well, or at least stop him from dying, when he was so often near death. As soon as we heard the cry we got up, my brother and I and my mother and father, and put on our clothes. We hurried out of the house and down the road for we were always afraid that we might someday be too late, and Mr. Sweet would get tired of dallying①.

10   When we got to the house, a very poor shack② really, we found the front room full of neighbors and relatives and someone met us at the door and said it was all very sad that old Mr. Sweet Little (for Little was his family name, although we mostly ignored it) was about to kick the bucket. My parents were advised not to take my brother and me into the "death room", seeing we were so young and all, but we were so much more accustomed to the death room than he that we ignored him and dashed in without giving his warning a second thought. I was almost in tears, for these deaths upset me fearfully, and the thought of how much depended on me and my brother (who was such a ham③ most of the time) made me very nervous.

11   The doctor was bending over the bed and turned back to tell us for at least the tenth time in the history of my family, that, alas, old Mr. Sweet Little was dying and that children had best not see the face of implacable④ death (I didn't know what "implacable" was, but whatever it was, Mr. Sweet was not!). My father pushed his rather abruptly out of the way saying, as he always did and very loudly for he was saying it to Mr. Sweet, "To hell with dying, man, these children want Mr. Sweet"—which was my cue to throw myself upon the bed and kiss Mr. Sweet all around the whiskers and under the eyes and around the collar of his nightshirt where he smelled so strongly of all sorts of things, mostly liniment⑤.

12   I was very good at bringing him around, for as soon as I saw that he was struggling to open his eyes I knew he was going to be all right, and so could finish my revival sure of success. As soon as his eyes were open he would begin to smile and that way I knew that I had surely won. Once, though, I got a tremendous scare, for he could not open his eyes and later I learned that he had had a stroke and that one side of his face was stiff and hard to get into motion. When he began to smile I could tickle him in earnest because I was sure that nothing would get in the way of his laughter, although once he began to cough so hard that he almost threw me off his

---

① dally: to be slow
② shack: a small roughly built house or hut
③ ham: an actor who overacts
④ implacable: impossible to change
⑤ liniment: 擦剂，药膏

stomach, but that was when I was very small, little more than a baby, and my bushy hair had gotten in his nose.

13   When we were sure he would listen to us we would ask him why he was in bed and when he was coming to see us again and could we play his guitar, which more than likely would be leaning against the bed. His eyes would get all misty and he would sometimes cry out loud, but we never let it embarrass us, for he knew that we loved him and that we sometimes cried too for no reason. My parent would leave the room to just the three of us; Mr. Sweet, by that time, would be propped up in bed with a number of pillows behind his head and with me sitting and lying on his shoulder and along his chest. Even when he had trouble breathing he would not ask me to get down. Looking into my eyes he would shake his white head and runs scratchy old finger all around my hairline, which was rather low down, nearly to my brows, and made some people say I looked like a baby monkey.

14   My brother was very generous in all this, he let me do all the revivaling—he had done it for years before I was born and so was glad to be able to pass it on to someone new. What he would do while I talked to Mr. Sweet was pretend to play the guitar, in fact pretend that he was a young version of Mr. Sweet, and it always made Mr. Sweet glad to think that someone wanted to be like him—of course, we did not know this then, we played the thing by ear, and whatever he seemed to like we did. We were desperately afraid that he was just gong to take off one day and leave us.

15   It did not occur to us that we were doing anything special; we had not learned that death was final when it did come. We thought nothing of triumphing over it so many times, and in fact became a trifle contemptuous of people who let themselves be carried away. It did not occur to us that if our father had been dying we could not have stopped it, that Mr. Sweet was the only person over whom we had power.

16   When Mr. Sweet was in his eighties I was studying in the university many miles from home. I saw him whenever I went home, but he was never on the verge of dying that I could tell and I began to feel that my anxiety for his health and psychological well-being was unnecessary. By this time he not only had a mustache but a long flowing snow-white beard, which I loved and combed and braided for hours. He was very peaceful, fragile, gentle, and the only jarring[①] note about him was his old steel guitar, which he still played in the old sad, sweet, down-home blues way.

17   On Mr. Sweets nineteth birthday I was finishing my doctorate in Massachusetts and had been making arrangements to go home for several weeks' rest. That morning I got a telegram telling me that Mr. Sweet was dying again and could I please drop everything and come home. Of course I could. My dissertation could wait and my teachers would understand when I explained to them when I got back I ran to the phone, called the airport, and within hours I was speeding along the dusty road to Mr. Sweet's. The house was more dilapidated than when I was last there, barely a shack, but it was overgrown with yellow roses, which my family had planted many years ago. The air was heavy and sweet and very peaceful. I felt strange walking through

---

① jarring: having a harshly unpleasant, perturbing effect on one's nerves, feelings, thoughts, etc.

the gate and up the old rickety[①] steps. But the strangeness left me as I caught sight of the long white beard I loved so well flowing down the thin body over the familiar quilt coverlet. Mr. Sweet!

18   His eyes were closed tight and his hands, crossed over his stomach, were thin and delicate, no longer scratchy. I remembered how always before I had run and jumped up on him just anywhere; now I knew he would not be able to support my weight. I looked around at my parents, and was surprised to see that my father and mother also looked old and frail. My father, his own hair very gray, leaned over the quietly sleeping old man, who, incidentally, smelled still of wine and tobacco, and said, as he'd done so many times, "To hell with dying, man! My daughter is home to see Mr. Sweet!" My brother had not been able to come as he was in the war is Asia. I bent down and gently stroked the closed eyes and gradually they began to open. The closed, wine-stained lips twitched[②] a little, then parted in a warm, slightly embarrassed smile. Mr. Sweet could see me and he recognized me and his eyes looked very spry and twinkly for a moment. I put my head down on the pillow next to his and we just looked at each other for a long time. Then he began to trace my peculiar hair line with a thin, smooth finger. I closed my eyes when his finger halted above my ear (he used to rejoice at the dirt in my ears when I was little), his hand stayed cupped around my cheek. When I opened my eyes, sure that I had reached him in time, his were closed.

19   Even at twenty-four how could I believe that I had failed? That Mr. Sweet was really gone? He had never gone before. But when I looked at my parents I saw that they were holding back tears. They had loved him dearly. He was like a piece of rare and delicate china which was always being saved from breaking and which finally fell. I looked long at the old face, the wrinkled forehead, the red lips, the hands that still reached out to me. Soon I felt my father pushing something cool into my hands. It was Mr. Sweet's guitar. He had asked them months before to give it to me; he had known that even if I came next time he would not be able to respond in the old way. He did not want me to feel that my trip had been for nothing.

20   The old guitar! I plucked the strings, hummed "Sweet Georgia Brown". The magic of Mr. Sweet lingered still in the cold steel box. Through the window I could catch the fragrant delicate scent of tender yellow roses. The man on the high old-fashioned bed with the quilt coverlet and the flowing white beard had been my first love.

STUDY QUESTIONS

A *Recalling*

1. Please describe the appearance of Mr. Sweet.
2. Please describe his personality.
3. What is the relationship like between Mr. Sweet and the children?
4. What is he sad about sometimes?
5. How do the children revive him?

---

① rickety: likely to fall or collapse, shaky
② twitch: to make a quick short sudden movement, usu. without conscious control

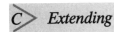

B　Interpreting

6. What makes Mr. Sweet a perfect playmate?

7. What do you know about the parents? And the neighbors?

8. What actually revives Mr. Sweet each time?

C　Extending

9. What is the essential thing in your life? Give your reasons.

VI. *Allegory of the Cave* by Plato

▶▶ ABOUT THE AUTHOR

Plato (Greek: *Πλάτων, Plátōn*, "broad"; 428/427 BC–348/347 BC) was a philosopher in Classical Greece. He was also a mathematician, student of Socrates, writer of philosophical dialogues, and founder of the Academy in Athens, the first institution of higher learning in the Western world. Along with his mentor, Socrates, and his student, Aristotle, Plato helped to lay the foundations of Western philosophy and science. In the words of A. N. Whitehead:

"The safest general characterization of the European philosophical tradition is that it consists of a series of footnotes to Plato. I do not mean the systematic scheme of thought which scholars have doubtfully extracted from his writings. I allude to the wealth of general ideas scattered through them."

▶▶ ABOUT *ALLEGORY OF THE CAVE*

The *Allegory of the Cave* can be found in Book VII of Plato's best-known work, *The Republic*, a lengthy dialogue on the nature of justice. Often regarded as a utopian blueprint, *The Republic* is dedicated toward a discussion of the education required of a Philosopher-King.

Unlike his mentor Socrates, Plato was both a writer and teacher. His writings are in the form of dialogues, with Socrates as the principal speaker. In the *Allegory of the Cave*, Plato described symbolically the predicament in which mankind finds itself and proposes a way of salvation. The *Allegory* presents, in brief form, most of Plato's major philosophical assumptions: his belief that the world revealed by our senses is not the real world but only a poor copy of it, and that the real world can only be apprehended intellectually; his idea that knowledge cannot be transferred from teacher to student, but rather that education consists in directing student's minds toward what is real and important and allowing them to apprehend it for themselves; his faith that the universe ultimately is good; his conviction that enlightened individuals have an obligation to the rest of society, and that a good society must be one in which the truly wise (the Philosopher-King) are the rulers.

The following selection is taken from the Benjamin Jowett translation (Vintage, 1991), from page 253 to 261.

Allegory of the Cave

1　　[Socrates] And now, I said, let me show in a figure how far our nature is enlightened or unenlightened: —Behold! Human beings living in a underground cave, which has a mouth open towards the light and reaching all along the cave; here they have been from their childhood, and have their legs and necks chained so that they cannot move, and can only see before them, being prevented by the chains from turning round their heads. Above and behind them a fire is blazing at a distance, and between the fire and the prisoners there is a raised way; and you will see, if you look, a low wall built along the way, like the screen which marionette① players have in front of them, over which they show the puppets.

2　　[Glaucon] I see.

3　　[Socrates] And do you see, I said, men passing along the wall carrying all sorts of vessels, and statues and figures of animals made of wood and stone and various materials, which appear over the wall? Some of them are talking, others silent.

4　　[Glaucon] You have shown me a strange image, and they are strange prisoners.

5　　[Socrates] Like ourselves, I replied; and they see only their own shadows, or the shadows of one another, which the fire throws on the opposite wall of the cave?

6　　[Glaucon] True, he said; how could they see anything but the shadows if they were never allowed to move their heads?

7　　[Socrates] And of the objects which are being carried in like manner they would only see the shadows?

8　　[Glaucon] Yes, he said.

9　　[Socrates] And if they were able to converse with one another, would they not suppose that they were naming what was actually before them?

10　　[Glaucon] Very true.

11　　[Socrates] And suppose further that the prison had an echo which came from the other side, would they not be sure to fancy when one of the passers-by spoke that the voice which they heard came from the passing shadow?

12　　[Glaucon] No question, he replied.

13　　[Socrates] To them, I said, the truth would be literally nothing but the shadows of the images.

14　　[Glaucon] That is certain.

15　　[Socrates] And now look again, and see what will naturally follow if the prisoners are released and disabused of their error. At first, when any of them is liberated and compelled suddenly to stand up and turn his neck round and walk and look towards the light, he will suffer sharp pains; the glare will distress him, and he will be unable to see the realities of which in his former state he had seen the shadows; and then conceive some one saying to him, that what he saw before was an illusion, but that now, when he is approaching nearer to being and his eye is turned towards more real existence, he has a clearer vision, —what will be his reply? And you may further imagine that his instructor is pointing to the objects as they pass and requiring him to name them, —will he not be perplexed? Will he not fancy that the shadows which he formerly saw are truer than the objects which are now shown to him?

---

① marionette: puppet

16   **[Glaucon]** Far truer.

17   **[Socrates]** And if he is compelled to look straight at the light, will he not have a pain in his eyes which will make him turn away to take and take in the objects of vision which he can see, and which he will conceive to be in reality clearer than the things which are now being shown to him?

18   **[Glaucon]** True, he now.

19   **[Socrates]** And suppose once more, that he is reluctantly dragged up a steep and rugged ascent, and held fast until he's forced into the presence of the sun himself, is he not likely to be pained and irritated? When he approaches the light his eyes will be dazzled, and he will not be able to see anything at all of what are now called realities.

20   **[Glaucon]** Not all in a moment, he said.

21   **[Socrates]** He will require to grow accustomed to the sight of the upper world. And first he will see the shadows best, next the reflections of men and other objects in the water, and then the objects themselves; then he will gaze upon the light of the moon and the stars and the spangled① heaven; and he will see the sky and the stars by night better than the sun or the light of the sun by day?

22   **[Glaucon]** Certainly.

23   **[Socrates]** Last of all he will be able to see the sun, and not mere reflections of him in the water, but he will see him in his own proper place, and not in another; and he will contemplate him as he is.

24   **[Glaucon]** Certainly.

25   **[Socrates]** He will then proceed to argue that this is he who gives the season and the years, and is the guardian of all that is in the visible world, and in a certain way the cause of all things which he and his fellows have been accustomed to behold?

26   **[Glaucon]** Clearly, he said, he would first see the sun and then reason about him.

27   **[Socrates]** And when he remembered his old habitation, and the wisdom of the cave and his fellow-prisoners, do you not suppose that he would felicitate② himself on the change, and pity them?

28   **[Glaucon]** Certainly, he would.

29   **[Socrates]** And if they were in the habit of conferring honors among themselves on those who were quickest to observe the passing shadows and to remark which of them went before, and which followed after, and which were together; and who were therefore best able to draw conclusions as to the future, do you think that he would care for such honors and glories, or envy the possessors of them? Would he not say with Homer, *Better to be the poor servant of a poor master*, and to endure anything, rather than think as they do and live after their manner?

30   **[Glaucon]** Yes, I think that he would rather suffer anything than entertain these false notions and live in this miserable manner.

31   **[Socrates]** Imagine once more, I said, such a one coming suddenly out of the sun to be replaced in his old situation; would he not be certain to have his eyes full of darkness?

32   **[Glaucon]** To be sure.

33   **[Socrates]** And if there were a contest, and he had to compete in measuring the shadows

---

① spangled: decorated with shining objects
② felicitate: to congratulate

with the prisoners who had never moved out of the cave, while his sight was still weak, and before his eyes had become steady (and the time which would be needed to acquire this new habit of sight might be very considerable) would he not be ridiculous? Men would say of him that up he went and down he came without his eyes; and that it was better not even to think of ascending; and if any one tried to loose another and lead him up to the light, let them only catch the offender, and they would put him to death.

34　　**[Glaucon]** No question.

35　　**[Socrates]** This entire allegory, I said, you may now append, dear Glaucon, to the previous argument; the prison-house is the world of sight, the light of the fire is the sun, and you will not misapprehend me if you interpret the journey upwards to be the ascent of the soul into the intellectual world according to my poor belief, which, at your desire, I have expressed whether rightly or wrongly God knows. But, whether true or false, my opinion is that in the world of knowledge the idea of good appears last of all, and is seen only with an effort; and, when seen, is also inferred to be the universal author of all things beautiful and right, parent of light and of the lord of light in this visible world, and the immediate source of reason and truth in the intellectual; and that this is the power upon which he who would act rationally, either in public or private life must have his eye fixed.

36　　**[Glaucon]** I agree, as far as I am able to understand you.

37　　**[Socrates]** Moreover, I said, you must not wonder that those who attain to this beatific[①] vision are unwilling to descend to human affairs; for their souls are ever hastening into the upper world where they desire to dwell; which desire of theirs is very natural, if our allegory may be trusted.

38　　**[Glaucon]** Yes, very natural.

39　　**[Socrates]** And is there anything surprising in one who passes from divine contemplations to the evil state of man, misbehaving himself in a ridiculous manner; if, while his eyes are blinking and before he has become accustomed to the surrounding darkness, he is compelled to fight in courts of law, or in other places, about the images or the shadows of images of justice, and is endeavoring to meet the conceptions of those who have never yet seen absolute justice?

40　　**[Glaucon]** Anything but surprising.

41　　**[Socrates]** Any one who has common sense will remember that the bewilderments of the eyes are of two kinds, and arise from two causes, either from coming out of the light or from going into the light, which is true of the mind's eye, quite as much as of the bodily eye; and he who remembers this when he sees any one whose vision is perplexed and weak, will not be too ready to laugh; he will first ask whether that soul of man has come out of the brighter light, and is unable to see because unaccustomed to the dark, or having turned from darkness to the day is dazzled by excess of light. And he will count the one happy in his condition and state of being, and he will pity the other; or, if he have a mind to laugh at the soul which comes from below into the light, there will be more reason in this than in the laugh which greets him who returns from above out of the light into the cave.

42　　**[Glaucon]** That is a very just distinction.

43　　**[Socrates]** But then, if I am right, certain professors of education must be wrong when they

---

① beatific: blissful, saintly

say that they can put a knowledge into the soul which was not there before, like sight into blind eyes.

44　　　　[Glaucon] They undoubtedly say this.

45　　　　[Socrates] Whereas, our argument shows that the power and capacity of learning exists in the soul already; and that just as the eye was unable to turn from darkness to light without the whole body, so too the instrument of knowledge can only by the movement of the whole soul be turned from the world of becoming into that of being, and learn by degrees to endure the sight of being, and of the brightest and best of being, or in other words, of the good.

46　　　　[Glaucon] Very true.

47　　　　[Socrates] And must there not be some art which will effect conversion in the easiest and quickest manner; not implanting the faculty of sight, for that exists already, but has been turned in the wrong direction, and is looking away from the truth?

48　　　　[Glaucon] Yes, such an art may be presumed.

49　　　　[Socrates] And whereas the other so-called virtues of the soul seem to be akin to bodily qualities, for even when they are not originally innate they can be implanted later by habit and exercise, the virtue of wisdom more than anything else contains a divine element which always remains, and by this conversion is rendered useful and profitable; or, on the other hand, hurtful and useless. Did you never observe the narrow intelligence flashing from the keen eye of a clever rogue —how eager he is, how clearly his paltry[1] soul sees the way to his end; he is the reverse of blind, but his keen eyesight is forced into the service of evil, and he is mischievous in proportion to his cleverness.

50　　　　[Glaucon] Very true.

51　　　　[Socrates] But what if there had been a circumcision[2] of such natures in the days of their youth; and they had been severed from those sensual pleasures, such as eating and drinking, which, like leaden weights, were attached to them at their birth, and which drag them down and turn the vision of their souls upon the things that are below—if, I say, they had been released from these impediments and turned in the opposite direction, the very same faculty in them would have seen the truth as keenly as they see what their eyes are turned to now.

52　　　　[Glaucon] Very likely.

53　　　　[Socrates] Yes, I said; and there is another thing which is likely or rather a necessary inference from what has preceded, that neither the uneducated and uninformed of the truth, nor yet those who never make an end of their education, will be able ministers of State; not the former, because they have no single aim of duty which is the rule of all their actions, private as well as public; nor the latter, because they will not act at all except upon compulsion, fancying that they are already dwelling apart in the islands of the blest.

54　　　　[Glaucon] Very true.

55　　　　[Socrates] Then, I said, the business of us who are the founders of the State will be to compel the best minds to attain that knowledge which we have already shown to be the greatest of all—they must continue to ascend until they arrive at the good; but when they have ascended and seen enough we must not allow them to do as they do now.

56　　　　[Glaucon] What do you mean?

① paltry: mean or contemptible
② circumcision: spiritual purification

57 ·   **[Socrates]** I mean that they remain in the upper world: but this must not be allowed; they must be made to descend again among the prisoners in the cave, and partake of their labors and honors, whether they are worth having or not.

58   **[Glaucon]** But is not this unjust? Ought we to give them a worse life, when they might have a better?

59   **[Socrates]** You have again forgotten, my friend, I said, the intention of the legislator, who did not aim at making any one class in the State happy above the rest; the happiness was to be in the whole State, and he held the citizens together by persuasion and necessity, making them benefactors of the State, and therefore benefactors of one another; to this end he created them, not to please themselves, but to be his instruments in binding up the State.

60   **[Glaucon]** True, I had forgotten.

61   **[Socrates]** Observe, Glaucon, that there will be no injustice in compelling our philosophers to have a care and providence of others; we shall explain to them that in other States, men of their class are not obliged to share in the toils of politics: and this is reasonable, for they grow up at their own sweet will, and the government would rather not have them. Being self-taught, they cannot be expected to show any gratitude for a culture which they have never received. But we have brought you into the world to be rulers of the hive, kings of yourselves and of the other citizens, and have educated you far better and more perfectly than they have been educated, and you are better able to share in the double duty. Wherefore each of you, when his turn comes, must go down to the general underground abode, and get the habit of seeing in the dark. When you have acquired the habit, you will see ten thousand times better than the inhabitants of the cave, and you will know what the several images are, and what they represent, because you have seen the beautiful and just and good in their truth. And thus our State which is also yours will be a reality, and not a dream only, and will be administered in a spirit unlike that of other States, in which men fight with one another about shadows only and are distracted in the struggle for power, which in their eyes is a great good. Whereas the truth is that the State in which the rulers are most reluctant to govern is always the best and most quietly governed, and the State in which they are most eager, the worst.

62   **[Glaucon]** Quite true.

63   **[Socrates]** And will our pupils, when they hear this, refuse to take their turn at the toils of State, when they are allowed to spend the greater part of their time with one another in the heavenly light?

64   **[Glaucon]** Impossible, for they are just men, and the commands which we impose upon them are just; there can be no doubt that every one of them will take office as a stern necessity, and not after the fashion of our present rulers of State.

65   **[Socrates]** Yes, my friend, I said; and there lies the point. You must contrive for your future rulers another and a better life than that of a ruler, and then you may have a well-ordered State; for only in the State which offers this, will they rule who are truly rich, not in silver and gold, but in virtue and wisdom, which are the true blessings of life. Whereas if they go to the administration of public affairs, poor and hungering after their own private advantage, thinking that hence they are to snatch the chief good, order there can never be; for they will be fighting about office, and the civil and domestic broils[①] which thus arise will be the ruin of the rulers

---

① broil: quarrel

themselves and of the whole State.

66   **[Glaucon]** Most true.

67   **[Socrates]** And the only life which looks down upon the life of political ambition is that of true philosophy. Do you know of any other?

68   **[Glaucon]** Indeed, I do not.

69   **[Socrates]** And those who govern ought not to be lovers of the task. For, if they are, there will be rival lovers, and they will fight.

70   **[Glaucon]** No question.

71   **[Socrates]** Who then are those whom we shall compel to be guardians? Surely they will be the men who are wisest about affairs of State, and by whom the State is best administered, and who at the same time have other honors and another and a better life than that of politics?

72   **[Glaucon]** They are the men, and I will choose them.

73   **[Socrates]** And now shall we consider in what way such guardians will be produced, and how they are to be brought from darkness to light, —as some are said to have ascended from the world below to the gods?

74   **[Glaucon]** By all means.

75   **[Socrates]** The process, I said, is not the turning over of an oyster-shell, but the turning round of a soul passing from a day which is little better than night to the true day of being, that is, the ascent from below, which we affirm to be true philosophy?

76   **[Glaucon]** Quite so.

▶ STUDY QUESTIONS

A > *Recalling*

1. What is the source of light in the cave?

2. What the persons and objects people in the cave see really are?

3. What are people in the cave compared to?

4. What will happen to the person who manages to go up the cave? What will happen to him when he comes down to the cave again?

5. According to Socrates, what are the two causes for the blinding of the eyes? Which one is welcomed?

6. According to Socrates, what is the brightest and best of the being?

7. What is the responsibility of philosophers?

8. How should the rulers treat their duty?

9. What is the correct process of education according to Socrates?

B > *Interpreting*

10. Why can't people in the cave see true light?

11. How will the person who sees the true light and the people in the cave look at each other? Why?

12. Why shouldn't we put knowledge into a person's head?

13. Why shouldn't the philosopher rulers love their task too much? What are the other honors and better life for them?

C▷ *Extending*

14. Compare Socrates' idea of knowledge with the Buddhist idea.
15. Compare Socrates' idea of kings with Confucian idea of kings.
16. Are you still in the cave? Please name persons who have seen the true light.

VII. *How Much Land Does a Man Need* by Leo Tolstoy

▶▶ ABOUT THE AUTHOR

Leo Tolstoy (1828–1910), was a Russian writer who primarily wrote novels and short stories. Tolstoy was a master of realistic fiction and is widely considered one of the world's greatest novelists. He is best known for two long novels, *War and Peace* (1869) and *Anna Karenina* (1877). Later in life, he also wrote plays and essays. Tolstoy is equally known for his complicated and paradoxical persona and for his extreme moralistic and ascetic views, which he adopted after a moral crisis and spiritual awakening in the 1870s, after which he also became noted as a moral thinker and social reformer. His literal interpretation of the ethical teachings of Jesus, centering on the Sermon on the Mount, caused him in later life to become a fervent Christian anarchist and anarcho-pacifist. His ideas on nonviolent resistance, expressed in such works as *The Kingdom of God Is Within You*, were to have a profound impact on such pivotal twentieth-century figures as Mohandas Gandhi and Martin Luther King, Jr.

How Much Land Does a Man Need

Translated by Ronald Wilks

I

1   An elder sister came to visit her younger sister in the country. The elder was married to a tradesman in town, the younger to a peasant in the village. As the sisters sat over their tea talking, the elder began to boast of the advantages of town life: saying how comfortably they lived there, how well they dressed, what fine clothes her children wore, what good things they ate and drank, and how she went to the theatre, promenades①, and entertainments.

2   The younger sister was piqued②, and in turn disparaged③ the life of a tradesman, and stood up for that of a peasant.

3   "I would not change my way of life for yours," said she. "We may live roughly, but at least we are free from anxiety. You live in better style than we do, but though you often earn more than you need, you are very likely to lose all you have. You know the proverb,'Loss and gain are brothers twain.' It often happens that people who are wealthy one day are begging their bread the next. Our way is safer. Though a peasant's life is not a fat one, it is a long one. We shall never grow rich, but we shall always have enough to eat."

---

① promenade: a formal dance
② pique: to affect with sharp resentment or irritation
③ disparage: to speak lightly, to belittle

4   The elder sister said sneeringly:

5   "Enough? Yes, if you like to share with the pigs and the calves! What do you know of elegance or manners! However much your good man may slave, you will die as you are living on a dung—heap① —and your children the same."

6   "Well, what of that?" replied the younger. "Of course our work is rough and coarse. But, on the other hand, it is sure; and we need not bow to any one. But you, in your towns, are surrounded by temptations; today all may be right, but tomorrow the Evil One may tempt your husband with cards, wine, or women, and all will go to ruin. Don't such things happen often enough?"

7   Pahom, the master of the house, was lying on the top of the oven, and he listened to the women's chatter.

8   "It is perfectly true," thought he. "Busy as we are from childhood tilling② Mother Earth, we peasants have no time to let any nonsense settle in our heads. Our only trouble is that we haven't land enough. If I had plenty of land, I shouldn't fear the Devil himself!"

9   The women finished their tea, chatted a while about dress, and then cleared away the tea-things and lay down to sleep.

10   But the Devil had been sitting behind the oven, and had heard all that was said. He was pleased that the peasant's wife had led her husband into boasting, and that he had said that if he had plenty of land he would not fear the Devil himself.

11   "All right," thought the Devil. "We will have a tussle③. I'll give you land enough; and by means of that land I will get you into my power."

II

12   Close to the village there lived a lady, a small landowner, who had an estate of about three hundred acres. She had always lived on good terms with the peasants, until she engaged as her steward④ an old soldier, who took to burdening the people with fines. However careful Pahom tried to be, it happened again and again that now a horse of his got among the lady's oats, now a cow strayed into⑤ her garden, now his calves found their way into her meadows—and he always had to pay a fine.

13   Pahom paid, but grumbled, and, going home in a temper, was rough with his family. All through that summer Pahom had much trouble because of this steward; and he was even glad when winter came and the cattle had to be stabled. Though he grudged⑥ the fodder⑦ when they could no longer graze on the pasture-land, at least he was free from anxiety about them.

14   In the winter the news got about that the lady was going to sell her land, and that the

---

① dung-heap: pile of excrement
② till: to plough
③ tussle: contest
④ steward: a person who manages other's property, or financial affairs
⑤ stray into: to wander, to roam into
⑥ grudge: to give unwillingly
⑦ fodder: food for cattle

keeper of the inn on the high road was bargaining for it. When the peasants heard this they were very much alarmed.

15   "Well," thought they, "if the innkeeper gets the land he will worry us with fines worse than the lady's steward. We all depend on that estate."

16   So the peasants went on behalf of their Commune, and asked the lady not to sell the land to the innkeeper; offering her a better price for it themselves. The lady agreed to let them have it. Then the peasants tried to arrange for the Commune to buy the whole estate, so that it might be held by all in common. They met twice to discuss it, but could not settle the matter; the Evil One sowed discord among them, and they could not agree. So they decided to buy the land individually, each according to his means; and the lady agreed to this plan as she had to the other.

17   Presently Pahom heard that a neighbor of his was buying fifty acres, and that the lady had consented to accept one half in cash and to wait a year for the other half. Pahom felt envious.

18   "Look at that," thought he, "the land is all being sold, and I shall get none of it." So he spoke to his wife.

19   "Other people are buying," said he, "and we must also buy twenty acres or so. Life is becoming impossible. That steward is simply crushing us with his fines."

20   So they put their heads together and considered how they could manage to buy it. They had one hundred roubles laid by. They sold a colt, and one half of their bees; hired out one of their sons as a laborer, and took his wages in advance; borrowed the rest from a brother-in-law, and so scraped[①] together half the purchase money.

21   Having done this, Pahom chose out a farm of forty acres, some of it wooded, and went to the lady to bargain for it. They came to an agreement, and he shook hands with her upon it, and paid her a deposit in advance. Then they went to town and signed the deeds; he paying half the price down, and undertaking to pay the remainder within two years.

22   So now Pahom had land of his own. He borrowed seed, and sowed it on the land he had bought. The harvest was a good one, and within a year he had managed to pay off his debts both to the lady and to his brother-in-law. So he became a landowner, ploughing and sowing his own land, making hay on his own land, cutting his own trees, and feeding his cattle on his own pasture. When he went out to plough his fields, or to look at his growing corn, or at his grass meadows, his heart would fill with joy. The grass that grew and the flowers that bloomed there, seemed to him unlike any that grew elsewhere. Formerly, when he had passed by that land, it had appeared the same as any other land, but now it seemed quite different.

III

23.   So Pahom was well contented, and everything would have been right if the neighboring peasants would only not have trespassed[②] on his corn-fields and meadows. He appealed to them most civilly, but they still went on: now the Communal herdsmen would let the village

---

① scrape: to gather with difficulty
② trespass: to enter another's land

cows stray into his meadows; then horses from the night pasture would get among his corn. Pahom turned them out again and again, and forgave their owners, and for a long time he forbore① from prosecuting any one. But at last he lost patience and complained to the District Court. He knew it was the peasants' want of land, and no evil intent on their part, that caused the trouble; but he thought:

24   "I cannot go on overlooking it, or they will destroy all I have. They must be taught a lesson."

25   So he had them up, gave them one lesson, and then another, and two or three of the peasants were fined. After a time Pahom's neighbours began to bear him a grudge for this, and would now and then let their cattle on his land on purpose. One peasant even got into Pahom's wood at night and cut down five young lime trees for their bark. Pahom passing through the wood one day noticed something white. He came nearer, and saw the stripped trunks lying on the ground, and close by stood the stumps②, where the tree had been. Pahom was furious.

26   "If he had only cut one here and there it would have been bad enough," thought Pahom, "but the rascal has actually cut down a whole clump③. If I could only find out who did this, I would pay him out."

27   He racked his brains as to who it could be. Finally he decided: "It must be Simon—no one else could have done it." Se he went to Simon's homestead to have a look around, but he found nothing, and only had an angry scene. However he now felt more certain than ever that Simon had done it, and he lodged a complaint. Simon was summoned. The case was tried, and re-tried, and at the end of it all Simon was acquitted④, there being no evidence against him. Pahom felt still more aggrieved, and let his anger loose upon the Elder and the Judges.

28   "You let thieves grease your palms⑤," said he. "If you were honest folk yourselves, you would not let a thief go free."

29   So Pahom quarrelled with the Judges and with his neighbors. Threats to burn his building began to be uttered. So though Pahom had more land, his place in the Commune was much worse than before.

30   About this time a rumor got about that many people were moving to new parts.

31   "There's no need for me to leave my land," thought Pahom. "But some of the others might leave our village, and then there would be more room for us. I would take over their land myself, and make my estate a bit bigger. I could then live more at ease. As it is, I am still too cramped⑥ to be comfortable."

32   One day Pahom was sitting at home, when a peasant passing through the village, happened to call in. He was allowed to stay the night, and supper was given him. Pahom had a

---

① forbear: refrain, hold back
② stump: the lower end of the tree after the main part has been cut off
③ clump: a small, close group of trees
④ acquit: to relieve from a charge of fault or crime
⑤ grease one's palm: to bribe sb, to influence through giving money to sb.
⑥ be cramped: be confined

talk with this peasant and asked him where he came from. The stranger answered that he came from beyond the Volga, where he had been working. One word led to another, and the man went on to say that many people were settling in those parts. He told how some people from his village had settled there. They had joined the Commune, and had had twenty-five acres per man granted them. The land was so good, he said, that the rye sown on it grew as high as a horse, and so thick that five cuts of a sickle made a sheaf[①]. One peasant, he said, had brought nothing with him but his bare hands, and now he had six horses and two cows of his own.

33   Pahom's heart kindled with desire. He thought:

34   "Why should I suffer in this narrow hole, if one can live so well elsewhere? I will sell my land and my homestead here, and with the money I will start afresh over there and get everything new. In this crowded place one is always having trouble. But I must first go and find out all about it myself."

35   Towards summer he got ready and started. He went down the Volga on a steamer to Samara, then walked another three hundred miles on foot, and at last reached the place. It was just as the stranger had said. The peasants had plenty of land: every man had twenty-five acres of Communal land given him for his use, and any one who had money could buy, besides, at fifty-cents an acre as much good freehold land as he wanted.

36   Having found out all he wished to know, Pahom returned home as autumn came on, and began selling off his belongings. He sold his land at a profit, sold his homestead[②] and all his cattle, and withdrew from membership of the Commune. He only waited till the spring, and then started with his family for the new settlement.

IV

37   As soon as Pahom and his family arrived at their new abode[③], he applied for admission into the Commune of a large village. He stood treat[④] to the Elders, and obtained the necessary documents. Five shares of Communal land were given him for his own and his sons' use: that is to say—125 acres (not altogether, but in different fields) besides the use of the Communal pasture. Pahom put up the buildings he needed, and bought cattle. Of the Communal land alone he had three times as much as at his former home, and the land was good corn-land. He was ten times better off than he had been. He had plenty of arable land and pasturage, and could keep as many head of cattle as he liked.

38   At first, in the bustle[⑤] of building and settling down, Pahom was pleased with it all, but when he got used to it he began to think that even here he had not enough land. The first year, he sowed wheat on his share of the Communal land, and had a good crop. He wanted to go on sowing wheat, but had not enough Communal land for the purpose, and what he had already used was not available; for in those parts wheat is only sown on virgin soil or on fallow[⑥] land.

---

① sheaf: bundle
② homestead: a dwelling with its land and buildings
③ abode: dwelling, a place where a person resides
④ stand treat: to undergo the process of application
⑤ bustle: busy and energetic activity
⑥ fallow: (of land) plowed and left unseeded for a season or more

It is sown for one or two years, and then the land lies fallow till it is again overgrown with prairie[①] grass. There were many who wanted such land, and there was not enough for all; so that people quarrelled about it. Those who were better off, wanted it for growing wheat, and those who were poor, wanted it to let to dealers, so that they might raise money to pay their taxes. Pahom wanted to sow more wheat; so he rented land from a dealer for a year. He sowed much wheat and had a fine crop, but the land was too far from the village—the wheat had to be carted more than ten miles. After a time Pahom noticed that some peasant-dealers were living on separate farms, and were growing wealthy; and he thought:

39　　　　"If I were to buy some freehold land, and have a homestead on it, it would be a different thing, altogether. Then it would all be nice and compact."

40　　　　The question of buying freehold land recurred to him again and again.

41　　　　He went on in the same way for three years; renting land and sowing wheat. The seasons turned out well and the crops were good, so that he began to lay money by. He might have gone on living contentedly, but he grew tired of having to rent other people's land every year, and having to scramble[②] for it. Wherever there was good land to be had, the peasants would rush for it and it was taken up at once, so that unless you were sharp about it you got none. It happened in the third year that he and a dealer together rented a piece of pasture land from some peasants; and they had already ploughed it up, when there was some dispute, and the peasants went to law about it, and things fell out so that the labor was all lost. "If it were my own land," thought Pahom, "I should be independent, and there would not be all this unpleasantness."

42　　　　So Pahom began looking out for land which he could buy; and he came across a peasant who had bought thirteen hundred acres, but having got into difficulties was willing to sell again cheap. Pahom bargained and haggled with[③] him, and at last they settled the price at 1,500 roubles, part in cash and part to be paid later. They had all but clinched the matter, when a passing dealer happened to stop at Pahom's one day to get a feed for his horse. He drank tea with Pahom, and they had a talk. The dealer said that he was just returning from the land of the Bashkirs, far away, where he had bought thirteen thousand acres of land all for 1,000 roubles. Pahom questioned him further, and the tradesman said:

43　　　　"All one need do is to make friends with the chiefs. I gave away about one hundred roubles' worth of dressing-gowns and carpets, besides a case of tea, and I gave wine to those who would drink it; and I got the land for less than two cents an acre. And he showed Pahom the title-deeds, saying:

44　　　　"The land lies near a river, and the whole prairie is virgin soil."

45　　　　Pahom plied[④] him with questions, and the tradesman said: "There is more land there than you could cover if you walked a year, and it all belongs to the Bashkirs. They are as simple as

---

① prairie: a land characterized by fertile soil and coarse grasses
② scramble: to compete or struggle with others for the possession of sth.
③ haggle with: to bargain with
④ ply sb. with questions: to ask sb a lot of questions

sheep, and land can be got almost for nothing."

46 "There now," thought Pahom, "with my one thousand roubles, why should I get only thirteen hundred acres, and saddle myself with a debt besides. If I take it out there, I can get more than ten times as much for the money."

V

47 Pahom inquired how to get to the place, and as soon as the tradesman had left him, he prepared to go there himself. He left his wife to look after the homestead, and started on his journey taking his man with him. They stopped at a town on their way, and bought a case of tea, some wine, and other presents, as the tradesman had advised. On and on they went until they had gone more than three hundred miles, and on the seventh day they came to a place where the Bashkirs had pitched their tents. It was all just as the tradesman had said. The people lived on the steppes, by a river, in felt- covered tents. They neither tilled the ground, nor ate bread. Their cattle and horses grazed in herds on the steppe①. The colts were tethered② behind the tents, and the mares were driven to them twice a day. The mares were milked, and from the milk kumiss③ was made. It was the women who prepared kumiss, and they also made cheese. As far as the men were concerned, drinking kumiss and tea, eating mutton, and playing on their pipes, was all they cared about. They were all stout and merry, and all the summer long they never thought of doing any work. They were quite ignorant, and knew no Russian, but were good-natured enough.

48 As soon as they saw Pahom, they came out of their tents and gathered round their visitor. An interpreter was found, and Pahom told them he had come about some land. The Bashkirs seemed very glad; they took Pahom and led him into one of the best tents, where they made him sit on some down cushions placed on a carpet, while they sat round him. They gave him tea and kumiss, and had a sheep killed, and gave him mutton to eat. Pahom took presents out of his cart and distributed them among the Bashkirs, and divided amongst them the tea. The Bashkirs were delighted. They talked a great deal among themselves, and then told the interpreter to translate.

49 "They wish to tell you," said the interpreter, "that they like you, and that it is our custom to do all we can to please a guest and to repay him for his gifts. You have given us presents, now tell us which of the things we possess please you best, that we may present them to you."

50 "What pleases me best here," answered Pahom, "is your land. Our land is crowded, and the soil is exhausted; but you have plenty of land and it is good land. I never saw the like of it."

51 The interpreter translated. The Bashkirs talked among themselves for a while. Pahom could not understand what they were saying, but saw that they were much amused, and that they shouted and laughed. Then they were silent and looked at Pahom while the interpreter said:

---

① steppe: an extensive plain, esp. one without trees
② tether: to fasten
③ kumiss: fermented mare's or camel's milk

52　　"They wish me to tell you that in return for your presents they will gladly give you as much land as you want. You have only to point it out with your hand and it is yours."

53　　The Bashkirs talked again for a while and began to dispute. Pahom asked what they were disputing about, and the interpreter told him that some of them thought they ought to ask their Chief about the land and not act in his absence, while others thought there was no need to wait for his return.

VI

54　　While the Bashkirs were disputing, a man in a large fox-fur cap appeared on the scene. They all became silent and rose to their feet. The interpreter said, "This is our Chief himself."

55　　Pahom immediately fetched the best dressing-gown and five pounds of tea, and offered these to the Chief. The Chief accepted them, and seated himself in the place of honour. The Bashkirs at once began telling him something. The Chief listened for a while, then made a sign with his head for them to be silent, and addressing himself to Pahom, said in Russian:

56　　"Well, let it be so. Choose whatever piece of land you like; we have plenty of it."

57　　"How can I take as much as I like?" thought Pahom. "I must get a deed to make it secure, or else they may say, 'It is yours,' and afterwards may take it away again."

58　　"Thank you for your kind words," he said aloud. "You have much land, and I only want a little. But I should like to be sure which bit is mine. Could it not be measured and made over to me? Life and death are in God's hands. You good people give it to me, but your children might wish to take it away again."

59　　"You are quite right," said the Chief. "We will make it over to you."

60　　"I heard that a dealer had been here," continued Pahom, "and that you gave him a little land, too, and signed title-deeds[1] to that effect. I should like to have it done in the same way."

61　　The Chief understood.

62　　"Yes," replied he, "that can be done quite easily. We have a scribe[2], and we will go to town with you and have the deed properly sealed."

63　　"And what will be the price?" asked Pahom.

64　　"Our price is always the same: one thousand roubles a day."

65　　Pahom did not understand.

66　　"A day? What measure is that? How many acres would that be?"

67　　"We do not know how to reckon it out," said the Chief. "We sell it by the day. As much as you can go round on your feet in a day is yours, and the price is one thousand roubles a day."

68　　Pahom was surprised.

---

① title-deed: a deed or document containing evidence of ownership
② scribe: a clerk

69   "But in a day you can get round a large tract of land," he said.

70   The Chief laughed.

71   "It will all be yours!" said he. "But there is one condition: If you don't return on the same day to the spot whence you started, your money is lost."

72   "But how am I to mark the way that I have gone?"

73   "Why, we shall go to any spot you like, and stay there. You must start from that spot and make your round, taking a spade with you. Wherever you think necessary, make a mark. At every turning, dig a hole and pile up the turf; then afterwards we will go round with a plough from hole to hole. You may make as large a circuit as you please, but before the sun sets you must return to the place you started from. All the land you cover will be yours."

74   Pahom was delighted. It was decided to start early next morning. They talked a while, and after drinking some more kumiss and eating some more mutton, they had tea again, and then the night came on. They gave Pahom a feather-bed to sleep on, and the Bashkirs dispersed for the night, promising to assemble the next morning at daybreak and ride out before sunrise to the appointed spot.

VII

75   Pahom lay on the feather-bed, but could not sleep. He kept thinking about the land.

76   "What a large tract I will mark off!" thought he. "I can easily go thirty-five miles in a day. The days are long now, and within a circuit of thirty-five miles what a lot of land there will be! I will sell the poorer land, or let it to peasants, but I'll pick out the best and farm it. I will buy two ox-teams, and hire two more laborers. About a hundred and fifty acres shall be plough-land, and I will pasture cattle on the rest."

77   Pahom lay awake all night, and dozed off only just before dawn. Hardly were his eyes closed when he had a dream. He thought he was lying in that same tent, and heard somebody chuckling outside. He wondered who it could be, and rose and went out, and he saw the Bashkir Chief sitting in front of the tent holding his side and rolling about with laughter. Going nearer to the Chief, Pahom asked: "What are you laughing at?" But he saw that it was no longer the Chief, but the dealer who had recently stopped at his house and had told him about the land. Just as Pahom was going to ask, "Have you been here long?" he saw that it was not the dealer, but the peasant who had come up from the Volga, long ago, to Pahom's old home. Then he saw that it was not the peasant either, but the Devil himself with hoofs and horns, sitting there and chuckling, and before him lay a man barefoot, prostrate on the ground, with only trousers and a shirt on. And Pahom dreamt that he looked more attentively to see what sort of a man it was lying there, and he saw that the man was dead, and that it was himself! He awoke horror-struck.

78   "What things one does dream," thought he.

79   Looking round he saw through the open door that the dawn was breaking.

80   "It's time to wake them up," thought he. "We ought to be starting."

81   He got up, roused his man (who was sleeping in his cart), bade him harness; and went to call the Bashkirs.

82   "It's time to go to the steppe to measure the land," he said.

83   The Bashkirs rose and assembled, and the Chief came, too. Then they began drinking kumiss again, and offered Pahom some tea, but he would not wait.

84   "If we are to go, let us go. It is high time," said he.

VIII

85   The Bashkirs got ready and they all started: some mounted on horses, and some in carts. Pahom drove in his own small cart with his servant, and took a spade with him. When they reached the steppe, the morning red was beginning to kindle. They ascended a hillock[①] (called by the Bashkirs a shikhan) and dismounting from their carts and their horses, gathered in one spot. The Chief came up to Pahom and stretched out his arm towards the plain:

86   "See," said he, "all this, as far as your eye can reach, is ours. You may have any part of it you like."

87   Pahom's eyes glistened: it was all virgin soil, as flat as the palm of your hand, as black as the seed of a poppy, and in the hollows different kinds of grasses grew breast high.

88   The Chief took off his fox-fur cap, placed it on the ground and said:

89   "This will be the mark. Start from here, and return here again. All the land you go round shall be yours."

90   Pahom took out his money and put it on the cap. Then he took off his outer coat, remaining in his sleeveless undercoat. He unfastened his girdle and tied it tight below his stomach, put a little bag of bread into the breast of his coat, and tying a flask of water to his girdle, he drew up the tops of his boots, took the spade from his man, and stood ready to start. He considered for some moments which way he had better go—it was tempting everywhere.

91   "No matter," he concluded, "I will go towards the rising sun."

92   He turned his face to the east, stretched himself, and waited for the sun to appear above the rim.

93   "I must lose no time," he thought, "and it is easier walking while it is still cool."

94   The sun's rays had hardly flashed above the horizon, before Pahom, carrying the spade over his shoulder, went down into the steppe.

95   Pahom started walking neither slowly nor quickly. After having gone a thousand yards he stopped, dug a hole and placed pieces of turf one on another to make it more visible. Then he went on; and now that he had walked off his stiffness he quickened his pace. After a while he dug another hole.

① hillock: a small hill

96   Pahom looked back. The hillock could be distinctly seen in the sunlight, with the people on it, and the glittering tires of the cartwheels. At a rough guess Pahom concluded that he had walked three miles. It was growing warmer; he took off his undercoat, flung it across his shoulder, and went on again. It had grown quite warm now; he looked at the sun, it was time to think of breakfast.

97   "The first shift is done, but there are four in a day, and it is too soon yet to turn. But I will just take off my boots," said he to himself.

98   He sat down, took off his boots, stuck them into his girdle, and went on. It was easy walking now.

99   "I will go on for another three miles," thought he, "and then turn to the left. The spot is so fine, that it would be a pity to lose it. The further one goes, the better the land seems."

100   He went straight on for a while, and when he looked round, the hillock was scarcely visible and the people on it looked like black ants, and he could just see something glistening there in the sun.

101   "Ah," thought Pahom, "I have gone far enough in this direction, it is time to turn. Besides I am in a regular sweat, and very thirsty."

102   He stopped, dug a large hole, and heaped up pieces of turf. Next he untied his flask, had a drink, and then turned sharply to the left. He went on and on; the grass was high, and it was very hot.

103   Pahom began to grow tired: he looked at the sun and saw that it was noon.

104   "Well," he thought, "I must have a rest."

105   He sat down, and ate some bread and drank some water; but he did not lie down, thinking that if he did he might fall asleep. After sitting a little while, he went on again. At first he walked easily: the food had strengthened him; but it had become terribly hot, and he felt sleepy; still he went on, thinking: "An hour to suffer, a life-time to live."

106   He went a long way in this direction also, and was about to turn to the left again, when he perceived a damp hollow: "It would be a pity to leave that out," he thought. "Flax[①] would do well there." So he went on past the hollow, and dug a hole on the other side of it before he turned the corner. Pahom looked towards the hillock. The heat made the air hazy: it seemed to be quivering, and through the haze the people on the hillock could scarcely be seen.

107   "Ah!" thought Pahom, "I have made the sides too long; I must make this one shorter." And he went along the third side, stepping faster. He looked at the sun: it was nearly half way to the horizon, and he had not yet done two miles of the third side of the square. He was still ten miles from the goal.

108   "No," he thought, "though it will make my land lopsided[②], I must hurry back in a straight line now. I might go too far, and as it is I have a great deal of land."

---

① flax: 亚麻
② lopsided: uneven

109   So Pahom hurriedly dug a hole, and turned straight towards the hillock.

IX

110   Pahom went straight towards the hillock, but he now walked with difficulty. He was done up with the heat, his bare feet were cut and bruised, and his legs began to fail. He longed to rest, but it was impossible if he meant to get back before sunset. The sun waits for no man, and it was sinking lower and lower.

111   "Oh dear," he thought, "if only I have not blundered trying for too much! What if I am too late?"

112   He looked towards the hillock and at the sun. He was still far from his goal, and the sun was already near the rim. Pahom walked on and on; it was very hard walking, but he went quicker and quicker. He pressed on, but was still far from the place. He began running, threw away his coat, his boots, his flask, and his cap, and kept only the spade which he used as a support.

113   "What shall I do," he thought again, "I have grasped too much, and ruined the whole affair. I can't get there before the sun sets."

114   And this fear made him still more breathless. Pahom went on running, his soaking shirt and trousers stuck to him, and his mouth was parched[①]. His breast was working like a blacksmith's bellows, his heart was beating like a hammer, and his legs were giving way as if they did not belong to him. Pahom was seized with terror lest he should die of the strain.

115   Though afraid of death, he could not stop. "After having run all that way they will call me a fool if I stop now," thought he. And he ran on and on, and drew near and heard the Bashkirs yelling and shouting to him, and their cries inflamed his heart still more. He gathered his last strength and ran on.

116   The sun was close to the rim, and cloaked in mist looked large, and red as blood. Now, yes now, it was about to set! The sun was quite low, but he was also quite near his aim. Pahom could already see the people on the hillock waving their arms to hurry him up. He could see the fox-fur cap on the ground, and the money on it, and the Chief sitting on the ground holding his sides. And Pahom remembered his dream.

117   "There is plenty of land," thought he, "but will God let me live on it? I have lost my life, I have lost my life! I shall never reach that spot!"

118   Pahom looked at the sun, which had reached the earth: one side of it had already disappeared. With all his remaining strength he rushed on, bending his body forward so that his legs could hardly follow fast enough to keep him from falling. Just as he reached the hillock it suddenly grew dark. He looked up—the sun had already set. He gave a cry: "All my labor has been in vain," thought he, and was about to stop, but he heard the Bashkirs still shouting, and remembered that though to him, from below, the sun seemed to have set, they on the hillock could still see it. He took a long breath and ran up the hillock. It was still light there. He

---

① parched: extremely dry

reached the top and saw the cap. Before it sat the Chief laughing and holding his sides. Again Pahom remembered his dream, and he uttered a cry: his legs gave way beneath him, he fell forward and reached the cap with his hands.

119   "Ah, what a fine fellow!" exclaimed the Chief. "He has gained much land!"

120   Pahom's servant came running up and tried to raise him, but he saw that blood was flowing from his mouth. Pahom was dead!

121   The Bashkirs clicked their tongues to show their pity.

122   His servant picked up the spade and dug a grave long enough for Pahom to lie in, and buried him in it. Six feet from his head to his heels was all he needed.

▶▶ STUDY QUESTIONS

A▷ Recalling

1. Who has stirred Pahom's desire for more land in the first place?
2. Describe how step by step Pahom enlarges his land.
3. What are the specific stimuli for Pahom to buy more land each time?

B▷ Interpreting

4. Please name the initial stimulus, the apparent stimulus and the real cause for Pahom's destruction.
5. Please compare the life of the Bashkirs with that of Pahom's.
6. How do you like the idea that it is the wife who stirs Pahom's desire?
7. What is the significance of the dream?
8. How much land does a man need?

C▷ Extending

9. Reflect on your own life. Are you, just like Pahom, keeping pursuing more and more and never to be contented?
10. How shall we live? What shall we pursue? Find some religion or philosophy to support yourself.

VIII. "Solitude" from *Walden* by Henry David Thoreau

▶▶ ABOUT THE AUTHOR

Henry David Thoreau (1817–1862) was an American author, poet, philosopher, abolitionist, naturalist, tax resister, development critic, surveyor, historian, and leading transcendentalist. He is best known for his book *Walden*, a reflection upon simple living in natural surroundings, and his essay *Civil Disobedience*, an argument for individual resistance to civil government in moral opposition to an unjust state.

Solitude (selected from *Walden*)

1   This is a delicious evening, when the whole body is one sense, and imbibes[1] delight through every pore. I go and come with a strange liberty in Nature, a part of herself. As I walk along the stony shore of the pond in my shirt-sleeves, though it is cool as well as cloudy and windy, and I see nothing special to attract me, all the elements are unusually congenial[2] to me. The bullfrogs trump[3] to usher[4] in the night, and the note of the whip-poor-will[5] is borne[6] on the rippling wind from over the water. Sympathy with the fluttering[7] alder[8] and poplar[9] leaves almost takes away my breath; yet, like the lake, my serenity is rippled but not ruffled[10]. These small waves raised by the evening wind are as remote from storm as the smooth reflecting surface. Though it is now dark, the wind still blows and roars in the wood, the waves still dash, and some creatures lull the rest with their notes. The repose is never complete. The wildest animals do not repose, but seek their prey now; the fox, and skunk[11], and rabbit, now roam the fields and woods without fear. They are Nature's watchmen—links which connect the days of animated life.

2   When I return to my house I find that visitors have been there and left their cards, either a bunch of flowers, or a wreath of evergreen, or a name in pencil on a yellow walnut leaf or a chip. They who come rarely to the woods take some little piece of the forest into their hands to play with by the way, which they leave, either intentionally or accidentally. One has peeled a willow wand, woven it into a ring, and dropped it on my table. I could always tell if visitors had called in my absence, either by the bended twigs or grass, or the print of their shoes, and generally of what sex or age or quality they were by some slight trace left, as a flower dropped, or a bunch of grass plucked and thrown away, even as far off as the railroad, half a mile distant, or by the lingering odor of a cigar or pipe. Nay, I was frequently notified of the passage of a traveller along the highway sixty rods off by the scent of his pipe.

3   There is commonly sufficient space about us. Our horizon is never quite at our elbows. The thick wood is not just at our door, nor the pond, but somewhat is always clearing, familiar and worn by us, appropriated and fenced in some way, and reclaimed from Nature. For what reason have I this vast range and circuit, some square miles of unfrequented forest, for my privacy, abandoned to me by men? My nearest neighbor is a mile distant, and no house is visible from any place but the hill-tops within half a mile of my own. I have my horizon bounded by woods all to myself; a distant view of the railroad where it touches the pond on the one hand, and of the fence which skirts[12] the woodland road on the other. But for the most part it is as solitary where I live as on the prairies. It is as much Asia or

---

① imbibe: to receive
② congenial: agreeable
③ trump: to blow the trumpet
④ usher in: to herald, to introduce
⑤ whip-poor-will: an American bird, so called in imitation of the special notes it utteres in the evening
⑥ be borne: here be carried
⑦ fluttering: moving in quick, irregular motions, vibrating
⑧ alder: 赤杨
⑨ poplar: 白杨
⑩ ruffled: disturbed
⑪ skunk: 臭鼬
⑫ skirt: to border

Africa as New England. I have, as it were, my own sun and moon and stars, and a little world all to myself. At night there was never a traveller passed my house, or knocked at my door, more than if I were the first or last man; unless it were in the spring, when at long intervals some came from the village to fish for pouts① —they plainly fished much more in the Walden Pond of their own natures, and baited their hooks with darkness—but they soon retreated, usually with light baskets, and left "the world to darkness and to me," and the black kernel② of the night was never profaned③ by any human neighborhood. I believe that men are generally still a little afraid of the dark, though the witches are all hung, and Christianity and candles have been introduced.

4　　Yet I experienced sometimes that the most sweet and tender, the most innocent and encouraging society may be found in any natural object, even for the poor misanthrope④ and most melancholy man. There can be no very black melancholy to him who lives in the midst of Nature and has his senses still. There was never yet such a storm but it was Æolian music⑤ to a healthy and innocent ear. Nothing can rightly compel a simple and brave man to a vulgar sadness. While I enjoy the friendship of the seasons I trust that nothing can make life a burden to me. The gentle rain which waters my beans and keeps me in the house today is not drear⑥ and melancholy, but good for me too. Though it prevents my hoeing⑦ them, it is of far more worth than my hoeing. If it should continue so long as to cause the seeds to rot in the ground and destroy the potatoes in the low lands, it would still be good for the grass on the uplands, and, being good for the grass, it would be good for me. Sometimes, when I compare myself with other men, it seems as if I were more favored by the gods than they, beyond any deserts that I am conscious of; as if I had a warrant and surety at their hands which my fellows have not, and were especially guided and guarded. I do not flatter myself, but if it be possible they flatter me. I have never felt lonesome, or in the least oppressed by a sense of solitude, but once, and that was a few weeks after I came to the woods, when, for an hour, I doubted if the near neighborhood of man was not essential to a serene and healthy life. To be alone was something unpleasant. But I was at the same time conscious of a slight insanity in my mood, and seemed to foresee my recovery. In the midst of a gentle rain while these thoughts prevailed, I was suddenly sensible of such sweet and beneficent society in Nature, in the very pattering of the drops, and in every sound and sight around my house, an infinite and unaccountable friendliness all at once like an atmosphere sustaining me, as made the fancied advantages of human neighborhood insignificant, and I have never thought of them since. Every little pine needle expanded and swelled with sympathy and befriended me. I was so distinctly made aware of the presence of something kindred to me, even in scenes which we are accustomed to call wild and dreary, and also that the nearest of blood to me and humanest was not a person nor a villager, that I thought no place could ever be strange to me again.

---

① pout: 鳕鱼
② kernel: the heart
③ profane: destroyed or violated
④ misantrope: a hatred of human kind
⑤ Æolian music: in Greek mythology, the Aeolian harp was the instrument of Æolus, god of wind. The ancient Greeks made Aeolian harps that were played by moving air.
⑥ drear: gloomy, sad or boring
⑦ hoe: to cultivate

5
　　"Mourning untimely consumes the sad;
　　Few are their days in the land of the living,
　　Beautiful daughter of Toscar."[1]

6　　　Some of my pleasantest hours were during the long rain-storms in the spring or fall, which confined me to the house for the afternoon as well as the forenoon, soothed by their ceaseless roar and pelting[2]; when an early twilight ushered in a long evening in which many thoughts had time to take root and unfold themselves. In those driving northeast rains which tried the village houses so, when the maids stood ready with mop and pail in front entries to keep the deluge[3] out, I sat behind my door in my little house, which was all entry, and thoroughly enjoyed its protection. In one heavy thunder-shower the lightning struck a large pitch pine across the pond, making a very conspicuous and perfectly regular spiral groove[4] from top to bottom, an inch or more deep, and four or five inches wide, as you would groove a walking-stick. I passed it again the other day, and was struck with awe on looking up and beholding that mark, now more distinct than ever, where a terrific and resistless bolt came down out of the harmless sky eight years ago[5]. Men frequently say to me, "I should think you would feel lonesome down there, and want to be nearer to folks, rainy and snowy days and nights especially." I am tempted to reply to such—This whole earth which we inhabit is but a point in space. How far apart, think you, dwell the two most distant inhabitants of yonder star, the breadth of whose disk cannot be appreciated by our instruments? Why should I feel lonely? Is not our planet in the Milky Way? This which you put seems to me not to be the most important question. What sort of space is that which separates a man from his fellows and makes him solitary? I have found that no exertion of the legs can bring two minds much nearer to one another. What do we want most to dwell near to? Not to many men surely, the depot, the post-office, the bar-room, the meeting-house, the school-house, the grocery, Beacon Hill[6], or the Five Points[7], where men most congregate, but to the perennial[8] source of our life, whence in all our experience we have found that to issue, as the willow stands near the water and sends out its roots in that direction. This will vary with different natures, but this is the place where a wise man will dig his cellar... I one evening overtook one of my townsmen, who has accumulated what is called "a handsome property"— though I never got a fair view of it—on the Walden road, driving a pair of cattle to market, who inquired of me how I could bring my mind to give up so many of the comforts of life. I answered that I was very sure I liked it passably[9] well; I was not joking. And so I went home to my bed, and left him to pick his way through the darkness and the mud to Brighton—or Bright-town—which place he would reach some time in the morning.

7　　　Any prospect of awakening or coming to life to a dead man makes indifferent all times and places. The place where that may occur is always the same, and indescribably pleasant

---

① James Macpherson (1736–1796) from *Croma*, poetry of "Ossian", supposed 3rd cent. Gaelic poet, later established as a forgery by Macpherson
② pelting: striking
③ deluge: a great flood of water
④ groove: a long, narrow cut
⑤ Thoreau lived at Walden from 1845 to 1847. *Walden* was not published until 1854.
⑥ Beacon Hill: fashionable section of Boston
⑦ the Five Points: former disreputable section of New York City, between the current New York City Hall and Chinatown
⑧ perennial: everlasting, perpetual
⑨ passably: fairly, moderately

to all our senses. For the most part we allow only outlying[①] and transient[②] circumstances to make our occasions[③]. They are, in fact, the cause of our distraction. Nearest to all things is that power which fashions their being. Next to us the grandest laws are continually being executed. Next to us is not the workman whom we have hired, with whom we love so well to talk, but the workman whose work we are.

8   "How vast and profound is the influence of the subtile[④] powers of Heaven and of Earth!"

9   "We seek to perceive them, and we do not see them; we seek to hear them, and we do not hear them; identified with the substance of things, they cannot be separated from them."

10   "They cause that in all the universe men purify and sanctify their hearts, and clothe themselves in their holiday garments to offer sacrifices and oblations[⑤] to their ancestors. It is an ocean of subtile intelligences. They are everywhere, above us, on our left, on our right; they environ us on all sides."[⑥]

11   We are the subjects of an experiment which is not a little interesting to me. Can we not do without the society of our gossips a little while under these circumstances—have our own thoughts to cheer us? Confucius says truly, "Virtue does not remain as an abandoned orphan; it must of necessity have neighbors."[⑦]

12   With thinking we may be beside ourselves in a sane sense. By a conscious effort of the mind we can stand aloof from actions and their consequences; and all things, good and bad, go by us like a torrent. We are not wholly involved in Nature. I may be either the driftwood in the stream, or Indra[⑧] in the sky looking down on it. I may be affected by a theatrical exhibition; on the other hand, I may not be affected by an actual event which appears to concern me much more. I only know myself as a human entity; the scene, so to speak, of thoughts and affections; and am sensible of a certain doubleness by which I can stand as remote from myself as from another. However intense my experience, I am conscious of the presence and criticism of a part of me, which, as it were, is not a part of me, but spectator, sharing no experience, but taking note of it, and that is no more I than it is you. When the play, it may be the tragedy, of life is over, the spectator goes his way. It was a kind of fiction, a work of the imagination only, so far as he was concerned. This doubleness may easily make us poor neighbors and friends sometimes.

13   I find it wholesome to be alone the greater part of the time. To be in company, even with the best, is soon wearisome and dissipating[⑨]. I love to be alone. I never found the companion that was so companionable as solitude. We are for the most part more lonely when we go abroad among men than when we stay in our chambers. A man thinking or working is always alone, let him be where he will. Solitude is not measured by the miles of space that intervene between a man and his fellows. The really diligent student in one of the crowded hives of Cambridge College is as solitary as a dervish[⑩] in the desert. The farmer can work alone in the field or the

---

① outlying: remote
② transient: not lasting, transitory
③ to make one's occasion: we only think the remote and transient things are important and meaningful.
④ subtile: a rare spelling of "subtle"
⑤ oblation: the act of making an offering
⑥ Confucius (1551BC–1479 BC) Chinese philosopher; three paragraphs in quotes are from *Doctrine of the Mean*.
⑦ Quoted from *Confucian Analects*
⑧ Indra: in Hinduism, chief of the Vedic gods, god of thunder & rain
⑨ dissipating: exhausting
⑩ dervish: a member of any of various Muslim ascetic orders

woods all day, hoeing or chopping, and not feel lonesome, because he is employed; but when he comes home at night he cannot sit down in a room alone, at the mercy of his thoughts, but must be where he can "see the folks", and recreate, and as he thinks remunerate① himself for his day's solitude; and hence he wonders how the student can sit alone in the house all night and most of the day without ennui② and "the blues"; but he does not realize that the student, though in the house, is still at work in *his* field, and chopping in *his* woods, as the farmer in his, and in turn seeks the same recreation and society that the latter does, though it may be a more condensed form of it.

14   Society is commonly too cheap. We meet at very short intervals, not having had time to acquire any new value for each other. We meet at meals three times a day, and give each other a new taste of that old musty cheese that we are. We have had to agree on a certain set of rules, called etiquette and politeness, to make this frequent meeting tolerable and that we need not come to open war. We meet at the post-office, and at the sociable, and about the fireside every night; we live thick and are in each other's way, and stumble over one another, and I think that we thus lose some respect for one another. Certainly less frequency would suffice for all important and hearty communications. Consider the girls in a factory—never alone, hardly in their dreams. It would be better if there were but one inhabitant to a square mile, as where I live. The value of a man is not in his skin, that we should touch him.

15   I have heard of a man lost in the woods and dying of famine and exhaustion at the foot of a tree, whose loneliness was relieved by the grotesque visions with which, owing to bodily weakness, his diseased imagination surrounded him, and which he believed to be real. So also, owing to bodily and mental health and strength, we may be continually cheered by a like but more normal and natural society, and come to know that we are never alone.

16   I have a great deal of company in my house; especially in the morning, when nobody calls. Let me suggest a few comparisons, that some one may convey an idea of my situation. I am no more lonely than the loon③ in the pond that laughs so loud, or than Walden Pond itself. What company has that lonely lake, I pray? And yet it has not the blue devils④, but the blue angels in it, in the azure tint of its waters. The sun is alone, except in thick weather, when there sometimes appear to be two, but one is a mock sun. God is alone—but the devil, he is far from being alone; he sees a great deal of company; he is legion⑤. I am no more lonely than a single mullein⑥ or dandelion⑦ in a pasture, or a bean leaf, or sorrel⑧, or a horse-fly, or a bumblebee⑨. I am no more lonely than the Mill Brook, or a weathercock⑩, or the north star, or the south wind, or an April shower, or a January thaw, or the first spider in a new house.

17   I have occasional visits in the long winter evenings, when the snow falls fast and the wind

---

① remunerate: to reward
② ennui: boredom
③ loon: a foolish person or a kind of bird
④ blue devils: here refers to melancholy.
⑤ legion: a great number of
⑥ mullein: a kind of plant
⑦ dandelion: 蒲公英
⑧ sorrel: 酸模，一种有酸味的植物，可用于烹调
⑨ bumblebee: 大黄蜂
⑩ weathercock: a weather vane in the form of a cock, 风向标

howls in the wood, from an old settler and original proprietor[1], who is reported to have dug Walden Pond, and stoned it, and fringed it with pine woods; who tells me stories of old time and of new eternity; and between us we manage to pass a cheerful evening with social mirth and pleasant views of things, even without apples or cider[2] —a most wise and humorous friend, whom I love much, who keeps himself more secret than ever did Goffe or Whalley[3]; and though he is thought to be dead, none can show where he is buried. An elderly dame[4], too, dwells in my neighborhood, invisible to most persons, in whose odorous herb garden I love to stroll sometimes, gathering simples and listening to her fables; for she has a genius of unequalled fertility, and her memory runs back farther than mythology, and she can tell me the original of every fable, and on what fact every one is founded, for the incidents occurred when she was young. A ruddy and lusty old dame, who delights in all weathers and seasons, and is likely to outlive all her children yet.

18   The indescribable innocence and beneficence of Nature—of sun and wind and rain, of summer and winter—such health, such cheer, they afford forever! And such sympathy have they ever with our race, that all Nature would be affected, and the sun's brightness fade, and the winds would sigh humanely, and the clouds rain tears, and the woods shed their leaves and put on mourning in midsummer, if any man should ever for a just cause grieve. Shall I not have intelligence with the earth? Am I not partly leaves and vegetable mould myself?

19   What is the pill which will keep us well, serene, contented? Not my or thy great-grandfather's, but our great-grandmother Nature's universal, vegetable, botanic medicines, by which she has kept herself young always, outlived so many old Parrs[5] in her day, and fed her health with their decaying fatness. For my panacea[6], instead of one of those quack[7] vials[8] of a mixture dipped from Acheron[9] and the Dead Sea[10], which come out of those long shallow black-schooner[11] looking wagons which we sometimes see made to carry bottles, let me have a draught of undiluted morning air. Morning air! If men will not drink of this at the fountainhead of the day, why, then, we must even bottle up some and sell it in the shops, for the benefit of those who have lost their subscription ticket to morning time in this world. But remember, it will not keep quite till noonday even in the coolest cellar, but drive out the stopples[12] long ere that and follow westward the steps of Aurora[13]. I am no worshipper of Hygeia[14], who was the daughter of that old herb-doctor Æsculapius[15], and who is represented on monuments holding a serpent in one hand, and in the other a cup out of which the serpent sometimes drinks; but

---

[1] proprietor: the owner of a business establishment
[2] cider: the juice pressed from apples
[3] William Goffe, Edward Whalley, indicted for killing Charles I of England, lived in hiding in America
[4] dame: a woman of rank or dignity
[5] old Parr: Thomas Parr was an Englishman said to have lived for 152 years.
[6] panacea: a remedy for all disease
[7] quack: false
[8] vial: a small container
[9] Acheron: in Greek mythology, a river in Hades
[10] the Dead Sea: large salt lake bordering Israel & Jordan
[11] schooner: a very tall glass, as for beer
[12] stopple: plug
[13] Aurora: in Roman mythology, goddess of the dawn
[14] Hygeia: in Greek mythology, goddess of health
[15] Æsculapius: in Greek mythology, god of medicine, father of Hygeia

rather of Hebe[1], cup-bearer to Jupiter[2], who was the daughter of Juno and wild lettuce[3], and who had the power of restoring gods and men to the vigor of youth. She was probably the only thoroughly sound-conditioned, healthy, and robust young lady that ever walked the globe, and wherever she came it was spring.

▶ STUDY QUESTIONS

A⟩ *Recalling*

1. What is evening in the woods like?
2. How can the speaker tell whether any visitor come in his absence?
3. How does the speaker look at the storm? And the lingering rain?(Paragraph 4)
4. Where should a wise man dig his cellar? (Paragraph 6)
5. How does the speaker treat events concerning himself? (Paragraph 12)
6. What keeps "me" company? (Paragraph 16)
7. Who are the two visitors in the long winter evening? What is special about them? (Paragraph 17)

B⟩ *Interpreting*

8. What is being alone and what is being lonely?
9. Why human society is often too cheap? What is the desired relationship between human beings according to the author?
10. How does Nature keep herself young?
11. What is the relationship between nature and man as suggested by the article?

C⟩ *Extending*

12. How do you look at nature? What is the position of human beings in nature?
13. What is expressed by Thoreau is called Transcendentalism. Have you come across any philosophy that has expressed similar ideas?

▶ FURTHER READING

Sophocles, *Oedipus the King*
Milan Kundera, *The Unbearable Lightness of Being*
J. D. Salinger, *The Catcher in the Rye*
Virginia Woolf, *To the Lighthouse*
Ralph Waldo Emerson, *The Oversoul*

▶ MOVIES RECOMMENDED

The Seventh Seal (1957), directed by Ingmar Bergman
Wild Strawberries (1957), directed by Ingmar Bergman
Oh My God! (2012), directed by Umesh Shukla
Into the Wild (2007), directed by Sean Penn
Life of Pie (2012), directed by Ang Lee

① Hebe: in Greek mythology, goddess of youth
② Jupiter: in Roman mythology, chief of the gods
③ Juno and wild lettuce: in Roman mythology, Juno is the queen of heaven, who conceived Hebe after eating lettuce.

References

Barnet, S., Berman, M., Burto, W. (eds) 1988. *Literature for Composition, Essays, Fiction, Poetry, and Drama.* Glenview: Scott, Foresman and Company.

Cassill, R. V. , Bausch, R. 2000. *The Norton Anthology of Short Fiction.* London: W. W. Norton & Company, Inc.

Ferrara, C., Flynn, G., Foerster, R., etc. 1991. *Enjoying Literature:* Signature Edition (Macmillan Literature Series). New York: Glencoe/Mcgraw-Hill.

Hunter, J. P. 1986. *The Norton Introduction to Poetry.* London: W. W. Norton & Company, Inc.

Kearns, G. 1984. *Appreciating Literature.* New York: Macmillan Publishing Company.

Mengello, L., Jedamus, J., etc. 1991. *World Literature*: Signature Edition. New York: Glencoe Division of Macmi-llan/McGraw-Hill Publishing Company.

Pickering, J. H. 1998. *Fiction 100, An Anthology of Short Stories.* Bergen/New York: Prentice-Hall, Inc. A Simon & Schuster/ A Viacom Company.

www. bartleby.com

www. wikipedia.org